Lecture Notes
in Business Information Processing

230

Series Editors

Wil van der Aalst
  Eindhoven Technical University, Eindhoven, The Netherlands
John Mylopoulos
  University of Trento, Povo, Italy
Michael Rosemann
  Queensland University of Technology, Brisbane, QLD, Australia
Michael J. Shaw
  University of Illinois, Urbana-Champaign, IL, USA
Clemens Szyperski
  Microsoft Research, Redmond, WA, USA

More information about this series at http://www.springer.com/series/7911

Andrzej Kobyliński · Beata Czarnacka-Chrobot
Jarosław Świerczek (Eds.)

Software
Measurement

25th International Workshop on Software Measurement
and 10th International Conference on Software Process
and Product Measurement, IWSM-Mensura 2015
Kraków, Poland, October 5–7, 2015
Proceedings

 Springer

Editors
Andrzej Kobyliński
Institute of Information Systems and
    Digital Economy
Warsaw School of Economics
Warsaw
Poland

Jarosław Świerczek
Polish Software Measurement Association
Warsaw
Poland

Beata Czarnacka-Chrobot
Institute of Information Systems
    and Digital Economy
Warsaw School of Economics
Warsaw
Poland

ISSN 1865-1348   ISSN 1865-1356   (electronic)
Lecture Notes in Business Information Processing
ISBN 978-3-319-24284-2   ISBN 978-3-319-24285-9   (eBook)
DOI 10.1007/978-3-319-24285-9

Library of Congress Control Number: 2015948855

Springer Cham Heidelberg New York Dordrecht London

Printed on acid-free paper

Springer International Publishing AG Switzerland is part of Springer Science+Business Media
(www.springer.com)

Preface

The pressure for more efficient software development and maintenance processes, delivering appropriate quality software within a certain budget and time frame, is constantly increasing. Software measurement is a key tool in helping to manage and to control software development and maintenance projects. Measurement is essential to any engineering activity, by increasing the scientific and technical knowledge for both the practice of software development and maintenance and for empirical research in software technology. For this reason, there appeared a need to organize a forum where new ideas from the world of academic research on software measurement could meet up with practical improvements from industry.

The IWSM Mensura conference is the result of the joining of forces of the International Workshop on Software Measurement (IWSM) and the International Conference on Software Process and Product Measurement (Mensura).

The International Workshop on Software Measurement (IWSM) has a long tradition that started at the beginning of the 1990s with a small working group in Germany with Prof. Reiner Dumke, Prof. Horst Zuse, and Christof Ebert. In the late 1990s, Prof. Alain Abran with his team from the University of Québec joined in. From the beginning, IWSM was organized in various German cities, and later, until 2006, IWSM alternated between the Montréal area in Canada and German cities (e.g., Magdeburg, Berlin, Regensburg, Mannheim, Königs Wusterhausen, and Potsdam).

Independent of the IWSM workshop, the International Conference on Software Process and Product Measurement (Mensura) was founded in 2006 by Prof. Juan J. Cuadrado Gallego from the University of Alcalá (Spain). The first meeting was held in Cádiz.

To foster research, practice, and exchange of experiences and best practices both conferences joined forces and held a joint conference on the Island of Mallorca (2007). Since then, both conferences have acted as a combined conference and the event is now traveling around the world: Munich (Germany, 2008), Amsterdam (Netherlands, 2009), Stuttgart (Germany, 2010), Nara (Japan, 2011), Assisi (Italy, 2012), Ankara (Turkey, 2013), and Rotterdam (Netherlands, 2014). This year, IWSM Mensura was organized in Cracow (Poland) by the Polish Software Measurement Association and the Warsaw School of Economics (SGH), the oldest and most prestigious Polish university of economics and business. This year, two anniversaries coincided: it was the 25th IWSM and the 10th Mensura and the 9th joint conference IWSM Mensura.

This year, the IWSM Mensura conference attracted 32 submissions from 25 countries from all continents. They were rigorously reviewed by 68 members of the Program Committee representing 26 countries. As a result, 13 full papers, presenting novel research and industrial results, written by authors originating from 17 countries were selected for publication in this volume.

Apart from the main conference, satellite events, i.e., workshops, sponsors' presentations, and a poster session, took place during the conference.

We would like to thank everyone who contributed to the IWSM Mensura conference. First of all we thank the authors for being ready to present their research, we appreciate the invaluable contribution of the members of the Program Committee, and we thank all the members of the local organization team for their help in the organization of the conference. We acknowledge the EasyChair development team for providing a convenient tool for organizing the process of reviewing and selecting the best papers and the Springer publishing team for their collaboration. Last but not least, we thank the Steering Committee and we hope that the IWSM Mensura 2015 conference in Cracow will be a memorable link in the IWSM Mensura conference series.

July 2015   Andrzej Kobyliński
                                                                         Beata Czarnacka-Chrobot
                                                                            Jarosław Świerczek

Conference Organization

General Chair

Andrzej Kobyliński   Warsaw School of Economics, Poland

Program Co-chairs

Beata Czarnacka-Chrobot   Warsaw School of Economics, Poland
Jarosław Świerczek   Polish Software Measurement Association, Poland

Program Committee

Silvia Abrahao   Universitat Politècnica de València, Spain
Alain Abran   ÉTS, University of Quebec, Canada
Mauricio Aguiar   TI Metricas, Brazil
Pierre Almén   ImproveIT, Sweden
Rafa Al-Qutaish   ÉTS, University of Quebec, Canada
Tiago Alves   Microsoft, Portugal
Sousuke Amasaki   Okayama Prefectural University, Japan
Lefteris Angelis   Aristotle University of Thessaloniki, Greece
Luigi Buglione   ÉTS, University of Quebec, Canada and Engineering.
         IT, Italy
Manfred Bundschuh   DASMA, Germany
Tom Cagley   David Consulting Group, USA
Ramiro Carballo   Spain
Laila Cheikhi   ENSIAS, Morocco
Marcus Ciolkowski   QAware GmbH, Germany
Beata Czarnacka-Chrobot   Warsaw School of Economics, Poland
Maya Daneva   NESMA, Netherlands
Ton Dekkers   NESMA, Netherlands
Onur Demirörs   ODTÜ, Turkey
Jean-Marc Desharnais   ÉTS, University of Quebec, Canada
Reiner Dumke   University of Magdeburg, Germany
Christof Ebert   Vector Consulting, Germany
Thomas Fehlmann   Euro Project Office AG, Switzerland
Filomena Ferrucci   Università di Salerno, Italy
Dan Galorath   Galorath, USA
Çigdem Gencel   Free University of Bolzano-Bozen, Italy
Marcela Genero   University of Castilla-La Mancha, Spain
Naji Habra   PReCISE Research Center University of Namur,
         Belgium

Harold van Heeringen	Sogeti Nederland B.V., Netherlands
Emilio Insfran	Universitat Politècnica de València, Spain
Jens Bæk Jørgensen	Mjølner Informatics A/S, Denmark
Alpay Karagöz	Innova IT Solutions, Turkey
Andrzej Kobyliński	Warsaw School of Economics, Poland
Eberhard Kranich	Euro Project Office AG, Germany
Rob Kusters	Technische Universiteit Eindhoven, Netherlands
Luigi Lavazza	Università degli Studi dell'Insubria, Italy
Jean-Louis Letouzey	Inspearit, France
Mathias Lother	Robert Bosch GmbH, Germany
Beatriz Marín	Universidad Diego Portales, Chile
Roberto Meli	DPO, Italy
Arlene Minkiewicz	PRICE Systems, LLC, UK
Eduardo Miranda	Carnegie Mellon University, USA
Yoshiki Mitani	Japan
Akito Monden	NAIST, Japan
Maurizio Morisio	Politecnico di Torino, Italy
Makoto Nonaka	Tokyo University, Japan
Rory O'Connor	Dublin City University & Lero-ISERC, Ireland
Olga Ormandjieva	Concordia University, Canada
Kai Petersen	Blekinge Institute of Technology/Ericsson AB, Sweden
Keith Phalp	Bournemouth University, UK
Geert Poels	Ghent University, Belgium
Grzegorz Poręcki	Polish Software Measurement Association, Poland
Nicolas Porta	Daimler TSS, Germany
Rudolf Ramler	Software Competence Center Hagenberg GmbH, Austria
Gabriela Robiolo	Universidad Austral, Argentina
Andreas Schmietendorf	Berlin School of Economics and Law and Otto-von-Guericke-Universität Magdeburg, Germany
Asma Sellami	ISIMS, Tunisia
Martin Shepperd	Brunel University, UK
Miroslaw Staron	University of Goetheborg, Sweden
Charles Symons	COSMIC, UK
Jarosław Świerczek	Polish Software Measurement Association, Poland
Ayça Tarhan	Hacettepe University, Turkey
Sylvie Trudel	Université du Québec à Montréal, Canada
Francisco Valdés Souto	SPINGERE, Mexico
Monica Villavicencio	ESPOL, Ecuador
Frank Vogelezang	NESMA, Netherlands
Stefan Wagner	University of Stuttgart, Germany
Dietmar Winkler	Vienna University of Technology, Austria
Chris Woodward	Chris Woodward Associates Ltd., UK

Organization Committee

Grzegorz Poręcki   Polish Software Measurement Association, Poland
Bogumiła Różyńska   Polish Software Measurement Association, Poland

IWSM Mensura Steering Committee

Alain Abran   École de Technologie Supérieure – ETS, Université du
                            Québec, Montréal, Canada
Onur Demirörs   Graduate School of Informatics, Middle East Technical
                            University, Ankara, Turkey

Sponsors

Contents

A Suite of Rules for Developing and Evaluating Software Quality Models

Anas Bassam AL-Badareen[1(✉)], Jean-Marc Desharnais[2],
and Alain Abran[2]

[1] Jerash University, Jerash, Jordan
anas_badareen@hotmail.com
[2] École de Technologie Supérieure, Montreal, Canada
{jean-marc.desharnais, alain.abran}@etsmtl.ca

Abstract. Software quality has become a critical and essential aspect in the success of many software companies and products. Since 1970, a number of software quality models have been proposed to evaluate the quality of general and specific domains of software products. These models suffer from the ambiguity of relationships among quality characteristics, sub characteristics and quality measures: there is no clear definition, rule or procedure on how the quality sub characteristics are derived from the main characteristics, how the quality measures could be identified and associated with quality characteristics and sub characteristics and how those could be validated. This study proposes a set of rules for the development and evaluation of software quality models.

Keywords: Software quality · Quality measures · Quality models · Model rules

1 Introduction

In the last few decades, the use of software products and software-intensive computer systems to perform a wide variety of business and personal functions has increased significantly [1]. High quality software and systems are essential to provide value and avoid any negative consequences that may occur. This is required to achieve personal satisfaction, business success, and human safety [1]. Therefore, quality is considered as one of the main assets that enhance the competitive global position for organizations [2]. To ensure that software quality has been achieved, measuring it is essential. However, for measuring adequately software quality it is necessary to have a sound quality model.

1.1 Software Quality Evaluation

Software quality represents the capability of software product to satisfy stated and implied needs when used under specified conditions [3]. Several methods are available for evaluating the quality of a software product, such as expert review, software measurement, and quality models [4].

© Springer International Publishing Switzerland 2015
A. Kobyliński et al. (Eds.): IWSM-Mensura 2015, LNBIP 230, pp. 1–13, 2015.
DOI: 10.1007/978-3-319-24285-9_1

A number of software quality models have been proposed to measure and control software products. A quality model is a set of characteristics, sub characteristics, quality measures, quality measure elements and relationships between them [3]. It aims to facilitate an objective communication between project managers and technical personnel regarding the quality objectives [5]. The quality characteristics and sub characteristics could represent either the users' views or technical personnel views depending of the quality measures chosen. Quality measures could be associated directly with quality characteristics or sub characteristics (see Fig. 1). Each quality characteristic or sub characteristic could be measured by identifying a set of base and derived measures to cover it, respectively referred to as quality measure elements (QME) and quality measures within ISO 25020 (see Fig. 1). Each base measure is measured independently and then some of these base measures are combined computationally to arrive at a derived measure which may next be combined again along with a corresponding quality characteristic or sub characteristic [1].

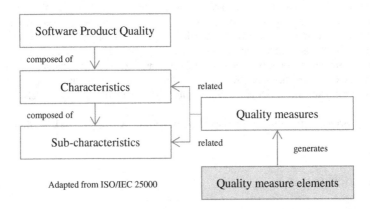

Fig. 1. Adaptation of the ISO 25000 software product quality measurement reference model

1.2 Software Quality Models

Research in software quality has been going on since the 1970s, when software development techniques started to be perceived as an engineering discipline [6]. McCall's model [7] is one of the oldest software quality models [8] that was developed to improve the quality of the software products and to make them measurable. Other models such as that of Boehm's [9], Murine's [10], or Azuma's [11] are derived from it. These derived models added new characteristics, redefined existing characteristics or redefined the relationships between the quality characteristics (characteristics, sub characteristics, quality measures).

According to Ortega [2], the best-known software quality models in chronological order of appearance are: McCall's [7], Boehm's [9], FURPS [12], ISO 9126-1 [13] and Dromey's [14], in addition to the new model of ISO 25010 [1] derived from ISO 9126.

However, ISO standards models of software quality did not eliminate the debate on quality models definitions and these models suffer from a lack of rationale in considering the quality characteristics and the relationships between them [6, 15, 16].

2 Problems Related to Software Quality Models

Several quality models have been proposed in order to evaluate general and specific types of software products [17]. For instance, many models were developed to evaluate the same types of software products. For example, Alvaro [18], Sharma [19] and Upadhyay [20] developed models for evaluating Component Based Software (CB), and Sung [21], Samoladas [22] and del Bianco [23] developed models for evaluating Open Source Software (OSS). Moreover, several comparisons have been made between same models and the same quality characteristics but with different outcomes: such as, Rawashdeh [24], Hamada [25], and Haiguang [26] who made comparisons between McCall's, Boehm's, and ISO 9126 models.

A key difference in the methods of developing and evaluating software quality models is the decomposition of the quality characteristics. The decomposition of the quality characteristics is conducted and evaluated in a subjective manner, based on different perspectives. Indeed, there is a lack of clear definitions for criteria decomposition [15] and most software quality models depend on taxonomic, hierarchical decomposition, and are not following guidelines, which can be arbitrary [16, 27–29]. Therefore, software quality models suffer from a lack of rationale for the relationships between quality characteristics and how the lowest levels properties are composed into an overall assessment of higher level quality characteristics [16].

Unclear decomposition of quality characteristics makes locating their sub characteristics and properties difficult, which leads to redundancy in the quality characteristics and overlapping between quality properties [15]. Consequently, Hofman [6] concludes that there is no commonly accepted model for software quality, and therefore, software engineering does not have yet tools to manipulate the quality level for a product.

3 Software Quality Model Components

ISO 25020 [30] presents the main structure of the ISO software quality model and the relationships between its components (see Fig. 1). The model consists of different levels: characteristic and sub characteristic in one part, and quality measures related to sub characteristics and characteristics. In this article we are not evaluating the relation between the quality measures elements (or base measures) to the quality measures (derived measures).

Quality characteristics are the top level of a software quality model and are often considered as the non functional requirements in software development: they are significant for both software users and project managers as they make the values of software quality meaningful and understandable. These characteristics are chosen during the requirements definition phase, and may be defined according to specific standards, regulations, or laws, and agreed upon by both the project development team and user representatives. The characteristics also address the technical personnel objectives regarding the quality.

The quality characteristics are decomposed into sub characteristics. The sub characteristics are independent and eventually measurable by quality measures. The quality measures could be meaningful to the technical personnel or the project managers and might correspond to more than one characteristic. It is necessary to know the quality measures used to facilitate an objective communication between project managers and technical personnel, and between the software development team and software users regarding the quality objective.

Therefore, to measure the quality characteristic or sub characteristic, it is necessary to identify a collection of quality measures that together aim to cover the characteristic or sub characteristic and obtain data for each quality measures. For information, these quality measures are calculated by applying a measurement function that is derived from quality measures elements (ISO/IEC 25021) [31] or base measures[1] [32].

The hierarchical decomposition of the quality model provides a convenient breakdown of product quality. The relationships identified among the components of the quality model are used to map the values of the low level components (quality measures) into high level components (quality characteristics) in order to present quantitatively the software quality. Therefore, any problem in these relations may lead to a misrepresentation of the quantification, which will cause a miscommunication between technical personnel, project managers and users [16]. Consequently, rules for mapping the quantification from the low level components (quality measures) into higher level components (characteristics) of the software quality model have to be defined.

4   Quality Characteristics Construction

The selected quality characteristics represent the requirements defined and agreed upon by the project stakeholders. These characteristics are defined according to certain conditions as follows:

1. The characteristic represents the requirements needed by at least one of the project stakeholders.
2. The characteristic is understandable and meaningful for each of the project stakeholders.
3. The characteristic is not part of, or required in, any other quality characteristic; it is only required directly by the stakeholders.
4. There are no two characteristics or more intended to achieve the same requirements regarding the software quality.
5. Two or more characteristics can be shared in some sub characteristics or quality measures.

---

[1] The quality measures are the equivalent of derived measures and the quality measure elements are equivalent of base measures within ISO 15939.

The quality characteristics are broad and cannot be measured directly. These characteristics are generally decomposed into sub characteristics. The sub characteristics (or characteristics) are related to quality measures in order to be able to measure the software product during the development life cycle objectively. A quality measure can be a candidate to measure more than one sub characteristic. Figure 2 illustrates the process of decomposing quality characteristics.

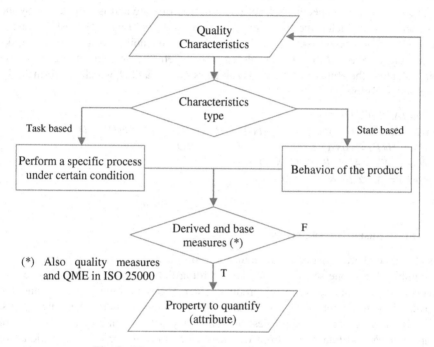

Fig. 2. The process of characteristic decomposition

The first step of decomposing the quality characteristic or sub characteristic is to identify its type. The quality characteristics or sub characteristics can be classified into two main types based on their objectives: task-based and state-based characteristics.

In the context of this article, the task-based characteristics represent the ability to perform a specific process under certain conditions, such as software maintainability and usability. For example, software maintainability represents the ability of modifying a software product after its delivery, and software usability represents the ability of performing specific tasks using the software product.

In the context of this article, the state-based characteristics represent the behavior of the software product when performing a certain task under specific conditions. For example, fault tolerance represents the state of the software product when failure occurs regarding the ability to work, and the efficiency represents the state of the software product when performing a specific task regarding the speed and the resource usage.

4.1 Task-Based Characteristic

In a task-based characteristic, the task represented by the characteristic is decomposed into several sub tasks. For example, the maintainability characteristic aims to evaluate the degree of performing the maintenance process. The maintenance process consists of four main sub tasks: system understanding, analyzing, modifying and testing. The total degrees of measuring the ability to achieve these sub tasks are the ability to perform the main task, which is the maintenance task.

The process F is a specific task (process) in the software and is represented by the characteristic F`, which is the ability to perform the task $Ab(F) = F$`. The task F consists of several sub processes/tasks, A, B, C and D, whereas the ability to achieve these tasks is represented by A`, $B$`, C` and $D$` respectively. Therefore, the ability to achieve the main task (F) is the ability to achieve its sub tasks A, B, C and D, which can formally be expressed as follows:

$F = \{A, B, C, D\}$
With $Ab(F) = F$`, $Ab(A) = A$`, $Ab(B) = B$`, $Ab(C) = C$`, $Ab(D) = D$`.
Then $Ab(F) = Ab(A) \& Ab(B) \& Ab(C) \& Ab(D)$,
Where, F` $= A$` $\& B$` $\& C$` $\& D$`,
$Ab(F) = A$` $\& B$` $\& C$` $\& D$`

4.2 State-Based Characteristic

In state-based characteristic, the different states of the system regarding a certain view are combined into one set. For example, regarding the reliability, fault tolerance represents the state of the software product when a certain failure occurs, and the recoverability represents the state of the software product after the failure occurs. Portability is a degree of effectiveness and efficiency with which a system, product or component can be transferred from one hardware, software or other operational or usage environment to another [1]. In the portability, coexistence represents the behavior of the software when the software environment is changed, and the adaptability represents the state of the software when the hardware environment is changed.

5 Rules of Software Quality Models

Software quality models aim to achieve two main objectives: evaluate the software product and make the evaluation results meaningful for the technical personnel, project managers, and software users. Therefore, the models of software quality are evaluated from two points of view: the ability to measure the software product accurately and exhaustively (Product Evaluation), and the ability to represent the measured values meaningfully (Quality Presentation).

5.1   Product Evaluation

Here, product evaluation is conducted at the different levels in the software quality model: quality measures, sub characteristics and characteristics. This process allows quantifying characteristics, sub characteristics and quality measures, which is the result of the actual values of the quality measure elements (QMEs) in Fig. 1. The quality of this process is affected by the suitability of the QMEs to the quality measures, and the suitability and accuracy of the quality measures to the quality characteristics and sub characteristics.

There is another criterion for measuring a quality model, the model coverage. This criterion shows whether the model includes all quality characteristics required to measure the software product. In general, the number of software characteristics measured in the software product is positively related with the accuracy of the quality representation.

Proposition 1

(a) *The highest number of quality characteristics that are considered in a software product, may result with accurate representation of the quality of a software product.*

(b) *The highest number of sub characteristics that are considered in quality characteristic, may result with a more accurate representation of the quality characteristic.*

(c) *The highest number of quality measures that are considered in sub characteristic, may result with a more accurate representation of the sub characteristic.*

Let QM denote a quality model, QC_i, $1 \leq i \leq n$ denotes a characteristic of the model, and n is the number of the characteristics in the model.

For a quality model $QM = \{QC_1 ... QC_n\}$, $n = |QM|$, *where QC is a quality characteristic in the model.*

For specific software products, the number of software characteristics does not always truly represent the model coverage. That is, software products are different in their characteristics, and not all characteristics exist in every software product. Therefore, for a specific software product, the model coverage measures only the suitable characteristics for a software product.

For a specific software product, the highest number of suitable characteristics considered may result with more representation of the quality of the software product.

For a quality characteristic, the highest number of suitable sub characteristics considered may result with more representation of the quality characteristics.

For a sub characteristic, the highest number of suitable quality measures considered may result with more representation of the sub characteristics.

Proposition 2

(a) *The highest number of suitable quality characteristics considered in a software product, may result with more accurate representation of the quality of software product.*

(b) *The highest number of suitable sub characteristics considered in a quality characteristic, may result with more accurate representation of the quality characteristic.*

(c) *The highest number of suitable quality measures considered in a sub characteristic, may result with more accurate representation of the sub characteristic.*

For a quality model $QM = \{QC_1 \dots QC_n\}$ and software product $P = \{PC_1 \dots PC_m\}$, where QM is a quality model, QC a quality characteristic considered in the model, P a software product, and PC a characteristic of software product.

The coverage of the Quality Model (QM) is only the number of characteristics considered in the model and which exist in the software product. This is represented graphically using a Venn diagram as shown in Fig. 3.

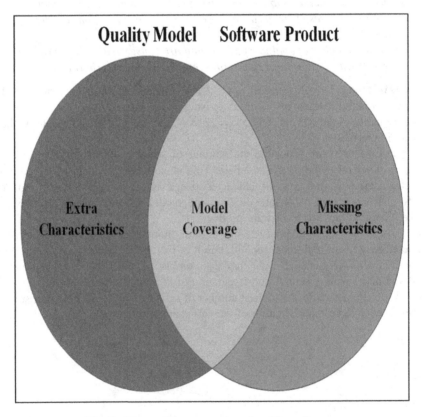

Fig. 3. The model coverage based on Venn diagram

The characteristics which are included in the quality model and which do not exist in the software product represent the extra characteristics in the model, $EC(QM) = QM\backslash P$. The characteristics which exist in the software product and are not considered in the quality model represent the missing characteristics, $MC(QM) = P\backslash QM$. The coverage of the model is only represented by the number of quality characteristics which exist in the software product and are considered in the quality model.

5.2 Quality Presentation

Every quality characteristic represents a set of sub characteristics and every sub characteristic may use a set of quality measures. The quality characteristics within each set are combined based on objectives. For example, the sub characteristics of the same set intend to evaluate the sub tasks of one task or present different states of the software product under specific conditions (depending of the objectives). While the root of the set (quality characteristic) presents the ability to achieve the main task represent the total state of the software product under specific conditions.

Example 1. *Software maintenance is a process of modifying a software product. The maintenance process requires to understand the software product, to analyze the software product to identify where the modification should be done, to develop the intended modification and to test the software product to verify whether the modification was made properly without any side effects. The maintenance task consists of the four sub tasks: understanding, analyzing, modifying and testing. The ability to perform these sub tasks is understandability, analyzability, modifiability and testability respectively. Therefore, the ability to perform the maintenance task (maintainability) is the ability to perform its sub tasks (understandability, analyzability, modifiability and testability).*

Example 2. *The reliability characteristic represents the state of the software product when a failure occurred. Software recoverability represents the state of the software product after the failure occurred and fault tolerance represents the state of the software product during the failure.*

Proposition 3

(a) *The group of quality characteristics within the same set (quality model) must fulfill the conditions of the set.*
(b) *The group of sub characteristics within the same set (quality characteristic) must fulfill the conditions of the set.*
(c) *The group of quality measures within the same set (sub characteristic) must fulfill the conditions of the set.*

The quality model is a set of quality characteristics, each quality characteristic is a set of quality sub characteristics and each quality sub characteristic is a set of quality measures. Let *QM, QC, QSC* and *QMS* denote a quality model, quality characteristic, quality sub characteristic and quality measure respectively. This proposition can be formalized as follows:

- $QM = \{QC_1.....QC_n\}$, for each $QC \subseteq QM$ intends to achieve x, where x is the rules/objective of the set (Quality Model), where $QC_m \nsubseteq QC_n$ and $QC_m \cap QC_n \geq \emptyset$
- $QC = \{QSC_1... QSC_n\}$, for each $QSC \subseteq QC$ intends to achieve x, where x is the rules/objective of the set (Quality Characteristic), where $QSC_m \nsubseteq QSC_n$ and $QSC_m \cap QSC_n \geq \emptyset$
- $QSC = \{QMS_1... QMS_n\}$, for each $QMS \in QSC$ intends to achieve x, where x is the rules/objective of the set(Quality Sub Characteristic), where $QMS_m \neq QMS_n$

The elements/subsets of the same set must fulfill the same conditions regarding the set, but none of these elements/subsets is part of other elements/subsets of the same set. This will result in an inappropriate representation of the element/subset.

Example 3. *As presented in Example 1, a modification is a sub task of a maintenance task, and therefore, the modifiability is a sub characteristic of the maintainability characteristic. However, the modifiability cannot be at the same level with the maintainability. Also the maintainability will not be completely represented by missing one of its sub characteristics (modifiability).*

Proposition 4

a) *For a set of quality characteristics, none of these characteristics is a part of measurement for other characteristic.*
b) *For a set of sub characteristics, none of these sub characteristics is a part of measurement for other sub characteristic.*
c) *For a set of quality measures, none of these measures is a part of measurement for other quality measure.*

- $QM = \{QC_1.....QC_n\}$, for each $QC \subseteq QM$, $QC_m \nsubseteq QC_n$, $QC_m \cap QC_n \geq \emptyset$ and $F(QC_m) \neq QC_n$
  $F(QC_m)$ is the rule of the quality characteristic QC_m
- $QC = \{QSC_1... QSC_n\}$, for each $QSC \subseteq QC$, $QSC_m \nsubseteq QSC_n$, $QSC_m \cap QSC_n \geq \emptyset$ and $F(QSC_m) \neq QSC_n$
  $F(QSC_m)$ is the rule of the quality sub characteristic QSC_m
- $QSC = \{QMS_1... QMS_n\}$, for each $QMS \in QSC$, $QMS_m \neq QMS_n$ and $F(QMS_m) \neq QMS_n$
  $F(QMS_m)$ is the rule of the quality measure QMS_m

Example 4. *Let a quality model QM consists of some quality characteristics A, B and C; the quality characteristic A consists of some sub characteristics D, E and F, and the sub characteristic D consists of some quality measures G, H and I.*

$QC = \{A, B, C\}, A = \{D, E, F\}, D = \{G, H, I\}.$

The following are the candidate relationships between the quality characteristics, sub characteristics and quality measures within the quality model:

1. *New characteristic (X) is added to the model, and it is defined as sub characteristic of D and sub of A at the same time. The problem occurs when the characteristic is represented twice in the set A, which results in an invalid relation.*
   A = {D, E, F, X}, D = {G, H, I, X}, then
   *A = {G, H, I, $\underline{X}$, E, F, $\underline{X}$}, **Invalid***

2. *The quality measure G is removed from sub characteristic D and retained in characteristic A. Characteristic A will not be affected as the required sub characteristics and measures are the same, but sub characteristic D misses one of its quality measures, and consequently, the sub characteristic D is not completely covered.*
   *D = {H, I} and A = {D, E, F, G}, **Invalid***

3. *The quality measure G is removed from the quality characteristic A, and retained in sub characteristic D. The quality characteristic A will not be affected, as it consists of the same sub characteristics and quality measures. The sub characteristic D is not missing any of its values and it will completely represent its meaning.*
   *D = {G, H, I}, A = {D, E, F} ⇒ {G, H, I, E, F}, **Valid***

4. *A new sub characteristic X is required in both quality characteristics B and C. The quality characteristics B and C are at the same level within the same set QM; therefore B∩C = X, **Valid***

6 Conclusions and Future Research

Since the first model of software quality (i.e., McCall's 1977) up until recently when the ISO 25010 model was released, software quality lacks a commonly accepted model or evaluation method. Software quality models were developed and evaluated based on different perspectives. The methods of developing and evaluating software quality models share a common problem, even though these models are used to develop and evaluate software quality models from different perspectives. They suffer from the ambiguity of decomposing quality characteristics and defining their relationships. There is no clear definition of how the quality sub characteristics and properties are derived from the main quality characteristics and how they can be validated. Software quality models have been developed in subjective manner, which make them debatable.

This study, has proposed a suite of rules for developing and evaluating software quality models. The defined rules allow developing clear, reasonable and testable software quality models. Moreover, the rules allow evaluating the attributes of software quality models.

As part of future research, it is also possible to propose a suite of quality measures for evaluating software quality models. It is suggested that a product evaluation collects the base measures for the number of quality characteristics that are required to be measured in the software product and included in the quality model. It is also possible to evaluate the quality aggregation (and correspondingly the presentation of the evaluation into a single aggregated number). The quality aggregation is the process of aggregating the actual values of the quality measures at the lower level of the model to the higher level (i.e., the quality characteristics level).

References

1. ISO/IEC: ISO/IEC 25010 Systems and software engineering - Systems and software Quality Requirements and Evaluation (SQuaRE) - System and software quality models. International Organization for Standardization, Geneva, Switzerland (2014)
2. Ortega, M., Pérez, M., Rojas, T.: Construction of a systemic quality model for evaluating a software product. Softw. Qual. J. **11**, 219–242 (2003)
3. ISO/IEC: Systems and software engineering —Systems and software Quality Requirements and Evaluation (SQuaRE) — Guide to SQuaRE. ISO/IEC FDIS 25000. International Organization for Standardization, Switzerland (2013)
4. Behkamal, B., Kahani, M., Akbari, M.K.: Customizing ISO 9126 quality model for evaluation of B2B applications. Inf. Softw. Technol. **51**, 599–609 (2009)
5. IEEE: IEEE standard for a software quality metrics methodology. IEEE Std 1061–1998 (R2009). The Institute of Electrical and Electronics Engineers, Inc, New York, USA (2009)
6. Hofman, R.: Behavioral economics in software quality engineering. Empir. Softw. Eng. **16**, 278–293 (2011)
7. McCall, J.A., Richards, P.K., Walters, G.F.: Factors in software quality. Rome Air Development Center, Air Force Systems Command, Griffiss Air Force Base (1977)
8. Pfleeger, S.L.: Software Engineering: Theory and Practice. Prentice Hall, Upper Saddle River (2001)
9. Boehm, B.W., Brown, J.R., Kaspar, H., Lipow, M., MacLeod, G.J., Merrit, M.J.: Characteristics of Software Quality, 1st edn. North-Holland, Elsevier Science Ltd (1978)
10. Murine, G., Carpenter, C.: Measuring software product quality. Qual. Prog. **7**, 16–20 (1984)
11. Azuma, M.: Software quality assurance. Vortragsmanuskript zum Vortrag **12** (1987)
12. Grady, R.B., Caswell, D.L.: Software Metrics: Establishing a Company-Wide Program. Prentice Hall, Upper Saddle River (1987)
13. ISO/IEC: ISO/IEC 9126-1: Software engineering-product quality-part 1: quality model. International Organization for Standardization, Geneva, Switzerland (2001)
14. Dromey, R.G.: Cornering the Chimera [Software quality]. IEEE Softw. **13**, 33–43 (1996)
15. Deissenboeck, F., Juergens, E., Lochmann, K., Wagner, S.: Software quality models: purposes, usage scenarios and requirements. In: ICSE 2009 - 7th Workshop on Software Quality (WoSQ' 2009), pp. 9–14. IEEE, Vancouver, Canada (2009)
16. Kitchenham, B., Pfleeger, S.L.: Software quality: the elusive target [Special issues section]. IEEE Softw. **13**, 12–21 (1996)
17. AL-Badareen, A.B., Selamat, M.H., A. Jabar, M., Din, J., Turaev, S.: Software quality models: a comparative study. In: Mohamad Zain, J., Wan Mohd, WMb, El-Qawasmeh, E. (eds.) ICSECS 2011, Part I. CCIS, vol. 179, pp. 46–55. Springer, Heidelberg (2011)
18. Alvaro, A., de Almeida, E.S., Meira, S.L.: A software component quality model: a preliminary evaluation. In: The 32nd EUROMICRO Conference on Software Engineering and Advanced Applications (EUROMICRO-SEAA 2006), vol. 32, pp. 28–37. IEEE, Cavtat/Dubrovnik, Croatia (2006)
19. Sharma, A., Kumar, R., Grover, P.S.: Estimation of quality for software components – an empirical approach. SIGSOFT Softw. Eng. Notes **33**, 1–10 (2008)

20. Upadhyay, N., Despande, B.M., Agrawal, V.P.: Towards a software component quality model. In: Meghanathan, N., Kaushik, B.K., Nagamalai, D. (eds.) CCSIT 2011, Part I. CCIS, vol. 131, pp. 398–412. Springer, Heidelberg (2011)
21. Sung, W.J., Kim, J.H., Rhew, S.Y.: A quality model for open source software selection. In: Sixth International Conference on Advanced Language Processing and Web Information Technology (ALPIT 2007), pp. 515–519, Henan, China (2007)
22. Samoladas, I., Gousios, G., Spinellis, D., Stamelos, I.: The SQO-OSS quality model: measurement based open source software evaluation. In: Russo, B., Damiani, E., Hissam, S., Lundell, B., Succi, G. (eds.) Open Source Development, Communities and Quality, vol. 275, pp. 237–248. Springer, Heidelberg (2008)
23. del Bianco, V., Lavazza, L., Morasca, S., Taibi, D.: Quality of open source software: the QualiPSo trustworthiness model. In: Boldyreff, C., Crowston, K., Lundell, B., Wasserman, A.I. (eds.) OSS 2009. IFIP AICT, vol. 299, pp. 199–212. Springer, Heidelberg (2009)
24. Rawashdeh, A., Matalkah, B.: A new software quality model for evaluating cots components. J. Comput. Sci. **2**, 373–381 (2006)
25. Hamada, A.A., Moustafa, M.N., Shaheen, H.I.: Software quality model analysis program. In: International Conference on Computer Engineering & Systems (ICCES 2008), pp. 296–300. IEEE, Cairo, Egypt (2008)
26. Haiguang, F.: Modeling and analysis for educational software quality hierarchy triangle. In: Seventh International Conference on Web-based Learning (ICWL 2008), pp. 14–18. IEEE, Jinhua, China (2008)
27. Broy, M., Deissenboeck, F., Pizka, M.: Demystifying maintainability. In: The 2006 International Workshop on Software Quality, pp. 21–26. ACM, Shanghai, China (2006)
28. Deissenboeck, F., Wagner, S., Pizka, M., Teuchert, S., Girard, J.F.: An activity-based quality model for maintainability. In: The 23rd IEEE International Conference on Software Maintenance (ICSM 2007), pp. 184–193. IEEE, Paris, France (2007)
29. Kitchenham, B., Linkman, S., Pasquini, A., Nanni, V.: The SQUID approach to defining a quality model. Softw. Qual. J. **6**, 211–233 (1997)
30. ISO/IEC: Software engineering — Software product Quality Requirements and Evaluation (SQuaRE) — Measurement reference model and guide. ISO/IEC 25020. International Organization for Standardization, Switzerland (2007)
31. ISO/IEC: System and software engineering – System and software product Quality Requirements and Evaluation (SQuaRE) – Quality measure elements. ISO/IEC 25021. International Organization for Standardization, Switzerland (2011)
32. ISO/IEC: Systems and software engineering — Measurement process. ISO/IEC 15939. International Organization for Standardization, Switzerland (2007)

The Effects of Duration-Based Moving Windows with Estimation by Analogy

Sousuke Amasaki[1]([✉]) and Chris Lokan[2]

[1] Okayama Prefectural University, Soja, Okayama, Japan
amasaki@cse.oka-pu.ac.jp
[2] School of Engineering and Information Technology, UNSW Canberra,
Canberra, ACT 2600, Australia
c.lokan@adfa.edu.au

Abstract. Context: Recent studies have revealed that estimation accuracy can be affected by only using a window of recent projects as training data for building an effort estimation model. The studies also showed that the effect and its extent could be affected by effort estimation methods and windowing policies (fixed size or fixed duration). However, a study of perhaps the most common situation — using Estimation by Analogy (EbA) for effort estimation, and only considering as training data projects completed recently in windows defined by duration — is lacking.
Objective: To investigate the effects on estimation accuracy of using the fixed-duration windowing policy, particularly in comparison to fixed-size windows, when using EbA.
Method: Using a single-company ISBSG data set studied previously in similar research, we examine the effects of using a fixed-duration windowing policy on the accuracy of estimates using EbA. As a preliminary step, we evaluate the effect of some changes to how we apply EbA itself.
Results: Fixed-duration windows can improve the accuracy of estimates with EbA. Some window sizes lead to statistically significant improvements. Reinforcing previous research, the effect is smaller and is seen in a narrower range of window sizes than when fixed-size windows are used.
Conclusions: Fixed-duration windows are helpful with this data set when using EbA. Variations in the settings for EbA can change the sizes at which windows are helpful. This suggests the need for reviewing optimal window sizes when adopting a new setting of EbA.

1 Introduction

Accurate effort estimation is an essential key to software project success. Many studies have sought to improve the accuracy of methods and models for estimating software development effort.

A software effort estimation model is developed from past project data. Most studies evaluate the accuracy of software effort estimation models using cross-validation. This approach uses data from all other projects to estimate the effort of a given project. For all but the last project, this means that data from projects that are still in the future are used when estimating the effort for the new project.

© Springer International Publishing Switzerland 2015
A. Kobyliński et al. (Eds.): IWSM-Mensura 2015, LNBIP 230, pp. 14–29, 2015.
DOI: 10.1007/978-3-319-24285-9_2

This makes no sense. Another evaluation approach exploits the reality that software projects can be arranged chronologically. It uses data from past projects as training data to predict new projects. Intuitively, it may also make sense to use only recent projects as a basis for effort estimation: older projects might be less representative of an organization's current practices. Lokan and Mendes [1] examined whether using only recent projects improves estimation accuracy. They used a window to limit the size of training data so that an effort estimation model used only recently finished projects. As projects finish, they replace old projects in the window. The results supported the advantage of the windowing approach.

Recent studies also showed the effect and its extent could be affected by windowing policies [2,3] and effort estimation models [4]. Lokan and Mendes [2,3] compared two types of window policies: fixed-size and fixed-duration. A fixed-size window policy determines the window size by the number of projects: the training set is the last N projects to finish before the target project starts. A fixed-duration policy determines the window size by calendar months: the training set is projects whose whole life cycle occurred during the last w months before the target project starts. They found that estimation accuracy could improve by using either window policy, but the policies affected the accuracy differently.

Amasaki and Lokan [4] examined the applicability of the windowing approach (using fixed-size windows) to Estimation by Analogy (EbA). The previous studies only used linear regression (LR), EbA and LR are both common approaches for estimating effort. The results showed difference in accuracy between using and not using the windowing approach. However, the effect of using a window was weaker with EbA than with LR.

This paper continues research into the use of windows with EbA. It focuses primarily on the effect of changing the windowing policy, from fixed size to fixed duration. This is relevant because arguably fixed-duration windows make more intuitive sense than fixed-size windows. In practice, we believe that people considering "windows of recent projects" think naturally in terms of window duration, not the number of training projects in the window. The use of windows of different durations with EbA has not previously been studied, but we believe it is commonly in estimators' minds.

First we must investigate the effect of changing some details of how we apply EbA in this paper, to improve its realism compared to [4].

We address the following questions:

RQ1. Is there a difference in the accuracy of estimates between EbA as used in [4] and EbA based on a more realistic situation, still using fixed-size windows?
RQ2. Is there a difference in the accuracy of estimates with and without windows, using the revised EbA, and using fixed-duration windows?
RQ3. How do these results compare with results based on fixed-size windows?

2   Related Work

Research in software effort estimation models has a long history. However, few studies evaluated software effort estimation models with consideration of the chronological order of projects.

Mendes and Lokan [5] compared estimates based on a growing portfolio with estimates based on leave-one-out cross-validation, using two different data sets. In both cases, the cross-validation estimates showed significantly superior accuracy. With cross-validation, all other projects in the data set — even some that were still in the future — are used as training data for a given project. Thus, estimates using cross-validation are based on unrealistic information. If estimates based on unrealistic information are significantly more accurate than estimates considering chronology (based on realistic information), the implication is that the apparent accuracy achieved when ignoring chronology does not reflect what an estimator would achieve in practice.

To the best of our knowledge, Kitchenham et al. [6] first mentioned the use of moving windows. As a result of an experiment, they argued that old projects should be removed from the data set as new ones came in so that the size of the dataset remained constant. MacDonell and Shepperd [7] investigated moving windows as part of a study of how well data from prior phases in a project could be used to estimate later phases. They found that accuracy was better when a moving window of the five most recent projects was used as training data, rather than using all completed projects as training data.

Lokan and Mendes [1] studied the use of moving windows with linear regression models (LR) and a single-company dataset from the ISBSG repository. Training sets were defined to be the N most recently completed projects. They found that the use of a window could affect accuracy significantly; predictive accuracy was better with larger windows; some window sizes were 'sweet spots'. Later they also investigated the effect on accuracy when using moving windows of various durations to form training sets on which to base effort estimates [2,3]. They showed that the use of windows based on duration can affect the accuracy of estimates, but to a lesser extent than windows based on a fixed number of projects.

Amasaki and Lokan [4] examined the applicability of the windowing approach to Estimation by Analogy (EbA) in addition to LR. They found ranges of window sizes for which it was significantly better to use a window, with both regression and estimation by analogy. The effect of using a window was stronger with regression. They focused on the effects of the fixed-size windowing approach and left as future work an investigation for the fixed-duration window approach.

This study builds on both [4] and [3]. It extends [4] by changing details of EbA to improve the realism in practical use. It also differs from [4] in using duration as the basis for defining window size. This study also extends [3] by adopting EbA instead of LR to explore the effects of moving windows.

3   Research Method

3.1   Dataset Description

The data set used in this paper is the same one analyzed in [1–4]. This data set is sourced from Release 10 of the ISBSG Repository. Release 10 contains data for 4106 projects; however, not all projects provided the chronological data we needed (i.e. known duration and completion date, from which we could calculate start date), and those that did varied in data quality and definitions. To form a data set in which all projects provided the necessary data for size, effort and chronology, defined size and effort similarly, and had high quality data, we removed projects according to the following criteria:

- The projects are rated by ISBSG as having high data quality (A or B).
- Implementation date and overall project elapsed time are known.
- Size is measured in IFPUG 4.0 or later (because size measured with an older version is not directly comparable with size measured with IFPUG version 4.0 or later). We also removed projects that measured size with an unspecified version of function points, and whose completion pre-dated IFPUG version 4.0.
- The size in unadjusted function points is known.
- Development team effort (resource level 1) is known. Our analysis used only the development team's effort.
- Normalized effort and recorded effort are equivalent. This should mean that the reported effort is the actual effort across the whole life cycle.
- The projects are not web projects.

In the remaining set of 909 projects, 231 were all from the same organization and 678 were from other organizations. We only selected the 231 projects from the single organization, as we considered that the use of single-company data was more suitable to answer our research questions than using cross-company data. Preliminary analysis showed that three projects were extremely influential and invariably removed from model building, so they were removed from the set. The final set contained 228 projects.

We do not know the identity of the organization that developed these projects.

Release 10 of the ISBSG database provides data on numerous variables; however, this number was reduced to a small set that we have found in past analyses with this dataset to have an impact on effort, and which did not suffer from a large number of missing data values. The remaining variables were size (measured in unadjusted function points), effort (hours), and four categorical variables: development type (new development, re-development, enhancement), primary language type (3GL, 4GL), platform (mainframe, midrange, PC, multi-platform), and industry sector (banking, insurance, manufacturing, other).

Table 1 shows summary statistics for size (measured in unadjusted function points), effort, and project delivery rate (PDR). PDR is calculated as effort divided by size; high project delivery rates indicate low productivity. In [1], the

Table 1. Summary statistics for ratio-scaled variables

Variable	Mean	Median	StDev	Min	Max
Size	496	266	699	10	6294
Effort	4553	2408	6212	62	57749
PDR	16.47	8.75	31.42	0.53	387.10

authors examined the project delivery rate and found it changes across time. This finding supports the use of a window.

The projects were developed for a variety of industry sectors, where insurance, banking and manufacturing were the most common. Start dates range from 1994 to 2002, although only 9 started before 1998. 3GLs are used by 86 % of projects; mainframes account for 40 %, and multi-platform for 55 %; these percentages for language and platform vary little from year to year. There is a trend over time towards more enhancement projects and fewer new developments. Enhancement projects tend to be smaller than new development, so there is a corresponding trend towards lower size and effort.

This study adopted the same range of window sizes as [3]. The smallest window size was based on the statistical significance of linear regression with windowed project data. The largest window size was based on the necessary number of testing projects for evaluation. The window ranges for the fixed-size policy is from 20 to 120 projects; those for the fixed-duration policy is 12 to 84 months.

3.2   Modeling Techniques

This study used Estimation by Analogy (EbA) to estimate efforts. EbA is a model-free method [8] and does not construct a model. Instead, EbA has several options to be optimized for a specific dataset [9].

In [4], the settings for EbA were as follows:

- Effort and Size were transformed to a natural logarithmic scale.
- The similarity between projects was based on Euclidean distance.
- An estimate was obtained from the arithmetic mean of logarithmic efforts of similar projects.
- Independent variables were selected with the wrapper approach [10], minimizing median MRE, on the basis of the whole dataset.

The last setting is unrealistic, in that only for the last project is the whole data set available. In practice, variables should be selected for each new estimation based on the past project data available at that time. The reason for doing a single variable selection based on the whole data set in [4] was that the wrapper approach was computationally expensive. A light weight variable selection method can resolve this problem. Furthermore, the application of EbA with these settings can be improved to improve the estimation accuracy.

This study mitigated these problems as follows:

- Select independent variables separately for every new project. This improves realism.
- Select independent variables with Lasso [11], minimizing the mean squared error. This involves less computation than using the wrapper approach.
- Adopt inverse rank weighted mean (IRWM) [12] to obtain estimates. This method was a simple method for better estimation.

The number of neighbors k we considered was $k = 1, 2, 3, 5$, as in [4].

3.3   Effort Estimation on Chronologically-Ordered Projects

This study evaluated the effects of moving windows of several sizes along with a timeline of projects' history. The effects were measured by performance comparisons between moving windows and a growing portfolio. A growing portfolio uses all past projects as the training set.

For a window of size w, this evaluation was performed as follows:

1. Sort all projects by start date
2. Find the earliest project p_0 for which using that window size could make a difference to the training set: that is, at least one project that had finished by the start of p_0 was "too old" to be included in the window.
3. For every project p_i in chronological sequence (ordered by start date), starting from p_0, form estimates using moving windows and using a growing portfolio.
   - For fixed-duration moving windows, the training set is the finished projects whose whole life cycle had fallen within a window of size w months prior to the start of p_i.
   - For fixed-size moving windows, the training set is the w projects that finished most recently prior to the start of p_i.
   - For the growing portfolio, the training set is all of the projects that had finished before the start of p_i.
4. Evaluate estimation results.

3.4   Performance Measures

Performance measures for effort estimation models are based on the difference between estimated effort and actual effort. As in previous studies, this study used MMRE and MMAE [13] for performance evaluation.

To test for statistically significant differences between accuracy measures, we used the Wilcoxon ranked sign test and set statistical significance level at $\alpha = 0.05$. We used the test as is because we focused on the significance of each window size, not all sizes.

Table 2. Accuracy with the modified EbA with $k = 5$ (growing and fixed-size moving windows)

Window size(N)	Testing projects	Growing MAE	Window MAE	p–val.	Growing MRE	Window MRE	p–val.
20	201	2936	2838	0.36	1.53	1.45	0.06
30	178	2656	2759	0.50	1.46	1.50	0.80
40	165	2582	2785	0.34	1.43	1.54	0.41
50	153	2572	2684	0.89	1.46	1.53	0.83
60	136	2486	2353	0.06	1.54	1.43	0.08
70	126	2341	2142	0.01	1.54	1.39	0.01
80	126	2341	2298	0.29	1.54	1.56	0.32
90	111	2449	2302	0.08	1.56	1.39	0.04
100	88	2501	2504	0.21	1.49	1.62	0.21
110	75	2243	2200	0.06	1.53	1.51	0.11
120	71	2251	2274	0.36	1.52	1.52	0.76

4   Results

4.1   The Effects of Changes in EbA

We begin by comparing estimation accuracy between EbA as used in [4] and EbA as adopted in this paper. The difference between them is the realism in practical use.

Table 2 shows the effect of fixed-size windowing with EbA as adopted in this paper, on mean absolute residuals and mean MRE. Here the number of neighbors was $k = 5$, which showed better performance than $k = 2$, the number used in [4]. The first column shows window sizes. The 2nd column shows the total number of projects used as a target project with the corresponding window size. The 3rd and 4th columns show accuracy measures of the growing portfolio and the moving windows based on MAE. The 5th column shows the p–value from statistical tests on accuracy measures based on MAE between the growing portfolio and the moving windows. The 6th and 7th columns show accuracy measures of the growing portfolio and the moving windows based on MRE. The 8th column shows the p–value from statistical tests on accuracy measures based MRE between the growing portfolio and the moving windows. The results were computed for every size; the tables only show every 10 sizes, due to space limitations. This is sufficient to show the essential trends.

Figure 1 shows the difference in mean MAE and mean MRE between the growing portfolio and moving windows with the modified EbA with $k = 5$. The x-axis is the number of projects in the window, and the y-axis is the subtraction of the accuracy measure value with a growing portfolio from that with moving windows at the given x-value (expressed in relative percentage terms). Smaller values of MAE and MRE are better, so the window is advantageous where the

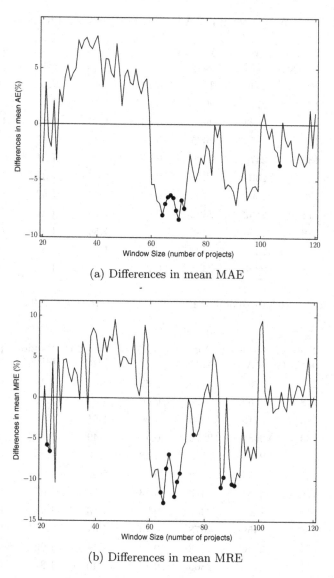

(a) Differences in mean MAE

(b) Differences in mean MRE

Fig. 1. Results with Fixed-size Window, modified EbA with $k = 5$

line is below 0. Circle points mean a statistically significant difference, in favor of moving windows.

Figure 1 and Table 2 revealed characteristics of moving windows compared to the growing portfolio:

- With windows of up to 60 projects, MAE showed no significant preference for any approach. The line starts below zero and quickly goes above zero (favoring the growing portfolio), but the difference was not significant as shown in

Table 3. Accuracy with EbA as used in [4] (repeated from [4])

Window size(N)	Testing projects	Growing MAE	Window MAE	p–val.	Growing MRE	Window MRE	p–val.
20	201	2943	3162	0.19	1.42	2.24	0.32
30	178	2711	2976	0.44	1.41	1.95	0.65
40	165	2623	2923	0.59	1.36	1.83	0.55
50	153	2575	2675	0.76	1.35	2.17	0.88
60	136	2479	2436	0.09	1.48	1.54	0.11
70	126	2305	2243	0.19	1.46	1.37	0.21
80	126	2305	2304	0.60	1.46	1.52	0.58
90	111	2662	2362	0.05	1.66	1.47	0.04
100	88	2735	2584	0.60	1.59	1.46	0.51
110	75	2467	2407	0.52	1.64	1.54	0.39
120	71	2465	2351	0.28	1.61	1.51	0.29

Table 4. Accuracy with the modified EbA with $k = 2$ (growing and fixed-size moving windows)

Window size(N)	Testing projects	Growing MAE	Window MAE	p–val.	Growing MRE	Window MRE	p–val.
20	201	2891	2918	0.82	1.57	1.48	0.55
30	178	2769	2926	0.66	1.53	1.51	0.57
40	165	2718	2950	0.96	1.51	1.80	0.62
50	153	2682	2872	0.43	1.49	1.86	0.31
60	136	2541	2505	0.18	1.56	1.48	0.26
70	126	2364	2362	0.41	1.58	1.70	0.47
80	126	2364	2479	0.83	1.58	1.65	0.51
90	111	2461	2382	0.33	1.53	1.41	0.19
100	88	2459	2878	0.73	1.37	1.81	0.86
110	75	2216	2702	0.73	1.41	1.92	0.91
120	71	2199	2805	0.17	1.40	1.87	0.16

Fig. 1(a). MRE showed a similar trend, except that moving windows were sometimes significantly advantageous around small window sizes, as shown in Fig. 1(b).

- For windows of 60 to 100 projects, moving windows are advantageous in MAE. There were several window sizes around 60 to 75 projects where the difference is significant, as shown in Fig. 1(a). The difference in MRE showed a similar trend, again with a significant advantage around 60 to 75 projects but also at several sizes around 90 projects.

- With windows of 100 projects or more, both measures showed no clear preference for windows or growing.

In summary, in this data set, moving windows improved estimation accuracy significantly with windows in the middle of the range of sizes investigated.

Comparing these results to [4], in the previous paper the effects of fixed-size moving windows were as follows:

- With a window of 20 to 55 projects, all measures were always better using the growing portfolio though the difference was not statistically significant.
- With a window of 90 or 91 projects, all measures were better using the moving windows and the difference is statistically significant. Although there were the only sizes where the difference was statistically significant, these were not just "lucky" window sizes: at nearly all window sizes from 61 to 120 projects, average values of all of the accuracy statistics were better with the moving windows.

Two things have changed between [4] and here: how EbA was applied, and the choice of the best value for k. To separate the effect of the two changes, we present two tables. Table 3 repeats the results from [4], for convenience. Table 4 presents an intermediate stage: it shows the accuracy with the modified EbA but with k held at 2. Thus the difference between Tables 3 and 4 shows the effect of modifying EbA, and the difference between Tables 4 and 2 shows the subsequent effect of changing k.

Most of the values in Table 4 are similar to or worse than the corresponding values in Table 3. This implies that the modification to EbA reduces the accuracy of the estimates. This may be because variable selection was done once in [4], using the entire data set; hence insights drawn from the whole data set were used in variable selection for every project, even early ones in the sequence. Less information is available for most projects in the modified approach, which could make the estimates less accurate.

However, most of the values in Table 2 are better than the corresponding values in Table 3. Increasing k from 2 to 5 more than overcomes the loss of accuracy in modifying the EbA approach.

Overall, the change in EbA, which is aimed at improving the realism of the estimation procedure and reducing computation effort, has also improved the estimation accuracy when combined with a change in k. Estimates are more accurate on average, and need fewer comparison projects for windows to be valuable: using the modified approach, windows were significantly better than the growing approach at windows of around 60 to 75 projects, according to MAE, and around 60 to 90 according to MRE, instead of 90 projects with the original method.

Table 2 and Fig. 1 present the best results for this data set, using windows defined as containing a fixed number of projects. In the next section we perform a similar experiment, using the same estimation method, but defining windows as covering fixed numbers of months.

Table 5. Accuracy with modified EbA with $k = 5$ (growing and fixed-duration moving windows)

Window size(N)	Testing projects	Growing MAE	Window MAE	p–val.	Growing MRE	Window MRE	p–val.
12	165	2582	2757	0.56	1.43	1.49	0.88
18	193	2834	2947	0.83	1.47	1.54	0.80
24	201	2936	2816	0.29	1.53	1.45	0.55
30	202	2940	2866	0.53	1.52	1.39	0.63
36	206	2940	2836	0.81	1.50	1.41	0.63
42	206	2940	2728	0.34	1.50	1.39	0.45
48	206	2940	2787	0.43	1.50	1.42	0.68
54	206	2940	2898	0.44	1.50	1.39	0.52
60	198	2951	2925	0.72	1.54	1.46	0.57
66	184	2776	2726	0.76	1.46	1.41	0.57
72	153	2572	2468	0.09	1.46	1.36	0.05
78	126	2341	2257	0.07	1.54	1.45	0.04
84	80	2461	2364	0.16	1.61	1.55	0.26

4.2   The Effects of Moving Windows of Fixed Duration

Table 5 shows the effect of the fixed-duration windowing, with the modified EbA with $k = 5$, on mean absolute residuals and mean MRE. Figure 2 shows the difference in mean MAE and mean MRE between the growing portfolio and moving windows. The notation is as same as in Fig. 1, except that the x-axis is now the window duration in months. The table and the figure reveal the following:

- With windows of up to 20 months, the growing portfolio was advantageous in terms of MAE. No difference was statistically significant. The advantage was not clear in MRE for that range.
- With windows of 20 to 50 months, the lines go down under the zero line and support the moving windows in terms of average differences in MAE and MRE. However, statistical tests showed no statistically significant differences. The lines then go back to close to zero.
- With windows of more than 55 months, moving windows are advantageous again. There were significant differences between 70 to 80 months, supporting the moving windows.

In [3], the authors used the same dataset, the same range of window durations, and linear regression to examine the effects of fixed-duration windows. Thus the difference between this work and [3] is the use of EbA instead of linear regression. The observations in [3] were:

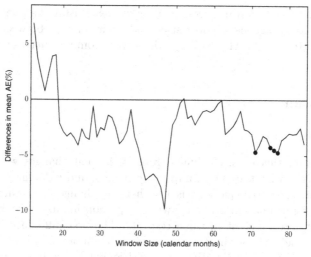

(a) Differences in mean MAE

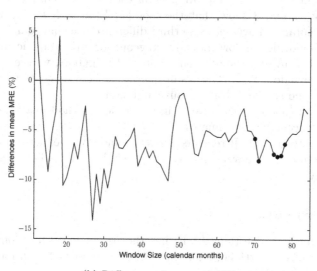

(b) Differences in mean MRE

Fig. 2. Results with Fixed-duration Windows, EbA with $k = 5$

- With windows up to 24 months, the growing portfolio was advantageous. Statistical tests sometimes supported the growing portfolio.
- With windows between 24 to 50 months, moving windows were advantageous. There were some window sizes where the difference was statistically significant.
- With larger windows, the difference got smaller, and there was no statistical difference between the growing portfolio and moving windows.

The observations in [3] and the results in this paper show different trends. The window durations at which windows are advantageous compared to the growing portfolio are larger with EbA than with LR, and the range of durations for which windows are advantageous is narrower with EbA than with LR. The difference in advantageous window sizes and their number between EbA and LR were reported in [4]. These observations were common between this study and [4].

5   Discussion

5.1   Answer to RQ1

The first part of this research differs from [4] in that changes were made in settings for EbA, with the aim of improving realism and reducing computation effort. Our first research question is whether the change in settings makes a difference to the estimation accuracy, while still adopting fixed-size windows.

The results are different in three respects. The first difference is a change in the optimal setting for the best number of neighbors, k. Previously $k = 2$ was best. The change in estimation method brought a new best setting $k = 5$. The second difference is an improvement in estimation accuracy. Comparison between Tables 2 and 3 show that the modifed EbA with $k = 5$ has better estimation accuracy on average. The third difference is a change in the window sizes at which moving windows are advantageous for estimation accuracy. With the changes to EbA and the optimal number of neighbors, we see a change of advantageous window sizes. The result shows a wider range of advantageous window sizes, and smaller advantageous window sizes.

We thus conclude that the change in estimation method made a difference, improving the accuracy of estimates.

This result updates [4]. It repeated the same underlying experiment, in which the key is the use of fixed-size windows and EbA, but with a better method for applying EbA.

5.2   Answer to RQ2

The second research question is whether the use of fixed-duration windows, instead of a growing portfolio, makes a difference to estimation accuracy when the new EbA is adopted.

Figure 2 showed the general trend that when using fixed-duration moving windows instead of a growing portfolio, the estimation accuracy improved as the window size increased. The differences are statistically significant at several surations between 70 to 80 months. The general trend looked similar to that with LR, as shown in [3], although the window sizes where the moving windows were significantly advantageous are different.

We thus conclude that fixed-duration windows can make a difference, and are effective to improve estimation accuracy.

5.3   Answer to RQ3

Table 2 and Fig. 1 present the results for this data set, using the modified EbA method and using windows defined as containing a fixed number of projects. Table 5 and Fig. 2 present the corresponding results when windows are defined as having fixed duration instead of containing a fixed number of projects.

From RQ1 and RQ2 we see that both windowing approaches can lead to significantly better estimation accuracy.

Figure 1 shows that at the window sizes where fixed-size windows lead to significantly better estimates than the growing portfolio, the improvement in MAE is around 7–9 % and the improvement in MRE is mostly around 12 %. With fixed-duration windows, as seen in Fig. 2, significant improvements in MAE are around 5 % and significant improvements in MRE are around 7–9 %. Thus the gains are smaller with fixed-duration windows.

With fixed-duration windows, the number of advantageous window sizes is smaller with EbA than with LR. This was also observed in [4]; this property was maintained in this study despite the changes to EbA and window policies. The degree of the improvement was weaker than that obtained with fixed-size windows. This characteristic was also observed in [3].

These observations imply that the use of fixed-size windows has more impact on estimation accuracy than the use of fixed-duration windows, at least with this dataset. The difference of datasets caused the difference of the effects of the moving windows as shown in [3]. Further study with other datasets is an area for future work.

5.4   What are the Practical Implications of this Study?

The implications of this study are as follows:

First, moving windows are suggested as an alternative approach to effort estimation for companies instead of using the whole history of past data. They have been shown now to be effective with the two most common estimation methods, LR and EbA. Research is still needed on the use of moving windows with other estimation methods.

Second, although it is more natural to think in terms of durations of windows rather than the number of projects in windows, in this data set the fixed-size window policy is more effective than the fixed-duration window policy. This has been shown using both LR and EbA. Practitioners may need to change their thinking, such that how many projects are available from which to learn might be more important than how recent the projects are.

Third, effective window sizes might be different even among practitioners. EbA resembles practitioners' thinking. Changes to how they arrive at an estimate may change the number of projects they should consider. This can result in a change to advantageous window sizes. This may partly explain why practitioners can make different estimates while drawing on the same repository of data about past projects.

6   Threats to Validity

This study has some threats to validity in common with previous studies.

First, we used only one dataset. The dataset is a convenience sample and may not be representative of software projects in general. Thus, the results may not be generalized beyond this dataset; this is true of all studies based on convenience samples. We trust that some potential sources of variation are avoided by the selection of a single-company dataset. Since the dataset is large and covers several years, we assume it is a fair representation of this organization's projects. The inclusion of the industry sector as an independent variable helps to allow for variations among sectors in the dataset. Experiments with other datasets are our major future work.

Second, this study applied EbA in a specific way. EbA has several options to be optimized for a specific dataset, as shown in [9], and high-quality models are dataset-driven in nature. Our choice of method might have missed more accurate or more realistic methods. Based on our past experience building models manually, we believe that the approach used here is acceptable, and the variable selection approach is more realistic than previously studied in [4].

7   Conclusions

This paper investigated the effect on the accuracy of effort estimation using EbA, when moving windows are used to retain only "recent" training data and the windows are of fixed durations.

The use of fixed-duration windows was able to improve the accuracy of estimates, in terms of both MAE and MRE, compared to the growing portfolio in which the entire history of training data is retained.

The advantage over a growing portfolio from using fixed-duration windows was smaller than the advantage from using fixed-size windows. The same was found in [3], in which LR was used rather than EbA as the estimation approach.

The paper has made these contributions:

– Changes were proposed and evaluated to how EbA was applied in [4], to improve its realism in practice and to reduce the computational effort. The changes improved the accuracy of estimates, and the useful window sizes were smaller so less data needed to be retained.
– Windows based on duration can improve the accuracy of estimation by analogy. This is useful because estimation by analogy is very common, and anecdotally filtering of projects based on recency is also very common. Past research has shown that fixed-duration windows help less than fixed-size windows, and windows help less with EbA than with LR. Evidence that duration-based windows can be effective with EbA is valuable.

The above observations were obtained using one specific approach to EbA, with one dataset. Our future work involves generalization with other settings: other companies' datasets and perhaps other options for EbA such as using recency as part of the distance metric [14] and greedy search for feature selection [15].

Acknowledgment. The authors would like to thank the anonymous reviewers for their thoughtful comments and helpful suggestions on the first version of this paper. This work was partially supported by JSPS KAKENHI Grant #25330083 and #15K15975.

References

1. Lokan, C., Mendes, E.: Applying moving windows to software effort estimation. In: Proceedings of ESEM 2009, pp. 111–122 (2009)
2. Lokan, C., Mendes, E.: Investigating the use of duration-based moving windows to improve software effort prediction. In: Proceedings of APSEC 2012, pp. 818–827 (2012)
3. Lokan, C., Mendes, E.: Investigating the use of duration-based moving windows to improve software effort prediction: a replicated study. Inf. Softw. Technol. **56**(9), 1063–1075 (2014)
4. Amasaki, S., Lokan, C.: The effects of moving windows to software estimation: comparative study on linear regression and estimation by analogy. In: 2012 Joint Conference of 22nd International Workshop on Software Measurement and the 7th International Conference on Software Process and Product Measurement (IWSM-MENSURA), pp. 23–32. IEEE, October 2012
5. Mendes, E., Lokan, C.: Investigating the use of chronological splitting to compare software cross-company and single-company effort predictions: a replicated study. In: Proceedings of EASE 2009 (2009)
6. Kitchenham, B., Pfleeger, S.L., McColl, B., Eagan, S.: An empirical study of maintenance and development estimation accuracy. J. Syst. Softw. **64**(1), 57–77 (2002)
7. MacDonell, S.G., Shepperd, M.: Data accumulation and software effort prediction. In: Proceedings of the 2010 ACM-IEEE International Symposium on Empirical Software Engineering and Measurement. ACM (2010)
8. Hastie, T., Tibshirani, R., Friedman, J.: The Elements of Statistical Learning: Data Mining Inference and Prediction. Springer, New York (2009)
9. Kocaguneli, E., Menzies, T., Bener, A., Keung, J.W.: Exploiting the essential assumptions of analogy-based effort estimation. IEEE Trans. Softw. Eng. **38**(2), 425–438 (2012)
10. Dejaeger, K., Verbeke, W., Martens, D., Baesens, B.: Data mining techniques for software effort estimation: a comparative study. IIEEE Trans. Softw. Eng. **38**, 2354–2364 (2011)
11. Tibshirani, R.: Regression shrinkage and selection via the lasso. J. Roy. Stat. Soc. Ser. B **58**, 267–288 (1996)
12. Mendes, E., Watson, I., Triggs, C., Mosley, N., Counsell, S.: A comparative study of cost estimation models for web hypermedia applications. Empirical Softw. Eng. **8**(2), 163–196 (2003)
13. Port, D., Korte, M.: Comparative studies of the model evaluation criterions MMRE and PRED in software cost estimation research. In: Proceedings of ESEM 2008. ACM (2008)
14. Kolodner, J.: Case-Based Reasoning. Morgan-Kaufmann, San Mateo (1993)
15. Kirsopp, C., Shepperd, M., Hart, J.: Search heuristics, case-based reasoning and software project effort prediction. In: GECCO 2002: Genetic and Evolutionary Computation Conference. AAAI (2002)

Software or Service? That's the Question!

Luigi Buglione[1,2(✉)], Alain Abran[2], Christiane Gresse von
Wangenheim[3], Fergal Mc Caffery[4], and Jean Carlo Rossa Hauck[3]

[1] Engineering Ingegneria Informatica Spa, Via R. Morandi 32, 00148 Rome, Italy
luigi.buglione@eng.it
[2] Ecole de Technologie Supérieure (ETS), Montréal, Canada
alain.abran@etsmtl.ca
[3] Federal University of Santa Catarina (UFSC), Florianópolis, Brazil
{gresse,jeanhauck}@gmail.com
[4] Regulated Software Research Group & Lero, Dundalk Institute of Technology,
Dundalk, Ireland
fergal.mccaffery@dkit.ie

Abstract. In Information and Communication Technology (ICT) a 'deliverable' may be either software (perceived as an 'output') or a service (perceived as an 'outcome'). On the one hand, the differences between software and service have led to the design of parallel models and lifecycles with more commonalities than differences, thereby not supporting the adoption of different frameworks. For instance, a software project could be managed applying best practices for services (e.g. ITIL), while some processes (e.g. Verification & Validation) are better defined in models of the Software Management domain. Thus, this paper aims at reconciling these differences and provides suggestions for a better joint usage of models/frameworks. To unify existing models we use the LEGO approach, which aims at keeping the element of interest from any potential model/framework for being inserted in the process architecture of the target Business Process Model (BPM) of an organization, strengthening the organizational way of working. An example of a LEGO application is presented to show the benefit from the joint view of the 'software + service' sides as a whole across the project lifecycle, increasing the opportunity to have many more sources for this type of improvement task.

Keywords: Software management · Service management · ISO 20000 · CMMI-DEV · CMMI-SVC · ITIL

1 Introduction

To classify items human beings create mental boundaries for distinguishing items, including adopting different terms: this is a classical approach for benchmarking purposes. For example, in the Automobile market SUVs or Crossovers are recognized as distinct car segments by adopting a number of criteria, for instance their length and main characteristics. Again, in the Telecom market smartphones, tablets or 'phablets' are now recognized as distinct kinds of products mainly according to their size etc. However, when classification rules become too strict we may risk losing the 'big picture'.

© Springer International Publishing Switzerland 2015
A. Kobyliński et al. (Eds.): IWSM-Mensura 2015, LNBIP 230, pp. 30–45, 2015.
DOI: 10.1007/978-3-319-24285-9_3

This can also be observed through the division of three main groups of processes (development, operation, maintenance) of a system throughout its lifetime. Here the first and the third group are often associated with the Software domain, while the second is associated with the Service domain. In this context CMMI-DEV [1] or ISO 15504-2 [2] now in the ISO 33000 series) are examples of process improvement models for the Software domain, while, ITIL [3], MOF[4], CMMI-SVC [5] or eTOM [6] are examples for the Service domain. Yet, a mix of 'components' from models of those two 'separated domains' is rarely observed. However, when analyzing the existing models/frameworks both at the process level and product level, the differences are not as sharp. For instance on the process level 16 out of the 22 processes within CMMI-DEV and CMMI-SVC are about the same, with very slight differences, mostly in the glossary adapted to the specific tasks to be performed [31].

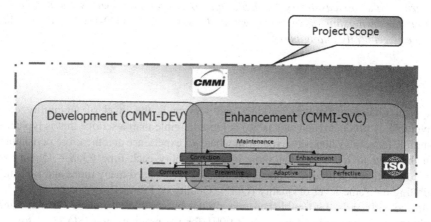

Fig. 1. Mixing CMMI constellations (DEV + SVC) into a unique 'project scope'

Looking at the product level, the quality model for a software product in the ISO 25010 standard [7], if the term 'software product' was substituted by 'service', the list of categories and sub-categories could still be a good fit for a pure service, with such a service not being necessarily an ICT-related service (e.g. a service should be designed to be maintainable, reusable, usable, reliable, etc.). A question that arises is: are software and services different or not? And, if not, how to preserve the best aspects from any existing model/framework/classification currently available within both communities?

Furthermore, how to lower the Total Cost of Ownership (TCO) for the management of a project? And could Knowledge Management (KM) be part of such a solution? In this respect, this paper attempts to answer these questions by introducing an improvement approach based on merging elements from different frameworks and models, having in mind one final goal: to reinforce the organization's Business Process Model (BPM) respecting, instead of upsetting, its architecture (Fig. 2).

This paper is structured as follows: Sect. 2 describes the main differences and commonalities as they are perceived by both communities of interest (software and service). Section 3 discusses how to merge best practices from other models as improvements to be integrated into an existing organizational BPM using the **LEGO** (Living EnGineering process) approach [8]. Section 4 presents an example using a typical ICT management case. Section 5 presents some conclusions and suggestions for improvements.

2   Software vs Service? Friends or Foes?

This section describes briefly the main differences and commonalities between products and services. According to ITIL and ISO 20000-1 [9]) *'a service is a means of delivering value to customers by facilitating outcomes customers want to achieve without the ownership of specific costs and risks'*. ISO 20000-1 adds a note that *'service is generally intangible'*.

2.1   Differences

A typical difference between product and service is the level of tangibility of a deliverable. A product (such as a table) is more tangible than a service that is typically intangible (e.g., the value perceived from whatever experience and therefore perishable, with the need to reproduce the same level of quality each time (QoS – Quality of Service)). Whereas a product – once produced – may be used many times and typically exhibiting the same level of quality (QoP – Quality of Product[1]).

In the early 90's, ISO published two similar but distinct standards for managing quality at the organizational level: ISO 9001 for the products and ISO 9002 for the services, whatever the application domain. Later, the so-called 'Vision 2000' project reconciled the two standards into a single one: ISO 9001:2000 indicated that while the formal term adopted in the document was 'product' it was intended as a 'product/service', with the ultimate aim being to achieve customer satisfaction. In particular, the ICS (International Classification for Standards) code distinguished the working sector for an organization to be audited[2]: EA33 is the code for those organizations managing software, while EA35 is the code for organizations managing services.

In relation to services for developing software ISO has published the ISO 20000 series, based upon ITIL (IT Infrastructure Library), the UK standard of best practices for the IT Service Management (ITSM) community. While some concepts are differentiated (e.g. service catalogue, risk register, capacity management), other elements (such as the process improvement approach based on the Deming's PDCA cycle) are the same in both standards. ITIL details the *'7-Step Improvement process'* stressing the

---

[1] http://asq.org/services/why-quality/overview.html.

[2] http://www.iso.org/iso/home/store/catalogue_ics.htm.

role of a proper Knowledge Management (KM) process for a more effective continuous improvement.

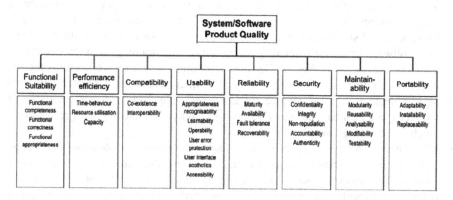

Fig. 2. ISO 25010:2011 quality model [7] – also for service?

2.2 Commonalities

There are different types of service. For instance, maintenance is a service; operation is a service, in addition to both developing and managing software also being a service. In order to understand how the 'boundaries' of both standards overlap, evidence from one set of standards can be mapped to evidence from the other one (e.g. taking ISO 20000-1 [9] requirement and applying them to a software development project or, alternatively, taking ISO 9001 requirements [10] and applying them to a pure service). Their differences seem to be mostly in the terminology adopted rather than the actual contents.

A 'service catalogue' is a library of services: applying the same concept to any type of asset library, it works well using libraries with software code for reuse. Furthermore, the ITIL definition in the Definitive Media Library (DML) where software and related documentation and licenses are stored makes use of the same configuration management process. Some specifications ('Service Asset and Configuration Management') do not change the inner content of the process but extend the common concept from software code to any kind of organizational asset (including HR-asset) needed as 'components' of a service, that is - conceptually speaking - wider than the software itself.

2.3 The Challenge – Possible Benefits

The commonalities appear to out-number the differences. Could this therefore indicate that an organization could be made more successful through using more knowledge from models/frameworks typically developed and adopted by each of the two communities? Here it follows a list of candidate drivers for stimulating a positive and effective change and possible benefits from the joint usage and vision of software + services as a whole within the 'project' umbrella:

- **Unique, Continuous Lifecycle and Process Flow:** what the final customer is asking for is a not a product itself, but the value that such a product (software or system) can provide to his users by its usage. Thus, the whole project can be split into a series of sub-projects (or iterations-sprints with several deliverables, outputs (e.g. software or a user manual) plus outcomes (e.g. training, positive perception after the usage), as in Fig. 1. Organizations often tend to have a group for the development part and another one for the maintenance part, creating possible logical breaks in terms of service continuity and value provided, while a customer would expect such continuity defined as 'availability' as stated in the agreed service levels to be as high as possible.

- **Glossary:** a Change Request (CR) is exactly the same as a Request for Change (RfC) or a Modification Request (MR): these are different terms for the same concept. This happens also for other terms: for instance, the internal 'capacity' of a service team can be associated to the 'productivity' levels needed to do a project estimate, etc. However, frequently words can create barriers that may be difficult to overcome and they may reduce the initial effectiveness when people with different professional paths work together. A common, shared glossary – including a list of most used acronyms – could help in speeding the communication among people within a team.

- **Knowledge Management (KM):** the input for improving anything is to know and, better, to know how to do better things. Most of the software process models assume that such knowledge is already part of a team, while often it is not. Thus, an organization stimulating creativity and knowledge sharing (e.g. the SECI model [14]) could have a greater probability to be effective on the market than its competitors.

- **Product/Service:** the more tangible product is the means for providing a service to the final users. In that sense, the management of a project should be more service-oriented because the focus in the mid-long term should be in measuring not only the ROI (Return on Investment) but also the VOI (Value on Investment). This includes also what is generated by intangibles.

2.4   A Short Example – Software + Service Together

A further example comes from project 'lifecycles'. The Agile approach was born in the mid '90 s for managing Telco projects with unstable requirements and short lead times for delivering the 'products'. When looking at an Agile Project Management (APM) method such as Scrum [11], it is possible to adapt it to a pure service using, for example, a revised version of user stories, US^2 (2nd generation of User Stories (US)) [12]. This is illustrated in Fig. 3: a US^2 card adds: (a) sizing FUR and NFR by functional and non-functional sizing units (fsu/nfsu) or – as in typical US cards – directly assigning the effort in person/days (or person/hours); (b) specifying a priority (after the INVEST grid evaluation [13], see below) according to the well-known

'MoSCoW' (Must or Should, Could or Would) criteria from BABOK [30] and Project Management guides; (c) the formal writing also of the non-functional side of a story, which is far from obvious in a typical US card.

US² **Title**: *Update User Profile*				
Id: 1.2	**Ver: 1.1**	**Priority:** M☐ S☐ C☐ W☐	**fsu:** ... **nfsu:** ...	**Effort** **(m/d):** ...
FUR	• User can update his/her own profile, included email, address, preferences and information about credit card(s)			
NFR	• Accessibility according to Section-508 standard • Browse with MS IE8			
US² **Acceptance Tests**				
1.	Successfully modify address, profession, hobbies, email, preferences, credit card data (positive)			
2.	Verify to insert another user's credit card data (negative)			

Fig. 3. US²-Type2, including both FURs and NFRs

There is also the possibility to have only NFR (including in this definition for sake of simplicity also the project-related tasks, as quality assurance, measurement, project planning and monitoring & control, etc.), in what we call a Type1 US² card (Fig. 4).

US² **Title**: *Install Mozilla Firefox v32.x*				
Id: 1.2	**Ver: 1.1**	**Priority:** M☐ S☐ C☐ W☐	**fsu:** ... **nfsu:** ...	**Effort** **(m/d):** ...
FUR	• ---			
NFR	• Install Firefox on all PCs			
US² **Acceptance Tests**				
1.	Verify browser compatibility with previous installed software			
2.	...			

Fig. 4. US²-Type1, including only NFRs

After the customer and provider create the single US² cards, as achieved in an agile context, their analysis and evaluation can be done through applying a grid based on criteria such as independent, negotiable, valuable, estimable, small and testable (INVEST) Grid. The process is fully defined in [13] and uses Table 1 as the basic template to use between a customer and a provider. The six attributes have been described using a four-point ordinal scale (0–3), as in the ISO 14598-x standards, where '0' means 'poor/absent', '1' means 'fair', '2' means 'good' and '3' 'excellent'. Each cell contains a description that proposes a rating for that attribute at that level.

Table 1. The INVEST Grid [13]

INVEST	Description	0	1	2	3
		Poor /Absent	Fair	Good	Excellent
I – **Independent**	User Stories should be as independent as possible	The start of construction of a US is tied to the completion of at least one other US	The completion of a US hinders the start of construction of at least one other US	The US can contain any constraint, but its release can be constrained by the completion of at least one other US	The US is fully independent, and it can be realized and released with any constraint
N – **Negotiable**	User Stories should be "open", reporting any relevant details as much as possible	The US contains enough detail to be a technical specification (Design phase), leaving no room to negotiate any element	The US is written with enough detail to be a functional specification (Analysis phase), leaving no room to negotiate any element	The US is written with informative content defining a User Requirement in a consolidated manner, yet shared between Customer and Provider	The US is written with the informative content typical of a high-level need, allowing feedback between customer and provider
V – **Valuable**	User Stories should provide value to end users in terms of the solution	The functional part (F) of the US does not contain all the functionalities requested by the customer	The functional (F) part of the US expresses mostly qualitative (Q) and technical (T) requirements about the system, and needs to be more developed in terms of functional requirements	The functional (F) part of the US expresses mostly the functional requirements requested by the Customer, but also includes qualitative (Q) and technical (T) requirements	The functional (F) part of the US correctly expresses only the functional requirements requested by the customer
E – **Estimable**	Each User Story must be able to be estimated in terms of relative size and effort	The US shows only its functional (F) part, filled in by the customer, but without sufficient detail to allow the provider to fill in the Q/T parts	The US shows only its functional (F) part, filled in by the customer, but validated with the provider	The US has been completed by the provider with respect to Q/T issues, but still needs to be validated jointly with the customer	All the useful parts of the US (F/Q/T) are shown, allowing the effort need to size and estimate it, and validated by both parts
S – **Small**	Each User Story should be sufficiently granular, and not defined at too high a level	The US is very large, and cannot be completed within a Sprint	The US is very large, and can be completed within a Sprint, but cannot accommodate the creation/delivery of other US	The size of the US is such that it can be completed within a Sprint, jointly with other US, but it is too small to create overhead about the Testing phase	The size of the US is such that it can be completed within a Sprint, jointly with other US, ensuring an appropriate balance between development and testing activities
T – **Testable**	Each User Story must be formulated in an effort to stress useful details for creating tests	The US does not include tips about Acceptance Tests	The US includes a formal indication of Acceptance Tests, but yet to be completed	The US includes an indication of Acceptance Tests which are complete, but yet to be validated	The US includes an indication of completed and validated Acceptance Tests

In a service management context the main goal is to release 'value' to a customer. This is a summary of 'utility' (*fit for purpose*) and 'warranty' (*fit for use*), where the first one covers functional user requirements (FUR[3]) and the second one for non-functional requirements (NFR[4]) (see Fig. 5).

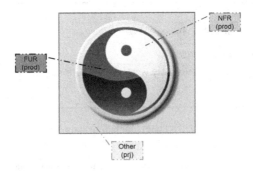

Fig. 5. Functional User Requirements (FUR) vs Non-Functional Requirements (NFR)

---

[3] A requirement that specifies a function that a system or system component must be able to perform (ISO/IEC/IEEE 24765:2010 [Systems and software Engineering Vocabulary]).

[4] A software requirement that describes not what the software will do but how the software will do it (ISO/IEC/IEEE 24765:2010 [Systems and software Engineering Vocabulary]).

There are two factors: (1) the ISO 25010 quality model for a software product can also be applied to a service for describing and managing the 'warranty'; (2) a service project could plan for each iteration ('sprint' in the Scrum glossary) to release firstly the 'core + enabling' services (in software this could be the 'development' part) and the following ones typically 'enhancing' services (in software this could be a series of enhancements).

3   Methodology

Our objective in this paper is to introduce a discussion and try to demonstrate that only one side of the story (software or service) may not deliver all the benefits an organization could achieve from a joint adoption. For instance, in two out of the three CMMI constellations, DEV and SVC, 16 out of 22 processes are the same [37, 38]: in this case would an organization run two separated process improvement initiatives or a single one by evaluating commonalities for a unique improvement plan? This corresponds to what BSI (British Standards Institution) called a 'publicly available specification' for an integrated management system ('PAS 99') [32]. For such an integration, our proposal is based on the **LEGO** (Living **EnG**ineering pr**O**cess) approach [8] proposed for stimulating organizations to improve their own processes: it suggests to take pieces (as LEGO bricks) from multiple candidate information sources and integrate them to form a unique, reinforced picture for a particular process or set of processes. It allows organizations to avoid searching conformity to 'external' models, when a model itself is an abstraction for trying to catch several instances at a time[5]. Again, any model/framework can represent only a part of the observed reality, not all of its possible views, since it needs to represent a single viewpoint at a time. In that way, enlarging the scope of potential useful elements for improving the organizational BPM, there could be more chances for success. LEGO has four main elements (Fig. 6):

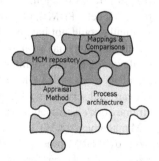

Fig. 6. The four elements of the LEGO approach

---

[5] Other related works are e.g. [27, 28, 33–35].

1. a 'Maturity & Capability Models' (MCM) repository (www.gqs.ufsc.br/mcm), from which relevant processes (i.e., MCMs) can be identified;
2. knowledge about the process architecture of each model, for understanding how to transform the desired elements from a certain model into the target format, especially when considering that the source models may have different architectures that need to be integrated into a single model;
3. mapping(s) & comparisons between relevant models, in order to understand the real differences or the deeper level of detail from 'model A' to import into 'model B';
4. a process appraisal method (PAM) to be applied on the target organization's BPM (Business Process Model).

The LEGO approach follows a four step process:

1. **Identify informative/business goals**: clearly identify your needs from the current BPM version and content.
2. **Query the MCM repository**: browse the MCM repository, setting up the proper filters in order to obtain the desired elements (processes; practices; etc.) to be inserted into the target BPM.
3. **Include the selected element(s) into the target BPM**: include the new element(s) in the proper position in the target BPM (e.g. process group, maturity level, etc.).
4. **Adapt & Adopt the selected element(s)**: according to the process architecture of both process models (the target and the source one), the selected elements may need to be adapted, tailoring such elements as needed.

Such an approach has been applied to several contexts and processes (e.g. requirement management [15], risk management [16], etc.), and it could be applied also to an improved BPM where some elements could have been missing.

4   Unification of Software + Service

This section presents an example on how to use jointly software and service models (what ISO calls a Process Reference Models (PRM)), picking up those information and best practices that one model eventually could not have yet foreseen, and to strengthen them. As already mentioned, an organization has to manage a project that could be often composed by pure software development and maintenance and pure services (e.g. incident management). Thus one of its goals will be how to lower the Total Cost of Ownership (TCO). Are really software and services so different or not? And if not, how keep the best from any model/framework/classification currently available from both communities? Can Knowledge Management (KM) be part of such solution? A real application should be done on your own BPM processes. Here, for sake of simplicity, ISO 15504-2 is selected as the target BPM to be reinforced and a series of Software and Service PRM as the sources to be investigated for picking up some interesting additional 'bricks' to be added, in case. Now a new application can be done considering the SPICE Knowledge Management process (RIN.3). KM was chosen because it is important to stress and discuss how to create and generate value for an organization. Having a proper KM process in place would help as a support process for many initiatives, and it is not yet part of CMMI-DEV/SVC but of another SEI-based model (People CMM): thus it can be proposed as an example, together with CMMI, as a target model for the positioning of 'missing pieces'. Table 2 presents a list of KM-related models/frameworks explored for finding Elements of Interest (EoI) to be inserted for reinforcing RIN.3.

Table 2. Some KM-related models/frameworks

Model/framework	Repr. Type	ML (#)	Architect-Type	Comments/notes
APQC KMMM [17]	Staged	5 [1–5]	Level-based	•
Siemens KMMM [18]	Staged	5 [1–5]	Level-based	• 8 Key Areas
ONTOKNOM [19]	Staged	5 [1–5]	Level-based	• Ontology included
(G-KMMM [20]	Staged	5 [1–5]	Matrix -based	• Assessment with questionnaire by ML
InfoSys KMMM [25]	Staged	5 [1–5]	Level-based	•
KPMG Knowledge Journey [21, 22]	Staged	5 [1–5]	Level-based	• 4 KPAs
K3 M [22]	Staged	8 [1–8]	Level-based	•
KMCA [23]	Staged	6 [0–5]	Level-based	• Added a 'zero' ML
ITIL v3 Refresh 2011 [3]	—	—	—	• Svc Mgmt Framework, 5 SLC phases → KM in the Svc Transition (ST) phase; 7-Step Improvement Process in CSI (Continual Svc Improvement) phase
Microsoft MOF v4 [4]	—	—	—	• Svc Mgmt Framework, 4 SLC phases → KM in the 'Manage' phase
COBIT [24]	—	—	—	• IT Governance Framework → 4 main phases (PO, AI, DS, ME)

The following preconditions, process and main results from the application of the LEGO process to the KM domain are proposed for a better process that may be applied in an organization:

1. **Identify informative/business goals:** improve the capability of the organization to collect, share, reuse and improve its knowledge by its employees and partners.
2. **Query the MCM repository:** Table 3 proposes the list of potential elements of interest (EoI) to consider for improving ISO 15504 KM process.

Table 3. KM MCM: Elements of Interest (EoI)

Model/ Framework	Elements of Interest (EoI)
APQC KMMM	• —
Siemens KMMM	• 8 Key Areas (Planning, Ext Knowledge, People, Informal Rules, Operation, Int. Knowledge, Technology, Formal Rules)
ONTOKNOM	• KM Maturity Model Ontology based on three components (Admin, Author, User)
KPMG KJourney	• 4 KPAs (People, Process, Content, Technology)
G-KMMM	• 3 KPAs (People/Org, Process, Technology)
K3 M	• More refined levels for a gradual implementation
	• Top-down retention measurement at ML3 and a formal Org Knowledge Base (ML4)
KMCA	• Separating 'behavior' and 'infrastructure' into the analysis
ITIL v3 KM	• Overall, global concept of SKMS (Service Knowledge Management System)
	• The four waves for KM: DIKW (Data, Information, Knowledge, Wisdom)
	• Goal-oriented KM, well linked with the Measurement perspective and the CSI (Continual Service Improvement) process
Microsoft MOF v4	• 'Plan' phase, POL (Policy) area, Process 2 (Create Policy), activity #5 (Create KM policies)
	• 'Operate' phase, CUS (Customer Service) area, Process 3 (Resolve the Request), activities asking to search, locate, verify knowledge base articles
	• 'Manage' phase, GRC (Governance, Risk, Compliance) area, Process 2 (Assess, Monitor & Risk), Activity #9 (Learn from prior effects and update the Knowledge Base) → Stressed the 'learning' activity as a 'risky' element whether not properly managed
COBIT v4.1	• PO2.1 (Enterprise Architecture Model)
	• PO2.4 (Integrity Management)
	• AI4.2 (Knowledge Transfer to Business Management)
	• AI4.3 (Knowledge Transfer to End Users)
	• AI4.4 (Knowledge Transfer to Operation and Support Staff)

3. **Include the selected element(s) into the target BPM:** looking at the analysis of potential EoI (Elements of Interest) in Table 3. Table 4 shows how our suggestions were introduced in the current RIN.3 process, describing a new possible improved process that may be mapped against your own QMS internal process(es) covering that subject.
4. **Adapt & Adopt the selected element(s):** after adapting the original RIN.3 process considering the proposed suggestions for improvement (see Table 4), the improved RIN.3 process should be mapped now against the related QMS internal process

Table 4. KM process - suggestions for improvements.

ISO/IEC 15504 KM Process	Suggested Improvements
RIN.3	KM BPs
BP 01 – Establish a KM system	• Distinguish the 'behavior' from the 'infrastructure' [KMCA]
	• Define/Refine which Information Systems are part of the overall SKMS in Architectural terms [ITIL] [COBIT PO2.1]
	• Define – according to the 'four waves of KM' – the layers and related IS for gathering and distributing data, information, knowledge and wisdom [ITIL]
BP02 - Create the Network of Knowledge contributors	• Create and update a list of (primary, secondary) stakeholders to consider as the main input for formulating requirements and for checking their validity [COBIT PO2.4]
BP 03 – Develop a KM strategy	• The strategy should have clear KM axes of interest well defined from the beginning, to be periodically updated [ITIL SS, Siemens KMMM; KPMG KJourney; G-KMMM]
	• The specification of which KM areas could be the most relevant to the organization for a proper generation of value is welcome [Siemens KMMM, G-KMMM, KPMG]
	• Consider KM process and its implication also from a Risk perspective [MOF]
	• A KM Ontology could help during the creation/periodical update of the organizational overall strategy [ONTOKNOM]
	• The KM Strategy must be goal-oriented, receiving feedbacks from previous improvements put in action [ITIL CSI; MOF Plan]
BP04 - Capture Knowledge	• Revise periodically the potential sources of data/information gathering, also considering new technologies (e.g. Social media and the possibility to interface organization's website and intranet) [MOF Operate CUS; SECI model [14])
BP 05 – Disseminate Knowledge Assets (KAs)	• Keep in mind several stakeholders, not only customers but mostly Users and their perceptions in the creation of value [COBIT AI4.x][ITIL CSI]
BP06 - Improve KAs	• KAs must be managed as one of the several organization's Configuration Items (CI) to be updated on a regular basis [ITIL ST]
	• KAs must be updated as part of a regular CSI (Continual Service Improvement) program [ITIL CSI]

covering that subject. Since many organizations adopt an ISO management system (e.g. ISO 9001), a cross-check for validating potential improvements from the design phase could be achieved through re-applying the related mapping document to their own internal process (e.g. using the N/P/L/F – Not/Partially/Largely/Fully achieved ordinal scale from CMMI or ISO 15504). Moving from ISO 15504, it could be used also the Mutafeljia & Stromberg's mapping [26] and/or the one by Peldzius and Ragaisis taking CMMI-DEV and ISO 15504 [29] as a basis. In this paper, our focus was limited to only the design phase. However, a case study with the application of hybrid-RIN processes will be included in a future paper.

The EoI presented in Table 3, as well as the included elements, respect the BPs of the RIN.3 process provided in Table 4 are not to be considered exhaustive: to the contrary, these two tables are to be considered as a starting point for the application of the LEGO approach in practice.

What can be easily observed reading the 'EoI' column is that any model can propose a series of elements and good practices, but just a single 'model' cannot include in one possible viewpoint every possible EoI, simply because they all were originated from different assumptions and rationales.

In particular this short example from ISO 15504 RIN.3 process stressed the need:

- to reinforce the list of work products/deliverables defined at the end of the ISO PRM with few more elements, not currently defined;
- to provide suggestions about the communication area, because – as in the SECI[6] model [14]– you can also have a great idea but being limited to few applications, while the larger the diffusion, the higher the probability to create/generate new joint ideas from the initial one, being refined little by little after an initial application;
- a list of stakeholders to be periodically contacted (e.g. panels) for providing opinions/ideas on new products-services or revision for current services provided to the market.

5   Conclusions and Next Steps

Software and Service are two sides of the same coin within an ICT project. Too often they are viewed as separated issues to be managed and improved by specific models and frameworks. After reviewing the main differences and commonalities, it could be valuable to an organization to start looking at them as friends and not as foes. A list of common items valid both from the software and service sides has been discussed (e.g. the way to manage requirements by User Stories), depicting the main challenges to properly manage them together as a whole.

The LEGO (Living EnGineering prOcess) approach has been presented as an effective way to take into account several information sources from the MCM (Maturity & Capability Models) belonging to the desired area/domain to be improved. LEGO has been applied in different ways over the past years to specific process areas (PA) to be

---

[6] SECI (Socialization – Externalization – Combination – Internalization).

improved as a 'vertical' improvement, while in this paper it was applied in a 'horizontal' way, trying to give continuity to a continuous flow (from the development of a software system till its maintenance) within the unique ICT project frame. The RIN.3 Knowledge Management process from the ISO 15504 PRM (Process Reference Model) has been considered as a small application example, considering models from both domains (software; service & governance) for picking up potential Elements of Interest (EoI) to be suggested for strengthening RIN.3.

An organization needs more and more to 'pick up' pieces from several frameworks and models in order to reinforce its own unique Business Process Model (BPM), while too often organizations search for compliance to 'external' models (e.g. one or more CMMI constellations) thinking such models could be the target instead of being simply suggestions for an internal improvement. But a model is and remains simply a model. Each model can have its way to look at a phenomenon but cannot capture all the potential interpretations and 'nuances' of a certain process/domain. Therefore the need to know more sources of information and try to summarize them in the best possible way but respecting the organization's BPM process architecture, that is the real target to improve. The papers about LEGO applications (e.g. [8, 15, 16, 39]) can be a starting point to learn and try to replicate the approach on 'your' own BPM and processes. The most challenging item can be how to filter the EoI (Elements of Interest) useful for being incorporated into your own BMP (target). This is why the issue dealt with in this paper was Knowledge Management and the way organizations typically deal with that process (or not). Too often such process seems to be too implicit in many medium-large organizations and could be confused with solely training.

LEGO represents a different way to improve processes from multi-source models than done in EnterpriseSPICE [27] or FAA iCMM [28] or other approaches (e.g. [33–35]) since LEGO stresses a dynamic perspective about how to find room for improvement in your own BPM, rather than considering a meta-model.

Next steps will be about the analysis of other points of contacts between the software and the service side of ICT projects, such as the measurability issue, where the knowledge coming from the software community could bring some useful tips for reinforcing the Service Level Management (SLM) process as well as how paradigms, such as DevOps [36], can help improving better and faster software and services by a more focused collaboration and communication about stakeholders. Again, a mapping of crossed terms and the way there are differently mentioned in the respective communities (e.g. a 'Change Request' is on software side the same concept and working item that a 'Request for Change' in the service side) will be created in order to facilitate such logical merging.

References

1. CMMI Product Team, CMMI for Development, Version 1.3, CMMI-DEV v1.3, Continuous Representation, CMU/SEI-2010-TR-033, Technical report, Software Engineering Institute, November 2010

2. ISO/IEC, IS 15504-2: 2003, Information technology – Process assessment – Part 2: Performing an assessment, October 2003
3. ITIL v3 Refresh 2011 suite, AXELOS (2011). http://goo.gl/Ets5Xb
4. Microsoft, Microsoft Operation Framework (MOF) v4.0 (2012). http://goo.gl/BvGg3i
5. CMMI Product Team, CMMI for Service, Version 1.3, CMMI-SVC v1.3, CMU/SEI-2010-TR-034, Technical report, Software Engineering Institute, November 2010
6. TM Forum, Business Process Framework (eTOM), v14.5 (2015). http://goo.gl/vTXjkh
7. ISO/IEC IS 25010:2011, Systems and software engineering – Systems and software Quality Requirements and Evaluation (SQuaRE) – System and software quality models, Geneve (2011)
8. Buglione, L., Gresse von Wangenheim, C., Hauck, J.C.R., McCaffery, F.: The LEGO maturity & capability model approach. In: Proceedings of the 5th World Congress on Software Quality, Shanghai (China), October 2011
9. ISO/IEC IS 20000-1:2011, Information technology – Service management – Part 1: Service management system requirements, Geneve (2011)
10. ISO, IS 9001:2008, Quality management systems – Requirements, Geneve (2008)
11. Schwaber, K.: Agile Project Management with Scrum, Microsoft Press (2004). ISBN 978-0735619937
12. Buglione L.: Agile-4-FSM. Improving estimates by a 4-pieces puzzle, Webinar, IFPUG Agile Interest Group, 17 May 2012. http://goo.gl/wtXWt
13. Buglione, L., Abran, A.: Improving the user story agile technique using the INVEST Criteria, IWSM-MENSURA 2013. In: 23th International Workshop on Software Measurement and 8th International Conference on Software Process and Product Measurement. IEEE/CS Proceedings, Ankara (Turkey), 23–26 October 2013, pp. 49–53 (2013)
14. Nonaka, I., Takeuchi, H.: The Knowledge-Creating Company: How Japanese Companies create the Dynamics of Innovation, OUP USA (1995). ISBN 978-0195092691
15. Buglione, L., Hauck, J.C.R., Gresse von Wangenheim, C., Mc Caffery, F.: Hybriding CMMI and requirement engineering maturity & capability models: Applying the LEGO approach for improving estimates. In: ICSOFT 2012, Proceedings of the 7th International Conference on Software Paradigm Trends, Rome (Italy), 24–27 July 2012
16. Buglione, L., Lami, G., von Wangenheim, C.G., Caffery, F.M., Hauck, J.C.R.: Leveraging reuse-related maturity issues for achieving higher maturity and capability levels. In: Favaro, J., Morisio, M. (eds.) ICSR 2013. LNCS, vol. 7925, pp. 343–355. Springer, Heidelberg (2013)
17. Hubert, C., Lemons, D.: A Knowledge Management Maturity Model – APQC's Stages of Implementation (2009)
18. Langen, M.: Holistic development of KM with the KM maturity model (KMMM). In: APQC Conference, 7–8 Dec 2000
19. Hefke, M., Kleiner, F.: An ontology-based software infrastructure for retaining theoretical Knowledge Management Maturity Models. In: 1st Workshop on Formal Ontologies Meet Industry, FOMI 2005, Verona, Italy (2005)
20. Peel, L.G., Teah, H.Y., Kankanhalli, A.: Development of a general knowledge management maturity model. In: Proceedings of the 10th Pacific Asia Conference on Information Systems (PACIS), 6–9 July, pp. 401–416. Kuala Lumpur, Malaysia
21. KPMG, Knowledge Management Assessment Exercise (1999). http://goo.gl/3c9mOR
22. WisdomSource, Knowledge Management Maturity (K3 M). WisdomSource News 2(1), 31, May 2004. http://goo.gl/WbaW7b
23. Freeze, R., Kulkami, U.: Knowledge management capability assessment: validating a knowledge assets measurement instrument. In: HICSS 2005 Proceedings of the Proceedings of the 38th Annual Hawaii International Conference on System Sciences, vol. 08, p. 251.1 (2005)

24. ISACA, COBIT v4.1 (2007). http://goo.gl/lOaHZv
25. Kochikar, V.P.: The knowledge management maturity model: a staged framework for leveraging knowledge. In: KM World 2000, Santa Clara, CA (2000). http://goo.gl/zl7tBV
26. Mutafeljia, B., Stromberg, H.: Process Improvement with CMMI v1.2 and ISO Standards, Auerback Publications (2008). http://goo.gl/BFUqq
27. ISO JTC1/SC7/WG10 Study Group, EnterpriseSPICE - An Integrated Model for Enterprise-wide Assessment and Improvement Technical report Issue 1 - September (2010). http://enterprisespice.com/
28. Ibrahim, L., Bradford, B., Cole, D., LaBruyere, L., Leinneweber, H., Piszczech, D., Reed, N., Rymond, M., Smith, D., Virga, M., Wells, C.: The Federal Aviation Administration Integrated Capability Maturity Model-, (FAA-iCMM), Version 2.0. An Integrated Capability Maturity Model for Enterprise-wide Improvement, FAA, September 2001
29. Peldzius, S., Ragaisis, S.: Investigation correspondence between CMMI-DEV and ISO/IEC 15504. Int. J. Educ. Inf. Technol. 5(4), 361–368 (2011). http://goo.gl/Dqupq9
30. IIBA, A Guide to the Business Analysis Body of Knowledge (BABOK) v3, International Institute of Business Analysis (2015)
31. Pipkin, J., Lunsford, G.H.: Synergism of the CMMI development and services constellations in an hybrid organization. In: CMMI Conference North America, May 2014. http://goo.gl/s7s9Is
32. BSI, PAS 99:2012 – Specification of common management system requirements as a framework for integration – Publicly Available Specification (2012). https://goo.gl/zWh5OZ (working draft)
33. SEI, PrIME project, Process Improvement in Multiple Envinronment. http://goo.gl/AK79wr
34. Jeners, S., Lichter, H., Dragomir, A.: Towards an integration of multiple process improvement reference models based on automated concept extraction. In: Winkler, D., O'Connor, R.V., Messnarz, R. (eds.) EuroSPI 2012. CCIS, vol. 301, pp. 205–216. Springer, Heidelberg (2012)
35. Andelfinger, U., Heijstek, A., Kirwan, P.: A Unified Process Improvement Approach for Multi-Model Improvement Environments, News @ SEI, 1 Apr 2006. http://goo.gl/ztuKl2
36. Andelfinger, U., Heijstek, A., Kirwan, P.: DevOps, Wikipedia. https://goo.gl/20PrLX
37. Stall, A., Forrester, E.: Using CMMI-DEV and CMMI-SVC Together – Where 'Build Stuff' Happens in CMMI-SVC, 2012 SEPG NA, Presentation, March 2012. http://goo.gl/z0PIuT
38. Gonzales, R.M.: CMMI®-DEV versus CMMI®-SVC analysis. In: 11th Annual CMMI Technology Conference and User Group, Denver (USA), 15 Nov 2011. http://goo.gl/dhldcC
39. Buglione, L., Gresse von Wangenheim, C., Mc Caffery, F., Hauck, J.C.R.: The LEGO strategy: guidelines for a profitable deployment. Comput. Standard Interfaces 36(1), 10–20 (2013). Elsevier

A Process to Improve the Accuracy of MkII FP to COSMIC Size Conversions: Insights into the COSMIC Method Design Assumptions

Aveek Dasgupta[1], Cigdem Gencel[2], and Charles Symons[3(✉)]

[1] Société Internationale de Télécommunications Aéronautiques (SITA), London, UK
aveek.dasgupta@sita.aero
[2] DEISER, Madrid, Spain
cigdem.gencel@deiser.com
[3] The Common Software Measurement International Consortium (COSMIC), Reigate, UK
cr.symons@btinternet.com

Abstract. Converting software sizes measured by one Functional Size Measurement (FSM) method to another is usually achieved by measuring the size of a sample of software items by both methods and deriving a statistical correlation curve that can be used for converting the whole set of measurements.

This paper describes a 'calculation method' to convert functional sizes measured by the MkII FSM method to COSMIC functional sizes. The method exploits some common features of both FSM methods and uses 'functional profiling' of measurements in order to form homogeneous datasets suitable for conversion. Applying the method to measurements of the same software by both FSM methods confirms that the calculated COSMIC sizes are more accurate than statistically-converted sizes.

Comparing the way in which the two methods measure functional size and the results of the conversion study yields significant, positive insights into the design assumptions of the COSMIC FSM method.

Keywords: Functional Size Measurement · Function Point Analysis · COSMIC · IFPUG · MkII FPA · Size conversion

1   Introduction

The objectives of this paper are:

(a) to present the results of measurements of the functional size of the same software items using the MkII[1] and COSMIC methods, and to use these to establish simple formulae for converting MkII sizes to COSMIC sizes under certain conditions (we will call this most commonly-used method the 'statistical method');

(b) to propose another method (the 'calculation method') with the aim of improved accuracy when applied to MkII to COSMIC size conversion, and to present the results of applying this method;

---

[1] 'MkII' is an abbreviation for 'Mark Two'.

A. Kobyliński et al. (Eds.): IWSM-Mensura 2015, LNBIP 230, pp. 46–61, 2015.
DOI: 10.1007/978-3-319-24285-9_4

(c) to present some very significant and positive conclusions on the COSMIC method of measuring functional size, that were an unexpected side-result of this study.

Section 2 of the paper describes the origins and nature of the MkII and COSMIC measurement data used for the analyses. Section 3 outlines the MkII and COSMIC Functional Size Measurement (FSM) methods in sufficient detail for the purposes of this paper.

Section 4 describes a typical process to develop a statistically-based functional size conversion method (the 'statistical method'). The results of applying the method to the available data are presented and the limitations of this method are discussed. We use an analysis of the distribution of functional sizes over the input, processing and output phases of software on the two methods ('IPO profiling') to show how these profiles vary with software from different domains and how profiling may be used to identify homogeneous datasets that are well-suited for developing size conversion formulae.

Section 5 describes the 'calculated method' for MkII to COSMIC size conversion that aims to improve on the accuracy obtainable via the statistical method and shows the results of applying the method to data from 13 Information System software items and to four Control System software items.

Section 6 draws conclusions from the findings in this paper about the effectiveness of the calculation method for MkII to COSMIC size conversion and on the effectiveness of the COSMIC method in its practical uses.

Appendix 2 gives some more detail on differences between how the two methods measure functional size. We suggest that if more measurement detail were available, it might be possible to further improve the accuracy of converted sizes.

2   Data Sources

Data analysed in this paper came from two sources. Dr Gencel supplied measurements of nine software items from four organisations (denoted as A to D in the following). Three of the software items are from the domain of 'Information Systems'; the other six are described as various types of 'Complex control systems' (avionics, real-time, embedded, etc.). Some of the data reported here has been analysed in earlier papers [1, 2].

Measurements of 13 software items from the domain of Information Systems were supplied by SITA (Société Internationale de Télécommunications Aéronautiques, www.sita.aero). SITA is the world's leading specialist in air transport communications and information technology. SITA is 100 % owned by the world's air transport industry and supplies systems and services to its customers in more than 200 countries and territories. The measurements (denoted by 'S' in the following) were of SITA software supporting airline and airport operations and management. The 22 pairs of MkII and CFP total size measurements are from projects to develop new software, except some measurements from SITA are for projects to develop major additions to existing systems. Effectively all data are measurements of new software. The data shown in Table 1 and plotted in Fig. 1 (which distinguishes the organisations supplying the data), were input to the analysis required by objective (a) of this paper.

Table 1. MkII and COSMIC total size measurements of 22 software items

Control system			Information system			Information system		
Org	MkII FP	COSMIC FP	Org	MkII FP	COSMIC FP	Org	MkII FP	COSMIC FP
A	4380	3524	S	249	148	S	1927	1418
A	435	279	S	482	359	S	2182	1664
A	348	251	S	506	364	S	2230	1693
A	1180	923	S	550	400	S	2341	1807
C	261	275	S	652	438	S	2455	1947
C	356	321	S	609	454	B	1346	1029
–	–	–	S	932	661	D	1538	1113
–	–	–	S	833	681	D	2998	1947

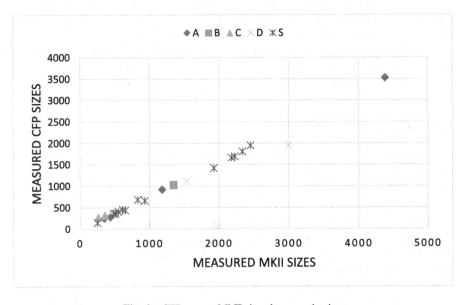

Fig. 1. CFP versus MkII sizes by organisation

To meet objective (b) we need to analyse measurements of the components of the total sizes as shown in Appendix 1. These details were available for all 22 measurements. Column headings are explained in Sect. 3.

3 Background to How the Two FSM Methods Measure Functional Size

FSM methods aim to measure a 'functional size' of the 'Functional User Requirements' (FUR) of software.

The first such method was Function Point Analysis, developed by Allan Albrecht of IBM in the mid-1970s [3]. Albrecht aimed to quantify software functionality in terms meaningful to the software's users. The International Function Point Users' Group (IFPUG) founded in 1986, adopted the FPA method.

The MkII method was developed in the late 1980s [4] to measure business application software. By 1998 the method was considered mature and was not developed further. The COSMIC FSM method was developed by a group of software metrics experts (the 'Common Software Measurement International Consortium') starting in 1998 to be applicable to business, real-time and infrastructure software. Both methods have been accepted as ISO/IEC standards [11, 12].

FUR for any software item can be decomposed into processes that the software must execute in response to data received about events in the world outside the software. The principal FSM methods all require that these processes be identified and measured. The IFPUG method refers to them as 'elementary processes' [5], the MkII method as 'logical transactions' [6] and the COSMIC method as 'functional processes' [7]. The IFPUG method defines an elementary process somewhat differently to how the MkII and the COSMIC methods define this concept. The latter two methods aim to define precisely the same concept, even though they use different words. The COSMIC definition has been refined for many more years than has the MkII definition, aiming to ensure consistent interpretation. We will therefore use the term 'functional process' for this concept for both the MkII and COSMIC methods.

The differences in the two methods' way of measuring functional size are in the selection of the *components* representing the Input, Process and Output phases of a functional process to be identified and counted, and in their weighting.

The size of a functional process in 'MkII FP' units is computed using Eq. (1).

$$\text{Size} = \{0.58 \times (\text{\# Input DET's})\} + \{1.66 \times (\text{\# ER's})\} + \{0.26 \times (\text{\# Output DET's})\}, \tag{1}$$

where

- # = 'count of';
- DET = 'data element type', and
- ER = 'Entity reference', i.e. a read or write reference by the functional process to an entity in the entity/relationship model of stored data used by the software being measured;
- the braces { } distinguish the input, process and output components of size.

Every MkII functional process must have at least one input and one output DET and one ER; its minimum size is therefore 2.5 MkII FP (0.58 + 1.66 + 0.26).

The size of a functional process in units of 'COSMIC Function Points' (CFP) is computed from the counts of its four types of 'data movements' as in Eq. (2).

$$Size = \{\# \, Entries\} + \{\# \, Reads + \# \, Writes\} + \{\# \, Exits\}. \qquad (2)$$

An Entry and an Exit each move a data group into and out of the software respectively. Reads and Writes move data from persistent storage into software, or vice versa, respectively. Every COSMIC functional process must be triggered by an Entry and it must have an outcome, i.e. either a Write or an Exit; its minimum size is therefore 2 CFP.

The DET's of a COSMIC data group all describe a single 'object of interest'. In general, MkII method entities for which data are stored correspond to COSMIC 'objects of interest'. Hence MkII 'entity references' correspond to COSMIC Read and/or Write data movements, subject to two exceptions described in the Appendix 2.

[In fact, describing the three components of the size of a functional process, as measured by either method, as representing its input, process and output phases is more a convenient label for discussion than an accurate description. In reality, the divisions of functionality, particularly between the input and process phases differ from this simple view, which we have had to use given the data that are available. See the Appendix 2 which discusses this point in more detail.]

For both methods, the size of a software item is obtained by summing the sizes of all its functional processes. Both methods have very similar rules for sizing changes to software but these are not relevant to this paper.

The set of three weights (0.58, 1.66, 0.26) for the MkII method were introduced because of the need to combine counts of two different concepts (DET's and ER's) to get a total size measure. The values of the weights were designed [8] to reflect the relative effort, averaged over all types of software projects, to develop the components. Weighting by relative effort was chosen because the MkII size scale was intended for use in comparing the performance of projects across different types of software using different technologies, etc., and for use in project estimating. (The sizes of the components of the IFPUG method were similarly calibrated based on relative effort.)

In practice, the MkII weights were obtained by a 'Delphi' exercise, asking representatives of 66 completed development projects to 'guestimate' the relative effort they had needed to deal with the input, processing and output phases of their software. As a final step of this calibration process, the weights were scaled so that the minimum size of a MkII logical transaction was 2.5 MkII FP which resulted in software sizes similar in magnitude to those measured by the IFPUG method.

The COSMIC size formula did not need any weights because all four components of a functional process size are sub-types of the same concept, a 'data movement', so their counts may be simply added together. Further, the method designers deliberately avoided introducing weights so that the size scale is completely independent of project effort and unquestionably conforms to the principles of functional size measurement published by ISO [10].

4   The 'Statistical Method' for Converting MkII FP to COSMIC Sizes

For an organisation that has many software size measurements using the MkII method and that wishes to start using the COSMIC method, conversion of the existing measurements to CFP sizes is very important to do as accurately as possible so as not to lose all the accumulated value and uses of those data.

The simplest way to convert existing MkII FP sizes to CFP sizes is to use the following process.[2]

- measure the CFP size of typically 10 or more software items that share a 'common profile' for which the organisation already has the corresponding MkII FP sizes;
- plot the pairs of (MkII FP, CFP) sizes on a scatter diagram and find the best-fitting correlation curve, ideally a straight line;
- (assuming a reasonable correlation of the two sets of sizes) use the straight line relationship to convert all existing MkII sizes to COSMIC sizes.

The choice of which measurements to include in the 'common profile' is critically important in order to develop a statistically-reliable method of size conversion. Criteria include the following.

- All software sizes are for new developments or for enhancements (but not mixed) and from the same domain, e.g. business applications. Organisations with a very large software portfolio should explore dividing it into sub-groups that might be expected to have more homogeneous size characteristics, e.g. operational versus MIS systems.
- The selected dataset should be selected for a limited size range, avoiding very small or large software sizes, well-outside the size range of the majority of measurements. Such outliers can easily distort the best-fitting correlation curve obtained by an Ordinary Least Squares (OLS) process, making it inaccurate for conversion of the majority of the sizes.
- A particular factor that is relevant to MkII to COSMIC conversion is that the minimum size of a functional process is 2.5 MkII FP or 2 CFP. For all practical purposes, this 'data point' can therefore be included as a constraint on the OLS fitted curve so that it passes through the origin of the graph at (0, 0). Hence in this paper, all graphs will only show straight line fits that are constrained to pass through the origin. (It is noticeable that the slopes of all fitted straight lines in the following are close to 0.8, the ratio of the minimum sizes on the two FSM methods.)

Applying the first 'common profile' criterion to the 22 pairs of size measurements in Table 1, we first decided to analyse the Control Systems and Information Systems data separately. The resulting fitted straight lines are shown in Fig. 2.

The fitted two straight lines are very close together, with high R-squared in spite of the diverse origins of the measurements. Nevertheless, the accuracy of converting from MkII FP sizes to COSMIC sizes using the OLS-fitted straight line might still not be good enough for practical purposes.

---

[2] This process has been applied several times [9] for the conversion of IFPUG to COSMIC functional size measurements but until now we are not aware of any published results of applying the process for MkII to COSMIC size conversion.

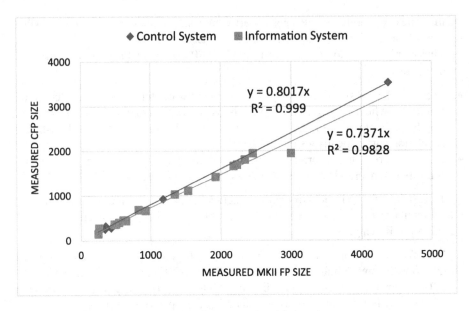

Fig. 2. CFP vs MkII sizes by domain

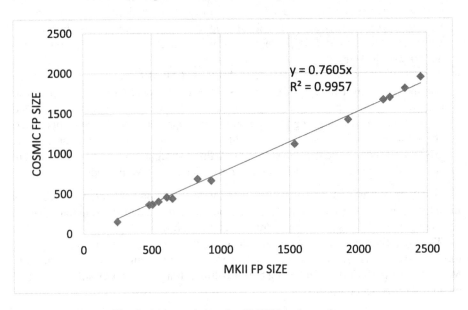

Fig. 3. Measured sizes for 13 SITA software items

To illustrate this point, we plotted the CFP versus MkII FP sizes for the subset of the 13 Information System data points from SITA, which should be a relatively homogenous data set,, shown in Fig. 3.

The slope of the line has changed slightly from the value for all Information Systems shown in Fig. 2 and the R-squared has improved significantly, which is promising for conversion. However, an important question remains: how accurate will the fitted line be when used to predict the CFP size from the measured MkII size *for each individual software item?*

To answer this question, we used this equation to predict the CFP sizes for the SITA software items from the measured MkII FP sizes. We then computed two parameters:

- the difference of the predicted CFP size from the measured CFP size, as a percentage of the measured CFP size, called the '% Diff.'
- the average of the absolute values of the '% Diff.' values for all 13 projects, called the 'AA% Diff.' (The absolute values are taken to eliminate the effect that some differences are positive and some negative. This parameter treats all software items as being equally important.)

The results for these 13 SITA software items in Table 2 show that this process can result in very significant errors in predicted CFP sizes, especially for the smaller sizes. Also there is a distinct bias to predicting CFP sizes that are higher than the measured CFP sizes.

Table 2. Measures of the inaccuracy of CFP sizes predicted from a conversion formula derived by conventional statistical analysis of measured MkII FP and CFP sizes

AA % Dff.	# under-sized items	# over-sized items	3 × highest % Diff errors
6.0 %	4	9	28 %, 13 %, 7.3 %

Ideally, one would seek more accurate converted COSMIC sizes than given by this statistical method.

At first glance, according to the second of our criteria for selection of a dataset of measurements for a conversion study, the data in Figs. 1 and 2 would suggest that the two highest data points (at about 3000 and 4380 MkII FP's) should be discarded as outliers. However, before making this decision, we analysed the profile of the software from another angle, using detailed data from the table in Appendix 1.

We computed the percentages of the contributions to total size of the input, process and output components as measured by both FSM methods, for all the software items. (We call this 'IPO profiling'). This analysis showed high homogeneity of the IPO profiles for the 13 SITA Information System software items and for the four Control System software items from organisation A. The three other Information System items and the two other Control System items had quite different profiles. Figure 4a shows the average profile of the 13 SITA Information System software items, as measured by the MkII and COSMIC methods. Figure 4b shows the corresponding result for the four Control System software items from organisation A.

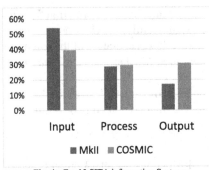 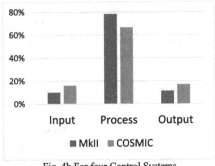

Fig. 4a. For 13 SITA information Systems   Fig. 4b For four Control Systems

Fig. 4. Percentage contributions of sizes of input, process and output phases to measured total software sizes

[Note re the four Control Systems, Fig. 4b shows that these systems have an unusual IPO profile, with a high proportion of size being accounted for by the processing phase relative to the input and output phases. These are air traffic control and avionics systems which must make many references to validate aircraft ID's and their flight plans, to store and retrieve statuses, etc.]

The conclusions from these analyses of both total sizes and of the IPO profiles are:

- the SITA Information System dataset is very homogeneous;
- the other three Information System software items (from organisations B and D) have a quite different IPO profiles from the SITA software, so should be kept separate. They were not analysed further;
- the four Control System software items have a common and distinctive IPO profile so may be analysed as one dataset. The other two Control System software items have quite different profiles, so should be kept separate. These were also not analysed further.

Note that the Information System data point at (2998 MkII FP, 1947 CFP) was omitted from this dataset not just because it was an outlier on the fitted straight line for all Information System software in Fig. 2, but because of its very different IPO profile from that shown in Fig. 4a.

Rejecting a data point because it is a statistical outlier to the fitted curve of a sample of measurements chosen to study size convertibility is dangerous. This is because we do not know without further investigation if the outlier data point is due to something unusual about either size measurement (in this case the MkII or the COSMIC size), or both. When using a fitted curve for conversion, we will only have the size measurements on the one scale (in this case MkII sizes). What we need is a test that can be applied to the measurements-to-be-converted for homogeneity, and that can identify any individual measurement as a potential outlier against the fitted curve, before applying its conversion formula. IPO profiling is an example of a useful and powerful test.

The very large Control System software item (4380 MkII FP, 3524 CFP) would also be a candidate for rejection as an outlier because it will dominate the OLS fitting of a straight line to organisation A's data. However we decided to explore using this small dataset of four software items as a further test of the conversion process that was devised for the SITA dataset.

5   Improving the Accuracy of Conversion of MkII FP to COSMIC CFP Sizes: The 'Calculation Method'

From the structure of the two FSM methods, we know that the CFP size of an individual software item converted from a MkII FP size using the fitted straight line process described in Sect. 4, may vary from the measured size because the software item has

- an exceptionally high or low count of DET's on its input and/or output compared with the average for all software resulting from the 'smoothing out' of the fitted straight line process;
- an exceptionally high or low count of entity references compared with the average for all software implied by the fitted straight line.

This suggests that a MkII to COSMIC size conversion process that takes into account exceptional distributions of the relative contributions of input, processing and output functionality to the overall size would lead to more accurate converted CFP sizes than using the OLS fitted straight line process. The following is such a process. (Entries, Exits, Reads and Writes are abbreviated as E, X, R and W respectively.)

(a) Take a set of software items with a 'common profile' and measure their MkII FP and CFP sizes, recording the numbers of their component DET's and ER's for the MkII sizes, and E's, X's, R's and W's for the COSMIC sizes.

(b) Sum these numbers for each component over the whole set, designating the totals as:

$\sum$ Input DET's, $\sum$ Output DET's and $\sum$ ER's, for the MkII FP counts
$\sum$ E's, $\sum$ X's, $\sum$ R's and $\sum$ W's for the COSMIC counts

(c) Compute the following ratios from these sums for the whole set:

AIDE = Average Input DET's per Entry = $(\sum$ Input DET's$)/\sum$ E's
AODX = Average Output DET's per Exit = $(\sum$ Output DET's$)/\sum$ X's
AERP = Average Entity Refs per (R + W) data movement = $\sum$ ER's/$(\sum$ R's + $\sum$ W's)

(d) Compute the CFP size of each individual software item using the sums of the DET's and ER's for the components of its measured MkII FP size and the Eq. (3) in order to obtain a 'Computed CFP size'.

Computed CFP = $(\sum$ Input DET's$)$/AIDE + $(\sum$ Output DET's$)$/AODX + $(\sum$ ER's$)$/AERP   (3)

This method was applied to the 13 SITA data points, with the results shown in Table 3.

Table 3. Measures of the inaccuracy of CFP sizes calculated by using a calculation method to convert from measured MkII FP sizes

AA % Diff.	# under-sized items.	# over-sized items	3 × highest % Diff errors
6.4 %	6	7	18 %, 11 %, 11 %

This calculation method for obtaining CFP sizes improves on the accuracy of the statistical method (cf results shown in Table 2) in that there is now no bias towards over-sizing or under-sizing, and the highest '% Diff.' figures for individual software items are substantially reduced. However, the absolute average of the % Diff.'s for all 13 projects is slightly worse than obtained by the statistical method.

We then noticed that the values of IDE, ODX and ERP for the *individual* software items (i.e. not the *average* value for all 13 software items) vary with MkII measured software size. Figure 5 shows that the values of IDE and ODX decline slowly with MkII size whereas the ERP values are practically constant. (The explanation for these trends seems to be related to the nature of SITA's systems.)

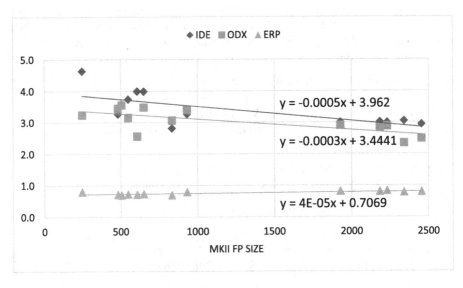

Fig. 5. Values of IDE, ODX and ERP versus actual MkII size for 13 SITA projects

If we now modify the process described above so that in step c) we compute the values of IDE, ODX and ERP for each individual software item from the three fitted lines shown in Fig. 5, and use them in Eq. (3) in step d) instead of the average values (AIDE, AODX and AERP) to calculate the CFP sizes, then we get the improvement in calculated CFP sizes that we have been seeking. Table 4 shows the results.

Table 4. Measures of the inaccuracy of CFP sizes obtained by using an improved 'calculated method' to convert from measured MkII FP sizes

AA % Dff.	# under-sized items.	# over-sized items	3 × highest % Diff errors
3.8 %	6	7	11 %, 8.9 %, 6.4 %

The average error on the calculated CFP size is now down to below 4 % and the maximum error is now well under half the maximum error obtained from using the statistical method to predict CFP sizes.

For the record, the result of applying this 'calculated method' to convert the sizes of the four Control software items from organisation A also shows similar improvement in accuracy through the three steps that were applied to the SITA dataset, as shown in Table 5. However this result from a set of only four data points has, of course, low statistical significance.

Table 5. Improvements in the accuracy of calculated CFP sizes over statistically-converted CFP sizes for four Control System software items

Conversion method	AA % Diff.	# under-sized items	# over-sized items	2 × highest % Diff. errors
OLS statistical straight line fit	9.7 %	1	3	25 %, 11 %
Calculated using AIDE, AODX, AERP values	8.6 %	2	2	17 %, 8.4 %
Calculated using individual IDE, ODX, ERP values[a]	6.6 %	2	2	12 %, 9.9 %

Using a process identical to that used to produce the IDE, ODX and ERP versus MkII FP sizes as shown in Fig. 5 for the SITA data.

6   Conclusions and Observations on the COSMIC Method Design Assumptions

The analyses in this paper demonstrate the limitations of statistically-based functional size conversion methods and that, in the case of MkII to COSMIC size conversion, a calculation conversion process based on a knowledge of the two methods' measurements of the input/process/output size profile can give significantly more accurate converted sizes.

Before starting on a FSM size conversion exercise, we recommend some form of 'profiling' of the measurements-to-be-converted to test for homogeneity and to identify potential outliers against the conversion curve. Refinement of a statistically-derived conversion formula by simply removing outliers without understanding why they are outliers could lead to unnecessary inaccuracy in size conversion.

The idea of functional profiling has been taken into account in selecting homogeneous sets of measurements to develop project effort estimation methods [13–15] but we are not aware of any previously-published size conversion studies that have used functional profiling to select homogenous sets of measurements-to-be-converted in order to improve conversion accuracy. The successful use of IPO profiling to test for homogeneity of datasets for MkII to COSMIC conversion suggests that IFPUG-to-COSMIC size conversion accuracy might also be improved by devising equivalent profiling tests that can be applied to IFPUG Unadjusted FP size measurements. An example might be to examine the ratio of the size contributions of their 'Elementary Processes' and so-called 'Data Functions' to total size.

This study has unexpectedly given new insight into the design assumptions of the COSMIC FSM method. A consequence of these assumptions is that it has always been legitimate to ask two important questions concerning the method's effectiveness as a size measure for its intended practical uses for software project performance measurement and estimating.

i.   First, does the fact that the COSMIC method ignores the detail of how many DET's are input and output to a functional process make a significant difference to the measured sizes? (The IFPUG and MkII methods take this detail into account.)

ii. Second, is the COSMIC method likely to be less suitable than other FSM methods for its intended practical uses because its size measurement scale has not been explicitly calibrated in relation to project effort (as were the scales of the IFPUG and MkII methods)?

The results of the data analyses in this paper help answer these two design questions.

The data in Figs. 4a and 4b show similar distributions of the input/process/output contributions to size when measured by the two methods. Further, the data in Fig. 2 show good correlations of total MkII and COSMIC sizes, especially bearing in mind the rather heterogeneous data available for analysis. These two findings suggest that it is unimportant to COSMIC size measurement that this method ignores the level of detail of the number of DET's on the input and output data, and that the method's design does not apply effort-related weights to the counts of data movement types. This conclusion is valid, of course, only based on the analysis of 13 Information System software data points and four Control System data points used in this study.

Subject to this limitation, these findings give independent confirmation that the design of the COSMIC method, as well as being theoretically well-founded, yields measures of functional size that should be valid and effective for software project performance measurement and for effort estimation – as we already have evidence from its use in the field for these purposes.

Acknowledgements. The authors are very grateful to SITA for supplying these data.

Appendix 1: Components of the MkII and COSMIC Size Measurements

		Components of MkII size			Total Mk II size	Components of COSMIC size				Total COSMIC size
Org.	Domain	# Input DET's	# Output DET's	# Entity Refs.		# Entries	# Exits	# Reads	# Writes	
S	Info	278	191	23	249	60	59	21	8	148
S	Info	411	369	89	482	126	107	93	33	359
S	Info	439	387	91	506	123	109	94	38	364
S	Info	490	466	87	550	131	148	87	34	400
S	Info	587	466	89	609	147	182	91	34	454
S	Info	622	564	87	652	156	162	108	12	438
S	Info	698	601	164	833	248	196	157	80	681
S	Info	874	711	145	932	268	209	110	74	661
S	Info	2016	1211	267	1927	671	417	280	50	1418
S	Info	1887	1381	439	2182	627	487	428	122	1664
S	Info	1888	1467	454	2230	630	510	418	135	1693
S	Info	2443	1273	357	2341	803	544	371	89	1807
S	Info	2241	1466	466	2455	764	591	402	190	1947
B	Info	563	1710	346	1346	157	381	336	155	1029
E	Info	545	1839	448	1538	256	330	375	152	1113
E	Info	1258	3385	836	2998	436	541	764	206	1947
A	Ctrl	665	2352	2038	4380	526	727	1946	325	3524
A	Ctrl	112	160	198	435	49	32	198	0	279
A	Ctrl	50	154	168	348	44	40	159	8	251
A	Ctrl	283	126	592	1180	184	51	588	100	923
C	Ctrl	133	234	74	261	69	115	45	46	275
C	Ctrl	152	112	144	356	80	79	99	63	321

Appendix 2: A More Detailed Examination of How the MkII and COSMIC Methods Measure the Input vs Processing Phases of a Functional Process

Data validation in the input phase of a functional process. The input phase of any functional process is normally considered to include validation of entered data, which can require significant amounts of functionality for business applications.

As represented by the MkII method, validation processes may require references to:

- the so-called 'System Entity'; this was introduced into the MkII method to simplify measurement by counting a single ER (entity reference) in any functional process that referenced fixed tables of simple codes and descriptions and other 'non-primary' entities, typically found in dialogues of on-line systems with GUI interfaces, and

- other 'primary' entities, e.g. to check if the data to be entered describes an occurrence of an entity about which data are already stored.

Consequently, the input phase is more closely accounted for by:

- the number of DET's on the input, <u>plus</u>
- (where required) reference to the System Entity and maybe references to other entities.

This is in contrast to the 'simple' view described in the main text which assumes all entity-references belong to the processing phase.

Similarly, for the COSMIC method, data entry is accounted for by the Entry data movements and by any Read data movements needed for validation of the input data. So in reality the functionality needed to handle data entry and validation, i.e. the Input phase, includes some of the Reads that have been considered as part of the Processing phase on the 'simple' view of the division of functionality across the three phases.

Differences between MkII 'entity references' and COSMIC 'data movements'. There are two significant differences between how the MkII method defines an 'entity' and its rules for counting ER's, and the equivalent COSMIC method's definition of an 'object of interest' and its rules for counting Reads and Writes of persistently-stored data groups.

- The COSMIC method requires that all objects of interest that need to be referenced to validate entered data must be identified and counted as Reads. The COSMIC method does not recognise the simplifying concept of a 'System Entity'. So a single reference to the System Entity in the measurement of a MkII functional process may, when measured by the COSMIC method, be replaced by one or more Reads of objects of interest. (For more on this topic of the MkII System Entity and the equivalent COSMIC objects of interest, see the respective method's documentation.)
- In the COSMIC method, a functional processes that is designed for batch-processing may need a Read and Write of the same object of interest. The MkII method rules would require the counting of one ER in such a functional process. (All software items on which size data are reported in this paper were designed for on-line, not batch, processing, so this difference has no influence on the results reported here.)

Potential for further refinement of the 'calculated' size conversion method. The data available to the authors do not distinguish whether the counts of entity references include any that were required for input data validation. For this reason we have to continue to adopt the simple view of the division of functionality across the three phases when analysing the available data.

If we had the measurements, or could make some reasonable assumptions about the proportion of MkII entity-references and COSMIC Reads devoted to the input phase, then it might be possible to develop an even more refined version of the 'calculated' conversion process described and used in the body of this paper.

References

1. Gencel, C., Demirors, O.: Functional size measurement revisited. ACM Trans. Softw. Eng. Methodol. (TOSEM) **17**(3), 71–106 (2008)
2. Demirors, O., Gencel, C.: Conceptual association of functional size measurement methods. IEEE Softw. **26**(3), 71–78 (2009)
3. Albrecht, A.: Measuring application development productivity. In: Proceedings of the Joint SHARE, GUIDE, and IBM Application Development Symposium, pp. 83–92 (1979)
4. Symons, C.R.: Function point analysis: difficulties and improvements. IEEE Trans. Softw. Eng. **14**(1), 2–11 (1988)
5. The IFPUG Counting Practices Manual, v4.3. www.ifpug.org
6. The MkII FPA Counting Practices Manual, v1.3.1. www.uksma.org
7. The COSMIC Measurement Manual, v4.0.1. www.cosmic-sizing.org
8. Symons, C.: Software Sizing and Estimating: MkII FPA. John Wiley & Sons Ltd, West Sussex (1991)
9. Guideline on how to convert between 'First Generation' Function Points and COSMIC Sizes
10. Information technology – software measurement – Functional size measurement. Part 1 Definition of concepts, ISO/IEC 14143/1:2011
11. Software engineering – COSMIC: a functional size measurement method, ISO/IEC 19761:2011
12. Software engineering – MkII Function Point Analysis – Counting Practices Manual, ISO/IEC 20968:2002
13. Abran, A., Gil, B., Lefebvre, E.: Estimation models based on functional profiles. International Workshop on Software Measurement – IWSM/MetriKon. Kronisburg, pp. 195–211. Shaker Verlag, Germany (2004)
14. Abran, A., Panteliuc, A.: Estimation Models Based on Functional Profiles. In: III Taller Internacional de Calidad en Technologias de Information et de Communications, Cuba, February 15–16 (2007)
15. Gencel, Ç., Buglione, L.: Do base functional component types affect the relationship between software functional size and effort? In: Cuadrado-Gallego, J.J., Braungarten, R., Dumke, R.R., Abran, A. (eds.) IWSM-Mensura 2007. LNCS, vol. 4895, pp. 72–85. Springer, Heidelberg (2008)

Applying Manufacturing Performance Figures to Measure Software Development Excellence

Andreas Deuter[1](✉) and Hans-Jürgen Koch[2]

[1] Ostwestfalen-Lippe University of Applied Sciences, 32657 Lemgo, Germany
andreas.deuter@hs-owl.de
[2] Phoenix Contact Electronics GmbH, 31812 Bad Pyrmont, Germany
hkoch@phoenixcontact.com

Abstract. The Internet of Things is going to digitize traditional manufacturing plants. Apart from being as functional and robust as ever, products required to run these plants will need to be smart and connected. They will have software inside. Producing companies monitor their manufacturing excellence related to these products by evaluating manufacturing performance figures such as delivery time and yield. However, for the time being, no figures for the software inside are measured with similar means.

Software performance figures have been investigated a lot in software research and in the IT industry. However, as they are software domain-oriented they are difficult to understand for leading managing minds of producing companies.

This article demonstrates that it is reasonable to apply manufacturing performance figures to measure software development excellence. This is a valuable element ensuring future business success of producing companies by enabling their managers to control excellence in software development processes.

Keywords: Software performance figures · Manufacturing performance figures · Added value · Sliced V-model

1 Introduction

Huge changes in traditional manufacturing are taking place driven by IT-technology. The Internet of Things as well as cyber-physical systems are going to render plants self-organized and reconfigurable. The manufactured goods find their ways through the plants automatically. Mass customization is the vision. It is the fourth industry revolution - the so-called Industry 4.0 [1].

These changes have far-reaching consequences for all manufactures running these plants. At the same time, also those companies producing the products required to run these plants efficiently are affected enormously. Today, their products range from pure hardware (connectors, cables, power supplies, etc.) to intelligent automation devices (PLC, HMI, Industrial Switches, etc.) and complex machinery. In order to fulfill the scenarios foreseen many of the new

© Springer International Publishing Switzerland 2015
A. Kobyliński et al. (Eds.): IWSM-Mensura 2015, LNBIP 230, pp. 62–77, 2015.
DOI: 10.1007/978-3-319-24285-9_5

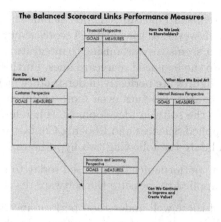

Fig. 1. The balanced scorecard principle [2]

products need to be intelligent. They will get or be equipped with much more software inside. It is inevitable that future innovation of manufacturing will be software-driven.

What are the consequences of these prospects for the producing companies? In order to compete and keep pace they will need to understand their software development excellence in the way they do understand their manufacturing excellence. Today, producing companies apply the balanced scorecard to measure their manufacturing excellence [2]. Kaplan and Norton say: "The balanced scorecard allows managers to look at the business from for four important perspectives." (Fig. 1). Manufacturing excellence as part of the internal business perspective is monitored by performance figures for cycle time, unit costs or yield.

Phoenix Contact, a leading supplier of electrical and electronic components for industrial applications, applies the balanced scorecard principle. Amongst others, it uses the manufacturing performance figures shown in Table 1 to measure the manufacturing excellence of the manufacturing lines for electronic devices.

With the increasing importance of software applied in electronic devices, the need to monitor the software development excellence is increasing as well.

Table 1. Manufacturing performance figures

Figure	Meaning
Readiness for delivery (%)	Ratio of agreed/actual delivery date
Complaints rate (%)	Ratio of produced/returned products
First pass yield (%)	Ratio of passed/failed end-tests
Order costs €	Costs to produce an order
Added value €	Production value minus related costs
Added value rate	Ratio of added value/order costs

The current balanced scorecard measures do not include the measurement of the software development. However, as the balanced scorecard principle is well established and well known, it seems very promising to integrate software development performance figures into the balanced scorecard ones. Furthermore, as the manufacturing performance figures are perfectly understood (which cannot be said for software performance figures) it seems even more promising to apply the same performance figures for the software development. Therefore, the Ostwestfalen-Lippe University of Applied Sciences and Phoenix Contact have started a design research activity to validate the following two hypotheses:

H1: The manufacturing performance figures used today to monitor manufacturing excellence can be applied to measure the software development excellence.

H2: The application of these well-understood performance figures creates value by increased management attention towards software development.

This article is structured as follows: Sect. 2 presents related work. Section 3 describes our design research and the details of the proposed approach. Section 4 explains its implementation and evaluation at Phoenix Contact. Section 5 outlines the conclusions and the future work.

2   Related Work

This section gives an overview about the known work on software performance figures and the transfer of manufacturing ideas to software. Before we start with this we explain the sliced V-model as it is the process model used for the proposed approach.

2.1   Sliced V-Model

In a recent work, the first author introduced the sliced V-model [3]. It maintains the strength of the traditional V-model originally defined by Boehm [4]. However, the sliced V-model eases the management of documentation, reduces team's Work In Progress (WiP) and more flexible regarding time. Within a sliced V-model documents are containers of work items. A work item is a small piece of information created during a phase of the software life cycle, e.g. a requirement or a test case. All work items and source code revisions belonging to a single requirement are linked together. This ensures easy traceability in software projects (Fig. 2). Furthermore, a defect is also tracked as a work item. The source code needed to fix this defect is linked to the defect work item.

The sliced V-model requires the application of an appropriate database system. Phoenix Contact uses the *Polarion* system [5]. There is a *Polarion* project for each software product. This projects contains all data over the complete software life cycle. Furthermore, defects found during internal testing activities and defects reported externally are tracked separately.

The team members enter their efforts in "task" work items. Each team members is asked not only to track tasks for implementing, but also for writing specifications, performing tests, etc.

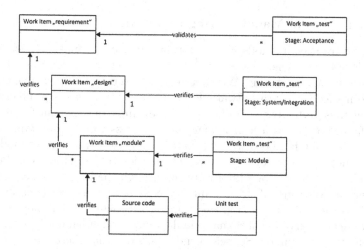

Fig. 2. The sliced V-model structure [3]

Baselines track the time-line of a single software version. A baseline is "a reference configuration from which to identify and to control changes" [6]. We set a baseline when the work on a new software version starts and when it is released. The difference between these dates is the duration as defined by Barry et al. [7].

2.2   Software Performance Figures

There are numerous articles, books and studies about software performance figures, metrics and measures. Fenton and Fleeger name a length of possible metrics, e.g. function points and defect density [8]. Applying suitable measures to understand software performance have already been investigated in the past. Kasunic names possible suitable software performance measures such as productivity, post-release defect density or requirement completion ratio [9]. Velocity is another practiced metric used preferable in agile developments [10]. Furthermore, there is published scientific literature to address software economics, e.g. by Boehm [11]. However, when we selected some figures and asked the managers at Phoenix Contact: "Do you understand the meaning of these performance figures?" they answered "Rather no". Especially, they struggle to understand the specific measuring units such as function points or lines of code. One may think that these performance figures could be explained in several sessions to these managers. But in our opinion, this is not a constructive way to make software performance transparent to them. Therefore, we have developed the idea of our alternative approach which includes important figures for software value. Managers do ask about money: "How do I know how much value is created by the software teams?".

2.3   Transfer from Manufacturing to Software

The idea to transfer methods and performance figures from manufacturing to software is not new. There have been enormous productivity increases over the last decades in manufacturing. Why not analyze and transfer applicable methods and performance figures to software development to increase its productivity as well? Kanban is probably the most prominent example of such transfer. It origins in manufacturing and is a lean management process to control manufacturing plants [12]. Kanban has been transferred to an agile software process model [13]. There are more transfers of lean manufacturing ideas to software, e.g. Petersen and Wohlin propose software improvement through the lean management [14].

Binder analyzed manufacturing quality models such as six sigma and their potential transfer to software [15]. He came to the conclusion that manufacturing and software are two different domains and quality models cannot be transferred. In opposite to that opinion, Schneidewind points out that there are indeed some methods used in manufacturing which can be transferred [16]. He names the Tagushi methods, statistical quality control and statistical process control using failure probability and failure counts as possible elements. However, our analyzes of related work to this topic indicates that there is very few research in this area.

Summarizing, we know that there are many software performance figures. However, at least in the environment of Phoenix Contact as a traditional manufacturing company, the middle and upper management is excellent in applying manufacturing performance figures and other business related figures such as turnover or margin. But, there is little understanding about software performance figures. As explained, we believe that this situation will not change in the near future. As there is no mapping today between these two worlds we fill this gap with our approach.

3   Proposed Approach

In order to proceed in a structured way, we follow the design research (DR) approach as depicted by Goldkuhl [17] (Fig. 3). In the previous sections we derived the problem analysis. This section builds the approach consisting of software performance figures and manufacturing ones. Section 4 addresses the evaluation.

Fig. 3. Design research approach [17]

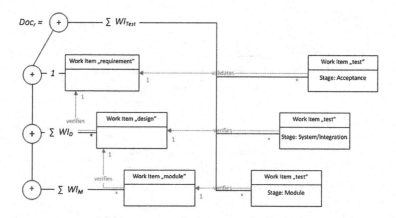

Fig. 4. Measuring the software documentation size of one requirement

3.1   Software Performance Figures

<u>Quantity:</u> The first author participated in the development of an approach to calculate software quantity in the sliced V-model [18]. The core idea is to calculate the sum of work items which are connected to a single requirement (Fig. 4) and the sum of code changes made to implement this requirement. As work items represent the documentation by this way we include the size of the development and the test documentation in the software size. We called it *software documentation size* and use the symbol Doc_r. The measuring unit is Work Items (WI). We apply the *churn* method [19] by using unified diff patches [20] to measure the source code changes. We call it *requirements churn*. We use the symbol Ch_r. The measuring unit is Kilobytes (KB). These calculations are repeated for each requirement implemented in a specific software version giving the software sizes for one software version represented with the symbols Doc_R and Ch_R.

<u>Quality:</u> Due to the mentioned defect organization in a sliced V-model project we can analyze the quality data. We measure the number of defects found during internal testing activities, DI, the number of defect reported externally, DX, and the sum of both, DS. Furthermore, we measure the size of source code changes made to fix all defects, which have been found during the internal testing activities. We call this size *internal defect churn*. We use the symbols Ch_{di} for one defect and Ch_{Di} for all defects found during testing activities (Fig. 5).

Furthermore, we measure the size of source code changes made to fix all defects, which have been found after the software releases. We call this size *external defect churn*. We use the symbol Ch_{dx} for one defect and Ch_{Dx} for all externally reported defects.

<u>Costs:</u> The development costs of a software version using the sliced V-model process are the sum of all efforts reported in the "task" work item multiplied with a company dependent hour rate. We do not consider further costs, e.g. indirect

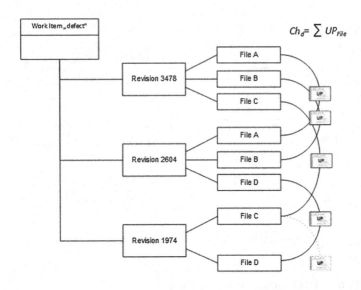

Fig. 5. Measuring the defect churn of one defect

costs in distributed environments. Equations (1) and (2) show the calculations.

$$DE = \sum_{i=1}^{n} TS_i \tag{1}$$

$$DC = DE * HR \tag{2}$$

with:

DE	Development effort
TS	Effort per "task" work item
n	Number of "task" work items
DC	Development costs
HR	Hour rate (company dependent)

The measuring unit for DE is hours (h) and for DC it is €.

<u>Duration:</u> The development duration is the number of elapsed days between the start baseline and the end baseline. Equation (3) shows the calculation.

$$DD = t_{B_e} - t_{B_s} \tag{3}$$

with:

DD	Development duration for a software version
t_{B_e}	Date when the work of software version starts
t_{B_s}	Release date of the software version

The measuring unit for DD is days (d).

<u>Productivity:</u> The productivity is the ratio between the software quantity and the development effort. It indicates the team's efficiency to develop software. As

we have defined two software sizes, there are also two figures for productivity. Equations (4) and (5) show the calculations.

$$P_D = \frac{Doc_R}{DE} \qquad (4)$$

$$P_C = \frac{Ch_R}{DE} \qquad (5)$$

with:

P_D Software documentation productivity
P_C Requirements churn productivity

Velocity: The velocity is the ratio between the software quantity and the development duration. It indicates how fast teams can deliver. As we have two software sizes, we also have two figures for velocity. Equations (6) and (7) show the calculations.

$$V_D = \frac{Doc_R}{DD} \qquad (6)$$

$$V_C = \frac{Ch_R}{DD} \qquad (7)$$

with:

V_D Software documentation velocity
V_C Requirements churn velocity

Defect Density: The defect density is the ratio between the total number of defects DS and the software quantity. It indicates the team's capability to deliver defect-free software. As we have two software sizes, we also have two figures for defect density. Equations (8) and (9) show the calculations.

$$DT_D = \frac{DS}{Doc_R} \qquad (8)$$

$$DT_C = \frac{DS}{Ch_R} \qquad (9)$$

with:

DT_D Software documentation defect density
DT_C Requirements churn defect density

Table 2 summarizes all software performance figures.

3.2 Manufacturing Performance Figures

Now we map the software performance figures to the manufacturing performance figures shown in Table 1.

Complaints Rate: The traditional complaints rate indicates how many products have been returned by customers. As most of the returns are due to quality

Table 2. Software performance figures

Figure	Symbol
Software documentation size	Doc_R
Requirements churn	Ch_R
Internal defect churn	Ch_{Di}
External defect churn	Ch_{Dx}
Defect numbers	DI, DX, DS
Development duration	DD
Development effort	DE
Development costs	DC
Productivity	P_D, P_C
Velocity	V_D, V_C
Defect density	DT_D, DT_C

issues, it indicates the ability to produce error-free products. In order to find a suitable mapping into the software world, we set the requirements churn size, the internal defect churn size and the external defect churn size into a relation. This relation also indicates the ability to develop error-free software. Equation (10) shows the calculation.

$$CR = 100\,\% * \frac{Ch_{Dx}}{Ch_R + Ch_{Di} + Ch_{Dx}} \qquad (10)$$

with:

    CR Complaints rate

First Pass Yield: The traditional first past yield indicates the percentage of products successfully passed the production end-tests. It indicates the amount of re-work in order to deliver all manufactured pieces. In order to find a suitable mapping into the software world, we set the requirements churn size and the internal defect churn size into a relation. This relation also indicates the amount of re-work before the release of a software version. Equation (11) shows the calculation.

$$FPY = 100\,\% * \frac{Ch_R}{Ch_R + Ch_{Di}} \qquad (11)$$

with:

    FPY First past yield

Order Costs: The traditional order costs consist of labor and material costs of a production lot. We do not consider material costs for software. Therefore, the software order costs are the development costs DC. Equation (12) shows the calculation.

$$OC = DC \qquad (12)$$

with:

OC Order costs

Added Value: The traditional added value is a monetary indicator of the value produced by own competencies and resources. Simplified said, it is the difference between the material costs of all product pieces and the product sales price. The software documentation size and the requirements churn size indicate the amount of software produced by the own teams to implement requirements. These figures also indicate the added value for software, as there are no other results produced. However, these are not monetary values. Therefore, we multiply Doc_R and Ch_R with added value factors. These added value factors are given in €. They are defined per work item and per churn KB separately. Historical project data can be analyzed to determine suitable values. Equation (13) shows the calculation.

$$AV = \frac{(Doc_R * AF_D)}{WI} + \frac{(Ch_R * AF_C)}{KB} \tag{13}$$

with:

AV Added value
AF_D Software documentation added value factor
AF_C Requirements churn added value factor

The so-defined software added value is a virtual monetary figure, because in difference to the traditional added value it is not charged to the customer. However, such mapping makes software value much more tangible for managers. It shows the potential business value created by the software teams. If this value would not contribute to the business success the related activities could be omitted at all.

Added Value Rate: The traditional added value rate is the ratio of the added value and the overall performance. It quantifies the value growth by the application of production means expressed as order costs. The added value rate for software quantifies the value growth per development costs. Equation (14) shows the calculation.

$$AVR = \frac{AV}{DC} \tag{14}$$

with:

AVR Added value rate

Readiness for Delivery: The traditional readiness for delivery indicates how many products were delivered on requested or confirmed time. It is a figure of producing companies' ability to deliver on-time. The velocities V_D and V_C indicate how fast teams can develop software. But, they are not figures measure the ability to deliver software on-time. Therefore, for the readiness for delivery manufacturing figure we cannot provide an appropriate mapping.

However, we believe that is required to indicate some information about "speed" also for software. Such figure should be expressed with a well-understood measuring unit (see discussion in Sect. 2.3). Therefore, we create a ratio between potential target and actual figures for the velocities V_D and V_C. As it is an indicator to deliver on-time, we call it "Readiness for delivery indicator". The measuring unit is %. Equation (15) shows the calculation.

$$RDI = 100\,\% * \frac{\frac{V_{Da}}{V_{Dt}} + \frac{V_{Ca}}{V_{Ct}}}{2} \tag{15}$$

with:

RDI	Readiness for delivery indicator
V_{Da}	Actual software documentation velocity
V_{Dt}	Target software documentation velocity
V_{Ca}	Actual requirements churn velocity
V_{Ct}	Target requirements churn velocity

The target values for V_D and V_D are defined for different software products individually. Initial values for target figures are determined by first sample measurements. If RDI exceeds 100 %, the target values will be adjusted.

4   Evaluation of the Approach

Phoenix Contact is highly interested in this approach. In order to evaluate it, we took two evaluation steps:

1. Verification: The approach is technically applicable in Phoenix Contact's environment.
2. Validation: The approach helps Phoenix Contact managers to better understand software development.

4.1   Verification

We implemented a reporting tool called "PQM". It generates the software performance figures and manufacturing performance figures in an automated way.

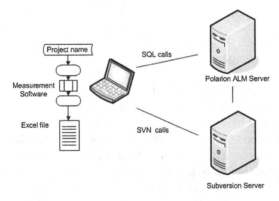

Fig. 6. The measurement setup

Table 3. Software performance figures (PQM)

Figure	V1.0	V1.2
Doc_R	170 WI	50 WI
Ch_R	2,737.238 KB	1,017.051 KB
Ch_{Di}	14.921 KB	17.303
Ch_{De}	2.964 KB	0 KB
DS	7 WI	2 WI
DD	680d	144d
DE	377 h	74h
DC	€ 26,390	€ 5,180
P_D	0.45 WI/h	0.68 WI/h
P_C	7.3 KB/h	13.7 KB/h
V_D	0.25 WI/d	0.34 WI/d
V_C	4.0 KB/d	7.1 KB/d
DT_D	0.042 Defect/WI	0.04 Defect/WI
DT_C	0.0025 Defect/KB	0.002 Defect/KB

PQM captures data from *Polarion* and *Subversion*, which is the version control system in use, and stores them in an Excel file (Fig. 6).

After implementing, we measured the PQM software development as a first test. PQM has been developed over around two years before the version V1.0 was released. There are only few tests performed so far. First measurements were taken for the PQM version V1.0, second measurement were taken for a version V1.2 internally released few month after V1.0. Table 3 shows the software performance figures for both versions.

We created the manufacturing performance figures based on the software performance figures. We defined a software documentation added value factor AF_D of € 50 per work item and a requirements churn added value factor AF_C of € 30 per KB. These are arbitrary values. We did not start an analysis on more

Table 4. Manufacturing performance figures (PQM)

Figure	V1.0	V1.2
Readiness for Delivery Indicator (RDI)	100 %	156.75 %
Complaints Rate (CR)	0,11 %	0 %
First Pass Yield (FPY)	99,45 %	98,32 %
Order Costs (OC)	€ 26,390	€ 5,180
Added Value (AV)	€ 91,150	€ 33,010
Added Value Rate (AVR)	3.45	6.37

appropriate values. As the version V1.0 was the first version measured its actual values for the velocities were declared as initial target values. For version V1.2 their target values are the actual values of V1.0. The version V1.2 has not been distributed. Therefore, no external defects have been reported. Table 4 shows the manufacturing performance figures taking these frame conditions into account.

There are discussable facts seen in the Tables 3 and 4. It is noticeable that the added value rate increased. In V1.2 more quantity was produced with less effort. A deeper look into the project showed that there was one source code file generated automatically. This generation does not consume any effort, but increase the churn figures a lot. Furthermore, for V1.2 a number of "test" work items were created without detailing or performing them. This increased the software documentation size, but again it did not consume much effort. It also increased the velocities in V1.2. Therefore, the readiness for delivery indicator RDI is here higher than 100 %.

4.2   Validation

In order to create more confidence in our approach we took also performance figures of a large Phoenix Contact software product. We call it SWB. This product exists already for many years. A lot of maintenance work is required for this product. As in the sliced V-model project of SWB the defects found internally and externally are not separately tracked we could not measure the complaints rate. Therefore, the first past yield contains the size of code changes made to fix both types of defects. We measured the order costs and the added value. We are not allowed to show these figures in this article. However, the AVR figures indicates the ratio between those two figures. The SWB manufacturing performance figures are shown in Table 5. We can demonstrate that our approach can be applied on a real-life software products.

Table 5. Manufacturing performance figures (SWB)

Figure	V1.0	V1.1
Readiness for Delivery Indicator (RDI)	100 %	46.89 %
Complaints Rate (CR)	-	-
First Pass Yield (FPY)	68,31 %	70,80 %
Order Costs (OC)	nn	nn
Added Value (AV)	nn	nn
Added Value Rate (AVR)	0.52	0.23

As next, we interviewed five Phoenix Contact managers. We selected following different roles: one low level software manager, one quality manager and three higher level managers, each of them running different departments. The quality manager and the higher level managers are not from the software domain. However, they are responsible to control and manage software departments. In these interviews we explained the content of the different tables. When we showed them the SWB manufacturing performance figures they could immediately start a discussion. For example, they were surprised to see that approximately 30 % of the source code changes are motivated by bug fixing. As a lot of maintenance work is required, these data are plausible. Also, the small added value rate provided discussions. However, as we used arbitrary added value factors we were encouraged to analyze potential realistic values. There were also plausible reasons for the reduction of the *RDI* figure in SWB V1.1. After this discussion, we asked them the following questions:

- Do you understand the approach?
- Do you use today manufacturing performance figures for your management tasks?
- Would you apply manufacturing performance figures for software development?
- Would this approach help you to better understand software?

The answers given in these interviews were overwhelming for us. All managers were strongly interested in this approach. They followed our opinion that the application of traditional manufacturing performance figures supports them to understand software development much better. Exemplary the following statements:

- "Applying performance figures I already know for software development, would be a great help for me in making better software product-related decisions. Honestly, I cannot tell today if we are improving in software development."
- "This approach will help me to consider our software development as a value center, rather than a cost center it is considered today. Especially, the added value figures are very promising."

All managers encouraged us to proceed in implementing the approach on a broader level.

5   Conclusion and Future Work

This article introduces a novel approach applying manufacturing performance figures to measure software development excellence. It is a two-step approach:

1. Measurement of software performance figures.
2. Mapping software performance figures to manufacturing performance figures.

We developed the approach as a design research activity. We evaluated the approach by taking performance figures of a reporting tool and of one Phoenix Contact software product. We interviewed several Phoenix Contact managers to proof that our approach is a valuable support for their management duties.

Assessing the hypotheses stated in Sect. 1, we conclude following:

H1 - Applicability of Manufacturing Performance Figures to Software:
Our approach demonstrates that is possible to use manufacturing performance

figures to monitor software development excellence. It is not simply a name mapping. It also maintains the meaning of the figures. However, our approach requires the measurement of software performance figures to gather the manufacturing ones.

H2 - Value Creation by Increased Management Attention: First interviews have shown that our approach eases the software understanding for managers unrelated to the software domain. For the first time, they could discuss about performance figures for software products. Therefore, as assumed, our approach increases the management attention towards software.

However, there are some threats to the validity of our approach. First of all, in order to generate exact figures, a high discipline in implementing the sliced V-model is required by the teams in their daily work. We have seen that if some rules of the sliced V-model are not followed, some performance figures cannot be generated.

Furthermore, there was only one iteration in our design research activity. In order to get a better understanding how managers will control software with our approach we will need a more broad-based field study. Therefore, the Ostwestfalen-Lippe University of Applied Sciences and Phoenix Contact have agreed on testing this approach on several software products for another year. We expect that we will get a better knowledge of the acceptance of our approach in the daily business of Phoenix Contact and by this a much more rigorous evaluation. We foresee that we may add, remove or adapt some of the performance figures explained in this article. Nevertheless, with our approach we have defined a clear starting point to transfer this new way of thinking into practice.

Our definition of the added value is rather straightforward. The great strength of this approach is its automated generation. Khurum et al. propose a systematic approach called software value map which could be taken into account for deeper analyses [21].

We did not find an adequate mapping regarding the "readiness for delivery" figure. A possible solution is to measure the duration between the agreed date to deliver a new function and its actual delivery date as part of a software version. However, in order to measure such figures from the database, we will need to extend the sliced V-model definition.

Today, producing companies have implemented an automated data collection of the performance figures of their manufacturing lines without any manual rework required. Our approach follows this key requirement for data collection. With our reporting tool we implemented an automated measurement of our performance figures. This is another important criterion towards the successful transfer of our novel approach into practice.

References

1. Kagermann, H., Wahlster, W., Helbig, J., eds.: Securing the Future of German Manufacturing Industry: Recommendations for Implementing the Strategic Initiative INDUSTRIE 4.0, Final Report of the Industrie 4.0 Working Group. Forschungsunion im Stifterverband für die Deutsche Wirtschaft e.V., Berlin, April 2013

2. Kaplan, R.S., Norton, D.P.: The balanced scorecard - measures that drive performance. Harvard Bus. Rev. **69**, 71–79 (1992)
3. Deuter, A.: Slicing the V-model - Reduced effort, higher flexibility. In: Proceedings of 8th International Conference on Global Software Engineering, ICGSE 2013, pp. 1–10 (2013)
4. Boehm, B.W.: Guidelines for verifying and validating software requirements and design specifications. In: Samet, P.A. (ed.) Euro IFIP, vol. 79, pp. 711–719. North Holland, Amsterdam (1979)
5. Polarion (2004). http://www.polarion.com. 04 April 2015
6. Deininger, W., Cottingham, C., Kanner, L., Verbeke, M.A.: Systems engineering data book (sedb) - a product baseline definition and tracking tool. In: 19th International Conference on Systems Engineering, 2008, ICSENG 2008, pp. 19–24 (2008)
7. Barry, E.J., Mukhopadhyay, T., Slaughter, S.A.: Software project duration and effort: An empirical study. Inf. Technol. Manag. **3**(1–2), 113–136 (2002)
8. Fenton, N., Pfleeger, S.L.: Software Metrics: A Rigorous and Practical Approach, 2nd edn. PWS Publishing Co., Boston (1997)
9. Kasunic, M.: A data specification for software project performance measures: Results of a collaboration on performance measurement. Technical report CMU/SEI-2008-TR-012, Software Engineering Institute, Carnegie Mellon University, Pittsburgh, Pennsylvania (2008)
10. Hartmann, D., Dymond, R.: Appropriate agile measurement: using metrics and diagnostics to deliver business value. In: Agile Conference, 2006, pp. 126-134, July 2006
11. Boehm, B.W.: Software Engineering Economics, 1st edn. Prentice Hall PTR, Upper Saddle River (1981)
12. Liker, J.: The Toyota Way, 1st edn. McGraw-Hill, New York (2004)
13. Hiranabe, K.: Kanban applied to software development: from agile to lean (2008). http://www.infoq.com/articles/hiranabe-lean-agile-kanban. 04 April 2015
14. Petersen, K., Wohlin, C.: Software process improvement through the lean measurement (spi-leam) method. J. Syst. Softw. **83**(7), 1275–1287 (2010)
15. Binder, R.: Can a manufacturing quality model work for software? Softw. IEEE **14**(5), 101–102, 105 (1997)
16. Schneidewind, N.: What can software engineers learn from manufacturing to improve software process and product? Intell. Inf. Manag. **1**, 98–107 (2009)
17. Goldkuhl, G.: Action research vs. design research: using practice research as a lens for comparison and integration. In: IT Artefact Design & Workpractice Improvement (ADWI 2013) (2013)
18. Deuter, A., Engels, G.: Measuring the software size of sliced V-model projects. In: Proceedings of International Workshop on Software Measurement and the International Conference on Software Process and Product Measurement, IWSM-Mensura 2014, pp. 233–242 (2014)
19. Sjoberg, D.I., Johnsen, A., Solberg, J.: Quantifying the effect of using kanban versus scrum: a case study. IEEE Softw. **29**, 47–53 (2012)
20. Jang, J., Agrawal, A., Brumley, D.: Redebug: finding unpatched code clones in entire os distributions. In: IEEE Symposium on Security and Privacy, pp. 48–62 (2012)
21. Khurum, M., Gorschek, T., Wilson, M.: The software value map - an exhaustive collection of value aspects for the development of software intensive products. J. Softw. Evol. Process **25**(7), 711–741 (2013)

Quantitative Functional Change Impact Analysis in Activity Diagrams: A COSMIC-Based Approach

Mariem Haoues[1(✉)], Asma Sellami[1], Hanêne Ben-Abdallah[2],
and Nourchène Elleuch Ben Ayed[2]

[1] Mir@cl Laboratory, University of Sfax, Sfax, Tunisia
mariem_haoues@yahoo.fr, asma.sellami@isimsf.rnu.tn
[2] Faculty of Computing and Information Technology,
King Abdulaziz University, Jeddah, Saudi Arabia
{hbenabdallah, nbenayed}@kau.edu.sa

Abstract. Change requests are inevitable in every phase of the Software Development Life Cycle (SDLC), and responding to a change request without jeopardizing the project success remains a challenge for software developers/managers. Expressing functional changes in terms of COSMIC Function Point units can be helpful in identifying changes leading to a potential impact on the software functional size; this latter can be used as a means to plan the project activities. This paper proposes to analyze the impact of functional changes on the size of UML activity diagrams, one artifact type produced early in the SDLC. The proposed analysis handles directly as well as indirectly affected elements in both modelling levels of the activity diagrams.

Keywords: COSMIC functional size measurement · Activity diagram · Functional change · Impact analysis · Functional user requirements change

1 Introduction

Functional requirements changes may occur at any phase of the Software Development Life Cycle (SDLC). Decisions taken about a change request may jeopardize the project success: Accepting a change request can lead to an additional cost and effort to produce the final product within the schedule, whereas rejecting a change request may produce a software that does not satisfy the user expectations. A judicious decision about a change request needs a thorough change impact analysis conducted over the various artifacts produced in all the phases of SDLC.

Many researches focused on change impact analysis in one SDLC phase like the design (*cf.* [1]) or the implementation (*cf.* [2]). Researches highlight that requirements changes occurring during later stages of the SDLC are costlier than those occurring in the early stages [3]. Consequently, some researchers looked into change prediction in an attempt to predict the risk of a change in the implementation phase (*cf.* [4]). Other studies focused on the requirements change in an early stage: analysis and design phases (*e.g.* [1, 5], and [6]). For example, [6] proposed a mechanism based on a formal

© Springer International Publishing Switzerland 2015
A. Kobyliński et al. (Eds.): IWSM-Mensura 2015, LNBIP 230, pp. 78–95, 2015.
DOI: 10.1007/978-3-319-24285-9_6

semantics of requirements relations and requirements change types to improve change impact analysis.

In the design phase, there are two types of impact change analysis: intra-dependency analysis which identifies changes among the same diagram (*cf.* [7]), and inter-dependency analysis which identifies changes among different diagrams (*cf.* [1]). Even though many researchers focused on the inter-dependency and/or intra-dependency analysis, there is not yet a study on the Functional Change (FC) impact in the Activity Diagram (UML-AD). In this paper, we focus on the intra-dependency analysis in UML-AD to propose a new approach for measuring the FC in terms of COSMIC Function Point (CFP) units and its impact on the size of the UML-AD.

The rest of this paper is organized as follows: Sect. 2 presents an overview of the COSMIC method and UML-AD, and it surveys some related works. In Sect. 3, we propose to use COSMIC to measure the FC in terms of CFP units and identify its impact on the functional size of UML-AD and UML-AD elements. Section 4 illustrates our approach through an example. Finally, Sect. 5 summarizes the presented work and outlines some of its extensions.

2 Background

2.1 Functional Size Measurement

Functional Size (FS) of software is defined as the size "derived by quantifying the functional user requirements" [8]. Functional User Requirements (FUR) represent "user practices and procedures that the software must perform to fulfill the user's needs, and exclude quality requirements and any technical requirements" [8]. Functional Size Measurement (FSM) methods based on FUR can be used to predict software project effort, control requirements, analyze project productivity, etc.

Several FSM methods have been proposed in the literature. The first generation of FSM methods was provided by Allan Albrecht in 1979 "Function Point Analysis" (FPA); it is supported by the "International Function Point Users Group" (IFPUG) and by ISO from 2003 - IFPUG (ISO/IEC 20926:2009). Other methods have since been proposed such as NESMA (ISO/IEC 24570:2005), MKII (ISO/IEC 20968:2002), FiSMA (ISO/IEC 29881:2010), and recently COSMIC (ISO/IEC 19761:2011). As argued in [9], IFPUG and MkII were primarily designed to measure business application software, whereas COSMIC can be used in different domains (*e.g.* business application, real-time, etc.). For a comparison between the IFPUG, MkII, and COSMIC methods, the reader is referred to [9].

As it is observed in Fig. 1, COSMIC identifies four types of data movements: Entry, eXit, Read, and Write. "Entry" data movement describes the move of data group from a functional user across the boundary into the functional process where it is required [8]. "eXit" data movement correspond to the move of data group from a functional process across the boundary to the functional user that requires it [8]. "Read" data movement represents the move of data group from persistent storage into the functional process which requires it [8]. Finally, a "Write" is a data movement that moves a data group lying inside a functional process to persistent storage [8]. Each data movement is equivalent to 1 CFP. The software functional size is computed by adding all data movements identified for every functional process.

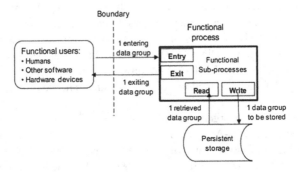

Fig. 1. Data movement types and their relationships with a functional process [8]

In the case of an enhancement project, the functional size of a functional change noted by FS(FC) is equal to the sum of the size of all data movements that are either new, changed or removed from the software [8]. In fact, COSMIC defines a FC as "any combination of additions of new data movements or of modifications or deletions of existing data movements" [8]. In addition, COSMIC provides rules to measure the FS (FC): After functionally changing a piece of software, its new total size equals: the original size, plus the functional size of all the added data movements, minus the functional size of all the removed data movements [8]. Note that, in COSMIC, modifying a data movement has no influence on the FS of the software.

2.2   Overview of UML Activity Diagram

A UML-AD involves the dynamic and functional behavior of a software system [10]. Figure 2 presents the meta-model of UML-AD where an activity is represented by a set of nodes 'Activity Node' interconnected by edges 'Activity Edge'. Subsets of the 'Activity Node' are 'Executable Node', 'Object Node', and 'Control Node'.

'Executable Node' is represented by 'Action'. According to [10], an action is "the fundamental unit of executable functionality". The textual description of an action is provided in [11] as follow:

```
<Number>    <Name>    <Partition    &&    [Object]>    ([<InputParameters>])
([<OutputParamaters>]) [<Pre_condition>] [<Post_condition>]
```

An activity can be invoked by using the 'Call Behavior Action' node, which means that the invoked activity is defined in more details in another activity diagram.

- *'Object Node'* contains data that are input to and output from *'Executable Node'*. Data can be moved from/to *'Object Node'* using *'Object Flow'* edges.
- *'Control Node'* specifies sequencing of *'Executable Node'* via *'Control Flow'* edges. *'Control Flow'* edges link between *'Actions'* or *'Activities'* and can move data using *'Pin'*.
- *'Pin'* is an object node that allows inputs and outputs values to actions.

The UML-AD meta-model depicted in Fig. 2 is inspired from [10]. It does not include all elements used in the UML-AD, because we keep only those that can be aligned with COSMIC concepts and represent an impact on the FS(UML-AD). As an example, we kept *'Call Behavior Action'* since it will be used differently compared to other actions, such as Time Event Action, Accept Event Action, etc. (see Sect. 3).

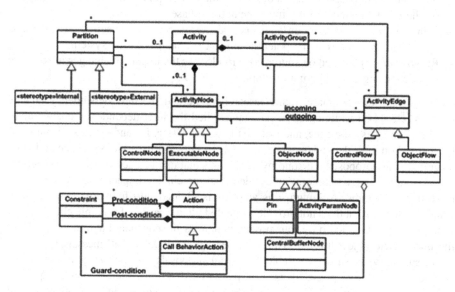

Fig. 2. A portion of activity diagram meta-model

2.3 Works on Change Impact Analysis

Despite all the attention taken in the requirements specification phase, requirements often change during all the software development lifecycle. For instance, customers may wish to alter the original design of software once the implementation is initiated (such as, adding some buttons after the inspection of a partially completed user interface; a new technology or market change may dictate adding new software requirements; designers may propose a functional change if they detect an error in the requirements specification, etc.). Thus, requirements change can be considered as a risk that needs to be addressed early in the SDLC. Risks of requirements change include for example; risk to the success and the completion of the project, reduce the product's quality, changes snowball, etc.

Change impact analysis is defined as "the process of identifying the potential consequences (side-effects) of a change, and estimating what needs to be modified to accomplish that change" [12]. In fact, each change must be accompanied by an impact analysis to determine the effect of this change on the software development progress. Surveying the problem of change impact analysis is a widely discussed subject in the literature. For instance:

- Bohner [12] provided causes for requirements change in different phases of the SDLC (requirement elicitation, design, implementation, and test).
- Chaumun et al. [13] focused on change assessment in object-oriented system. They provided the impact of changes defined at the design phase i.e. classes and mapped on the C ++ language in the implementation phase.
- Briand et al. [3] focused on analysis and design phases to keep UML diagrams up-to-date and to assess the potential impact of changes in the system.
- Russo et al. [2] focused on source code to identify the impact of changes in software products using colored commit graphs.

During the design phase, many researchers studied the intra-dependency change analysis (e.g. [14]) while other researchers studied the inter-dependency change analysis between class, sequence, and statechart diagrams (e.g. [1] and [15]). Inpirom et al. [7] focused on inter-dependency change analysis between use case, sequence and class diagrams. They proposed a taxonomy of changes that can be occurred in each diagram. Based on this change taxonomy, they identified the change impact in each element of these three diagrams. Although, this analysis is divided into four directions (Parent, Child, In, and Out), it does not provide a detailed identification of possible changes. For example, they identified only four possible changes in sequence diagram (Add object life line, Delete object life line, Add call message, and Delete call message).

In summary, as shown in Table 1, current proposals for analyzing the impact of changes in the design phase focused on particular diagrams, such as class, sequence, and statechart diagrams. Despite its importance in the requirements specification and design phases, the activity diagram has not been treated.

Table 1. Summary of the proposals focused on changes in UML Diagrams

	Inpirom et al. [7]	Briand et al. [1]	Hoa et al. [16]	JayPrakash [15]	Vargas et al. [14]	Briand et al. [17]	Chaumun et al. [13]
UML diagrams	Class	Class	Class	Class	Class	Class	Class
	Sequence	Sequence	Sequence	Sequence		Sequence	
		Statechart		Statechart			
	Use Case					Use Case	

3   Functional Changes in UML-AD

3.1   Classification of Functional Change Impact in UML-AD

A UML-AD is used to illustrate the behavior of a software system early in the SDLC at both the functional and dynamic levels. The functional level is first used to describe the services provided by the system, and the dynamic level is used to detail the dynamic operations of the system. In terms of the UML-AD meta-model, the functional level is modeled through the activity nodes, activity edges, etc. Each activity is detailed in the dynamic level, it is modeled through actions, partitions, activity edges, object nodes, etc.

In this paper, we focus on the intra-dependency functional change analysis in the UML-AD. When a functional change occurs in the UML-AD, it can affect the functional and/or dynamic level. Then, the impact of this change should be classified into one or a combination of the following impact directions:

1. Internal impact: the functional change affects only the element subject of the change and it does not propagate to any other element in the UML-AD. It can happen at either levels. For example, the modification of a "Pre-condition" in an activity.
2. Intra-level impact: the functional change affects elements within the level of the element subject of the change (*e.g.* functional level). For example, when an activity *A* invokes another activity *B* by a *'Call Behavior Action'* node. In other words, to continue the execution of activity *A*, it is required to execute activity *B*.
3. Inter-level impact: the functional change affects elements within the higher and/or lower level of the element subject of the change. This type of change induces changes that affect not only the element subject of the change but also the structurally related elements. When the changed element is at the functional (dynamic) level, then we have a *child* impact *(parent* impact). For example, the deletion of an activity generates a series of deletions to all of its actions, objects node, and activity edges, which causes a *child* impact. The addition of an action with data recovery from an object node will induce a change on the corresponding activity, causing a *parent* impact.

The more impact directions a functional change causes, the more delicate/costly it may be and vice versa. To determine the functional change in terms of CFP units, we move from the functional level, where activities, *i.e.* functional processes are identified, to the dynamic level where each activity is decomposed into actions. Indeed, as we next propose, the COSMIC measurement method can be applied adequately in dynamic level where the sub-processes may be identified [8].

3.2   Identification of COSMIC Data Movements in UML-AD

As it is described in our previous work [18], to identify the data movements in the UML-AD, we need to map COSMIC concepts onto UML-AD elements [18]. It is to be noted that data groups are encapsulated into 'Pin' in the UML-AD. If a 'Pin' provides a constant value, then it is not considered as a data group.

Read (R) and Write (W) DATA Movements in UML-AD. The identification of Read and Write data movements are provided in activities at the second level (dynamic level). Figure 3 presents the Read and Write data movements in an activity A. Note that (a) and (b) notations are equivalent according to [10].

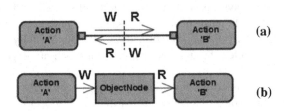

Fig. 3. Read/Write data movements in an activity

Entry (E) and eXit (X) Data Movements in UML-AD. Unlike Read and Write data movements, Entry and eXit data movements can be depicted in the first and the second levels. In fact, in the functional level, when a data exchange is needed between activity A and activity B, then it should be accounted for since each activity is associated to a Functional Process (FP). And, according to the COSMIC method, a data exchange between FPs is measured as data movements (Entry/eXit). For example, in Fig. 4 where A requests data from B through passed parameters, the data movements are an eXit followed by an Entry. 1 CFP is added to the functional size of each activity (A and B) measured in the dynamic level.

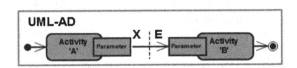

Fig. 4. Entry/eXit data movements in UML-AD

In the second level, Entry and eXit data movements are depicted in activities (Figs. 5 and 6). The call of an activity should be taken into account. As it is showed in Fig. 5, activity A calls two activities (B and C) using two *'Call Behavior Action'* nodes. Entry and eXit data movements are identified as provided in Fig. 5.

Actions in an activity exchange data through control and object flows. Control flow can lead to an Entry or eXit data movements if they move data encapsulated into 'Pin' as depicted in Fig. 6. Whereas, object flow corresponds to Read and Write data movements as provided in Fig. 3. Moreover, *'Exception Handlers'* correspond to 'Error messages' in COSMIC. It is equivalent to one eXit data movement. 'Confirmation messages' correspond also to one eXit data movement.

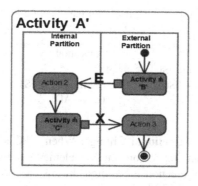

Fig. 5. Entry/eXit data movements in the case of *'Call Behavior Action'* in an activity *A*

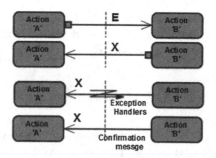

Fig. 6. Entry/eXit data movements inside an activity

3.3 Functional Size of UML-AD Elements When a Functional Change is Submitted and Classified into Impact Directions

As discussed in Sect. 3.1, we propose three possible FC impact directions (internal, intra-level, and inter-level) in UML-AD when FC requests are submitted. Recall that in COSMIC method, a FC includes addition, modification or deletion of a data movement. In this section, we propose to determine the FS of UML-AD elements after a FC. Appendix A gives measurement formulas used to measure the functional size of UML-AD, as it is proposed in our previous work [18].

Internal Impact of a Functional Change in UML-AD. Internal impact change is considered only within the element subject of the change and it does not propagate to any other element in the UML-AD. Table 2 determine the functional size of the element subject of the change (UML-AD) when a functional change is required. In this case, we can add, modify or delete an activity *A* in UML-AD, where:

- *FSf(UML-AD)*: functional size of *UML-AD* after the change
- *FSi(UML-AD)*: functional size of *UML-AD* before the change
- *FS(A)*: functional size of the activity *A*.

Table 2. Functional size of UML-AD in the case of a FC - internal impact

	FC in UML-AD		
UML-AD	Addition (A)	Modification (A)	Deletion(A)
	FSf(UML-AD) = FSi (UML-AD) + FS(A)	FSf (UML-AD) = FSi (UML-AD)	FSf(UML-AD) = FSi (UML-AD) - FS(A)

Intra-Level Impact of a Functional Change. When a FC affects an element in the UML-AD and lead to an impact on another element in the same level then the intra-level impact change direction is required. In this case, we have only one possibility: 'Activity => Activity'. Table 3 presents how to determine the FS of an activity A when A calls activity B by a *'Call Behavior Action'* in order to continue its execution, where:

- *FSf(A)*: the functional size of the activity A after the change
- *FSi(A)*: the functional size of the activity A before the change
- *FS(B)*: the functional size of the activity B.

Table 3. Functional size of an activity A in the case of an intra-level impact of a FC

	FC in an activity A		
Activity A	Addition (B)	Modification (B)	Deletion(B)
	FSf(A) = FSi(A) + FS(B)	FSf(A) = FSi(A)	FSf(A) = FSi(A) - FS(B)

Inter-Level Impact of a Functional Change. A FC that affects an action may lead to an impact not only on the FS of the affected action but also the FS of the related activity. Since actions are represented in the dynamic level and activities are represented in the functional level, we can say that this change propagates from the dynamic to the functional level (*parent* impact). It is to be noted that a FC in an action may lead to an impact only if it affects either: [<Pre_condition>], [<Input-Parameters>], or [<Output-Paramaters>]. Table 4 presents the functional size of an action *act* and activity A when a functional change is needed, where:

- *FSf(act)*: the functional size of *act* after the change
- *FSi(act)*: the functional size of *act* before the change
- *FSf(A)*: the functional size of A after the change
- *FSi(A)*: the functional size of A before the change.

Moreover, when a FC affects an ActivityEdge (*object flow* or *control flow*) in an activity A, it may lead to an impact on the FS of A and the FS of its actions. In this case, 'inter-level impact' (*parent*) direction is required. For example, when the FC is the addition of an *object flow* between two actions (*acti* and *actj*) in activity A then we should add 2 CFP to the FS(A), and 1 CFP to the FS of *acti* and *actj* (see Fig. 3). When a FC affects a *control flow* in activity A, then it will have an impact on the FS(A) only if it is generated with a 'guard-condition' or if it includes a 'Pin'. It will also have an

Table 4. Functional size of an action and its related activity in the case of the inter-level impact (*parent*) of a functional change

		FC in an action		
		Addition (act)	Modification (act)	Deletion(act)
Pre Cond	Action (act)	FSf(act) = FSi (act) + 1CFP	FSf (act) = FSi (act)	FSf(act) = FSi(act) - 1CFP
	Activity A (act's parent)	FSf(A) = FSi(A) + 1 CFP	FSf(A) = FSi (A)	FSf(A) = FSi(A) -1 CFP
Input Parameters	Action (act)	if [act ⊄ param-int] then FSf(act) = FSi (act) + 1CFP else FSf(act) = FSi (act)	FSf (act) = FSi (act)	if [act ⊄ param-int] then FSf (act) = FSi(act) - 1 CFP else FSf(act) = FSi (act)
	Activity A (act's parent)	if [act ⊄ param-int] then FSf(A) = FSi (A) + 1 CFP else FSf(A) = FSi(A)	FSf(A) = FSi (A)	if [act ⊄ param-int] then FSf(A) = FSi (A) - 1 CFP else FSf(A) = FSi(A)
Output Paramaters	Action (act)	if [act ⊄ param-out] then FSf(act) = FSi (act) + 1 CFP else FSf(act) = FSi (act)	FSf (act) = FSi (act)	if [act ⊄ param-out] then FSf(act) = FSi(act)-1 CFP else FSf(act) = FSi (act)
	Activity A (act's parent)	if [act ⊄ param-out] then FSf(A) = FSi(A) + 1 CFP else FSf(A) = FSi(A)	FSf(A) = FSi (A)	if [act ⊄ param-out] then FSf(A) = FSi(A) - 1 CFP else FSf(A) = FSi(A)

impact on the FS of the action preceded by the decision node or regrouping the input/output parameters 'Pin' (see Fig. 6). Table 5 presents the FS of activity A and its actions (*acti* and/or *actj*) when a FC affects an ActivityEdge. Where:

- *FSf(acti)*, *FSf(actj)*: the functional size of *acti* and *actj* after the change
- *FSi(acti)*, *FSi(actj)*: the functional size of *acti* and *actj* before the change
- *FSf(A)*: functional size of activity A after the change
- *FSi(A)*: functional size of activity A before the change

It is to be noted that in functional level, the deletion of an activity will necessary generate the deletion of all its actions (dynamic level). In this case, 'inter-level impact' (*child*) direction is required (Table 6). The addition of an activity requires only the internal-impact direction as provided in Table 2. The modification of an activity is

Table 5. Functional size of an action and its related activity in the case of inter-level impact (*parent*) of a functional change

		FC in an Activity		
		Addition (A-Edge)	Modification (A-Edge)	Deletion (A-Edge)
Object flow	Action (acti)	FSf(acti) = FSi (acti) + 1CFP	FSf (acti) = FSi (acti)	FSf(acti) = FSi (acti)-1 CFP
	Action (actj)	FSf(actj) = FSi (actj) + 1CFP	FSf (actj) = FSi (actj)	FSf(actj) = FSi (actj)-1 CFP
	Activity A (act's parent)	FSf(A) = FSi (A) + 2 CFP	FSf(A) = FSi (A)	FSf(A) = FSi(A) -2CFP
Control flow [guard_cond]	Action (acti)	FSf(acti) = FSi (acti) + 1CFP	FSf (acti) = FSi (acti)	FSf(acti) = FSi (acti) - 1CFP
	Activity A (act's parent)	FSf(A) = FSi (A) + 1CFP	FSf(A) = FSi (A)	FSf(A) = FSi(A) -1CFP
Control flow with [Pin]	Action (acti)	FSf(acti) = FSi (acti) + 1CFP	FSf (acti) = FSi (acti)	FSf(acti) = FSi (acti) -1CFP
	Activity A (act's parent)	FSf(A) = FSi (A) + 1CFP	FSf(A) = FSi (A)	FSf(A) = FSi(A) -1CFP

presented in Table 4, and Table 5. Table 6 presents the FS of the UML-AD and *act* (action in *A*) after a FC proposed the deletion of an activity *A*. Where:

Table 6. Functional size of an activity and its related actions in the case of inter-level impact (*child*) of a functional change

		FC = Deletion of an Activity A
Action with [Pre-condition]	**UML-AD**	FSf(UML-AD) = FSi(UML-AD) - FS(A)
	Action act (A's child)	FSf(act) = FSi(act) - 1 CFP
Action with [Input-Parameters]	**UML-AD**	FSf(UML-AD) = FSi(UML-AD) - FS(A)
	Action act (A's child)	FSf(act) = FSi(act) - 1 CFP
Action with [Output-Paramaters]	**UML-AD**	FSf(UML-AD) = FSi(UML-AD) - FS(A)
	Action act (A's child)	FSf(act) = FSi(act) - 1 CFP

- *FSf(UML-AD)*: functional size of *UML-AD* after the change
- *FSi(UML-AD)*: functional size of *UML-AD* before the change
- *FSf(act)*: the functional size of *act* after the change
- *FSi(act)*: the functional size of *act* before the change.

3.4   Functional Change Impact Analysis in UML-AD

Measuring the FS before and after a FC is required, but it is not enough to identify the impact of a FC on the FS(UML-AD). In some cases, the measurement value of FS (UML-AD) is the same before and after the FC. For example, a FC involving a set of modifications of data movements, or the addition and deletion of the same number of data movements. Thus, it is required to identify the status of the FC based on its FS.

Given the FC status, we can expect what should be happen after the submission of the FC. In fact, in COSMIC [8], "very small" changes to a piece of software means "a few data movements". COSMIC also considers that "The minimum size of a change to a piece of software is 1 CFP" [8]. In this context, we need a numerical threshold to help us to determine "how important is a functional change?". Assuming that this numerical threshold should not be a fixed value, we believe it will depend on the average value R of the functional sizes of all activities in the UML-AD. In other words, depending on the FS of UML-AD and the number of activities in UML-AD, we can determine R.

$$R = \frac{FS(UML-AD)}{n}$$

Where:

- *FS(UML-AD)*: functional size of the UML-AD, and
- n: the number of activities in UML-AD.

As illustrated in Fig. 7, the identification of the FC status in UML-AD depends on its FS compared to R. The matrix as presented in Fig. 7 is divided into three zones representing "Major", "Moderate", and "Minor" FC status. A FC with the status "Major" can lead to a *potential* impact on the software development progress. However, a FC that can be handled without any impact on the software development progress is considered as very small change with the status "Minor", while "Moderate" change may produce a *low* change in the software development progress. More specifically:

FC Status in UML-AD	Minor	Moderate	Major
FS(FC)	= 1 CFP	≥ 2CFP and ≤ R CFP	> R

Fig. 7. FC Status identification in UML-AD

- If the FS(FC) = 1 CFP, then the FC will be classified as "Minor" change. Since, COSMIC considers that "The minimum size of a change is 1 CFP" [8].
- If the FS(FC) > R, it will have a "Major" impact on the FS(UML-AD). Since the FC includes a number of data movements that exceed the ratio R.
- If 2 CFP ≤ FS(FC) ≤ R, the FC will be classified as "Moderate".

Analyzing the impact of FC will be helpful in decisions taken to answer the FC request (accepted, rejected, or deferred). It allows also managers to assess how much flexibility they have to justify acquiring additional cost or delaying the software project. Moreover, the benefit of quantifying the "Minor", "Moderate", and "Major" change is to help managers to determine whether the proposed FC can be really accomplished with a minor/moderate changes or not. These two change status are "in scope" change according to [19]. Whereas, "Major" change status is classified as an "out-of-scope" change according to [19]. Thus, "Major" changes should be accompanied with certain adjustment to the budget, schedule, etc.

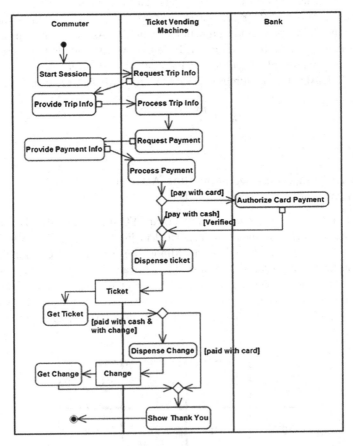

Fig. 8. "Ticket Vending Machine" activity diagram before change [20]

4 Illustrative Example

Figure 8 presents the activity diagram of the "Ticket Vending Machine" process [20]. This activity includes three partitions: Commuter, Ticket vending machine, and Bank. It allows a Commuter to buy a ticket. When a Commuter asks for a ticket, the Ticket vending machine will then request for trip information. Based on the provided trip info, Ticket vending machine will calculate payment due and request payment options. If payment by card was selected, Bank will participate by authorizing the payment via card. After payment is completed, ticket is dispensed to the Commuter. Ticket vending machine show the message "Thank You" at the end of the activity.

In order to illustrate the proposed impact change analysis in UML-AD, we propose the functional change as showed in Fig. 9: Add a decision node after the action "Authorize Card Payment" with guard conditions "[Verified]" and "[not Verified]". If [Verified] then "Dispense Ticket" action is executed, else if [not Verified] then return to "Process Payment" action.

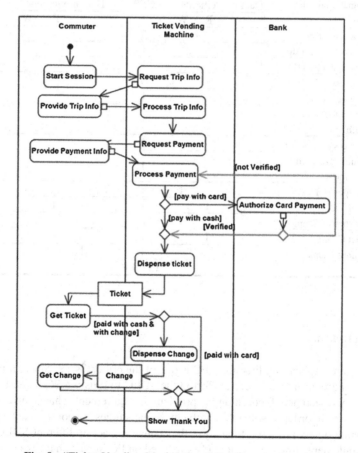

Fig. 9. "Ticket Vending Machine" activity diagram after change

The proposed FC lead to the addition of a guard condition, which lead to the addition of 1 CFP to the FS ("Ticket Vending Machine") activity, according to [18]. Then, the FS(FC) = 1 CFP. In fact, R = 13/1 = 13 CFP. Moreover, it affects the action "Process Payment". In this case, the 'inter-level impact (*parent*)' direction is required. In fact, the FC that affects the action "*Process Payment*" will lead to an impact on action's parent i.e. "Ticket Vending Machine" activity.

As provided in Table 7, the FS ("Ticket Vending Machine") before the change is equal to 13 CFP, and after the change the FS ("Ticket Vending Machine") is equal to 14 CFP. The inter-level impact (*parent*) on the FS of the activity ("Ticket Vending Machine") is performed as provided in Table 7. As it is depicted in Fig. 7, this FC is considered as a "**Minor**" change since FS(FC) = 1 CFP.

Table 7. Measurement results (Activity "Ticket Vending Machine") before and after change

FP	Functional sub-process	Before the change					After the change				
		Data movements				CFP	Data movement				CFP
		E	X	R	W		E	X	R	W	
Activity "Ticket Vending Machine"	Start Session					0					0
	Request Trip Info	1				1	1				1
	Provide Trip Info	1				1	1				1
	Process Trip Info					0					0
	Request Payment	1				1	1				1
	Provide Payment Info	1				1	1				1
	Process Payment					0		1			1
	Authorize Card Payment	1				1	1				1
	Dispense Ticket	2			1	3	2			1	3
	Get Ticket		1			1			1		1
	Dispense Change	1			1	2	1			1	2
	Get Change		1			1			1		1
	Show Thank You	1				1	1				1
Total =						**13 CFP**					**14 CFP**

5 Conclusion

In the software engineering literature, FC is one of the critical issue. Since, it may lead to project failure or induce an extra effort in the SDLC to satisfy a FC request. For this reason, many researchers focused on the problem of requirements change and proposed many solutions in order to solve this problem. Some studies proposed to anticipate the change, while others proposed to analyze the change impact in different SDLC phases (design, implementation, etc.). Our studies focused on FC impact analysis in the design phase. The herein presented work focused on the analysis of FC impact in the UML Activity Diagram (UML-AD) by using COSMIC-FSM method.

Our approach deals with the change impact along three directions (Internal, Intra-level, and Inter-level) and two levels (functional and dynamic). It provides for an analysis of the FC on the element subject of change as well as the overall UML-AD in terms of CFP units. We can provide the FC status ("Minor", "Moderate", or "Major") based on its FS. This analysis identifies also if the FC can be handled without changes to other UML-AD elements or if it cannot be accepted without compensating changes to other UML-AD elements. FS(FC) can be used also to compare the impact of the same FC on two distinct activity diagrams. In fact, regarding the ratio R, the same FC can be a "Minor" change in one UML-AD and a "Major" change in another UML-AD.

Further works include the extension of the proposed approach to other UML diagrams such as a structural diagram. Moreover, the focus of this paper is only on the intra-dependency analysis of a FC in UML-AD, in further work we focused on inter-dependency analysis. The extended approach can be helpful to software managers since it will provide guidelines to help in making appropriate decisions related to the FC purpose (*e.g.* enhancing the existing system, re-developing the system, etc.) and fast-track review of the proposed changes.

Appendix A

As proposed in our previous work [18], the FS(UML-AD) is computed as follows:

$$FS\ (UML-AD) \ = \ \sum_{i=1}^{n} FS\ (A_i) \tag{1}$$

Where:

- n: the number of activities in the activity diagram UML-AD (functional level).
- $FS(A_i)$: the functional size of the activity A_i in UML-AD (dynamic level).

To measure the functional size of an activity Ai, we use formula (2) [18].

$$FS(A_i) \ = \ FScond\ (Pcond\ A_i) + \sum_{j=1}^{m} FS(act_{ij}) \tag{2}$$

Where:

- $FS(Ai)$: the FS of the activity Ai $(1 \leq i \leq n)$
- m: the number of actions detailing the activity Ai (dynamic level).
- $FS(actij)$: the FS of an action actij (dynamic level).
- $FScond(Pcond\ Ai)$: the FS of the pre-condition of Ai. (1CFP if it exists).

To measure the FS of an action (actii), we use formula (3) [18].

$$FS(act_{ij}) = FScond \; (Pcond \; act_{ij}) + FSparam \; (Param \; act_{ij}) \qquad (3)$$

Where:

- $FScond(Pcond \; act_{ij})$: the FS of the pre-condition of act_{ii} (1 CFP if it exists).
- $FSparam(Param \; act_{ij})$ = 1 CFP if act_{ij} includes input or output parameters).

To measure the functional size of a guard condition, we use formula (4) [18].

$$FScond \; (CondGuard) = \begin{cases} 1 \; CFP & if \; act_{ij} \; has \; a \; guard \; condition \\ 0 & otherwise. \end{cases} \qquad (4)$$

References

1. Briand, L.C., Sullivan, Y., Labiche, L.O., Sowka, M.M.: Automated impact analysis of UML models. J. Syst. Softw. **79**, 339–352 (2005)
2. Russo, B., Steff, M.: What can changes tell about software processes? In: International Workshop on Emerging Trends in Software Metrics, Hyderabad, India, pp. 1–7 (2014)
3. Mala, D.J., Geetha, S.: Object Oriented Analysis and Design Using UML (2013)
4. Germán, D.M., Robles, G., Hassan, A.E.: Change impact graph: determining the impact of prior code changes. In: International Working Conference on Source Code Analysis and Manipulation, Beijing, China, September 2008
5. Fu, Y., Li, M., Chen, F.: Impact propagation and risk assessment of requirement changes for software development projects based on design structure matrix. Int. J. Proj. Manage. **30**, 263–373 (2012)
6. Goknil, A., Kurtev, I., Van den Berg, K., Spijkerman, W.: Change impact analysis for requirements: a metamodeling approach. Inf. Softw. Technol. **56**, 950–972 (2014)
7. Inpirom, A., Prompoon, N.: Diagram change types taxonomy based on analysis and design models in UML. In: IEEE International Conference on Software Engineering and Service Science, Beijing, pp. 283–287 (2013)
8. COSMIC (The Common Software Measurement International Consortium), The COSMIC Functional Size Measurement Method, Version 4.0.1, Measurement Manual (2015)
9. Gencel, C., Demirors, O.: Functional size measurement revisited. ACM Trans. Softw. Eng. Methodol. **17**(3), 71–106 (2008)
10. Object Management Group. Unified Modeling Language (UML) Version 2.5 (2012)
11. Sellami, A., Haoues, M., Ben-Abdallah, H.: Automated COSMIC-based analysis and consistency verification of UML activity and component diagrams. In: Filipe, J., Maciaszek, L.A. (eds.) ENASE 2013. CCIS, vol. 417, pp. 48–63. Springer, Heidelberg (2013)
12. Bohner, S.A.: Software change impacts-an evolving perspective. In: International Conference on Software Maintenance (2002)
13. Chaumun, M.A., Kabaili, H., Keller, R.K., Lustman, F.: A change impact model for changeability assessment in object-oriented software systems. In: European Working Conference on Software Maintenance and Reengineering (2002)
14. Vargas, R.T., Nugroho, A., Chaudron, M., Visser, J.: The use of UML class diagrams and its effect on code change-proneness. In: International Workshop on Experiences and Empirical Studies in Software Modelling (2012)

15. JayPrakash, L.T.: impact analysis of UML design changes using model slicing. In: CPSM, Eindhoven, pp. 1–10, September 2013
16. Hoa, K.D., Winikoff, M.: Supporting change propagation in UML models. In: International Conference on Software Maintenance, Timisoara, pp. 12–18, September 2010
17. Briand, L.C., Labiche, Y., Soccar, G.: Automating impact analysis and regression test selection. In: International Conference on Software Maintenance, pp. 252–261 (2002)
18. Sellami, A., Haoues, M., Ben-Abdallah, H.: Analyzing UML activity and component diagrams - an approach based on COSMIC functional size measurement. In: International Conference on Evaluation of Novel Approaches to Software Engineering (2013)
19. Fairly, R.E.: Managing and Leading Software Projects. IEEE Computer Society, Hoboken (2009)
20. The Unified Modeling Language, UML Activity Diagram Example: Ticket Vending Machine (2014). http://www.uml-diagrams.org/

Application of Function Points and Data Mining Techniques for Software Estimation - A Combined Approach

Przemysław Pospieszny[✉], Beata Czarnacka-Chrobot, and Andrzej Kobyliński

Institute of Information Systems and Digital Economy, Warsaw School of Economics,
ul. Madalińskiego 6/8, 02-513 Warsaw, Poland
p.pospieszny@gmail.com, {bczarn,kobyl}@sgh.waw.pl

Abstract. Project estimation is recognized as one of the most challenging processes in software project management on which project success is dependable. Traditional estimation methods based on expert knowledge and analogy tend to be error prone and deliver overoptimistic assessments. Methods derived from function points are good sizing tools but do not reflect organizations' specific project management culture. Due to those deficiencies in recent years data mining techniques are explored as an alternative estimation method. The aim of this paper is to present a combined approach of functional sizing measurement and three data mining techniques for effort and duration estimation at project early stages: generalized linear models, artificial neural networks and CHAID decision trees. The estimation accuracy of these models is compared in order to determine their potential usefulness for deployment within organizations. Moreover a merged approach of combining algorithms' results is proposed in order to increase prediction accuracy and overcome possibility of overfitting occurrence.

Keywords: Project estimation · Effort and duration estimation · Software measurement · Functional size measurement · Function points · Data mining · Predictive algorithms

1 Introduction

For centuries human activities were organized into temporary endeavors focused on delivering unique products, services or results [1]. The development and popularization of project management as a formal discipline that supports and provides tools for achieving the final outcome occurred in the 1960s. At that time project methodologies and techniques were applied widely for delivering complex initiatives by such organizations as NASA and IBM, additionally, major project management organizations were established, like Project Management Institute (PMI) and International Project Management Association (IPMA). Over the years these bodies have been responsible for the definition of numerous standards, practices and tools that support the development of final product and enhance project success rate.

© Springer International Publishing Switzerland 2015
A. Kobyliński et al. (Eds.): IWSM-Mensura 2015, LNBIP 230, pp. 96–113, 2015.
DOI: 10.1007/978-3-319-24285-9_7

In the current fast-paced world, information technology systems, which mostly are delivered as projects, play a significant role. Foremost they enable automation of different organizational processes and allow rational decision-making due to delivering accurate and comprehensive information. As a result, they may lead to cost reduction and the increased efficiency of processes within institutions [2].

The success of software initiative is dependent on delivering the final outcome within the assumed timeframe, budget and scope. These factors are considered as project constraints and part of project iron triangle, where any change to one of them during project execution impacts negatively others. They are defined at the initial stage of the initiative in order to put together a business case and estimate profitability of developing and implementing the system within the organization. In recent years a high rate (approx. 60 %) of software projects can be observed struggling with delivering products within their assumed timeframe, budget and scope [3, 4]. This often leads to project overruns or even cancelation because of unbalanced business cases, due to the development cost overcoming the potential benefits of implementing the solution, or that time to market does not guarantee achieving a competitive advantage. There are many grounds for failure mentioned, including problems like poor communication, lack of skills within the project team or no project management methodology in place [5–8]. Nevertheless the most important reason that determines project success is considered to be improper planning conducted at an early stage of the initiative lifecycle [9]. During that time, project boundaries are defined, such as the effort and duration needed to develop the final product, therefore inaccurate estimation of those two may often result in an over-optimistic budget and schedule, and ultimately lead to project failure.

The process of estimation of effort and duration during project initiation and planning is a very complex task, mostly due to the high uncertainty and lack of information available in terms of the product that the initiative needs to deliver. Available techniques and tools, which are in place and are commonly used for that purpose, are mostly based on estimation by analogy or expert knowledge. They rely on common sense and subjective judgment; therefore in the hands of inexperienced project managers may provide inaccurate estimations. More mature organizations that undertake software projects use a parametric models based on source line of code (SLOC), but they are technology sensitive and difficult to apply at early stages of the project, due to an issue of relation of SLOC to functional requirements [8]. An other approach employed is function points measurement (FPM), that overcomes the above mentioned problems, and provide accurate software size measurement even at project initiation. Nevertheless, product development methods derived from FPM may deliver imprecise results in terms of the effort and duration needed because of applying mathematical formulas for this purpose that do not take into consideration factors like existing project management methodology or details of organizational culture that highly impact budget and timeframe of projects. Therefore it is considered as an excellent software sizing method, but there is a necessity for an additional estimation approach that would utilitize the system size represented in function points, and based on that information provide accurate effort and duration predictions.

In the past 20 years, data mining techniques have been applied for numerous disciplines, especially for tasks where uncertainty and risk occurrence is substantial, such as credit scoring or customer retention. In terms of project management, researchers in the past decade explored its potential application and proved its outstanding prediction capability for estimating effort and duration at initial project phases, but also for monitoring the use of earned value analysis and system's maintenance cost. Despite numerous publications in the area, there are few studies of real-life applications, mostly because researchers focus on the efficiency of particular data mining algorithms rather than proposing an implementation approach.

The aim of this paper is to present a combined application of function points and data mining techniques for this crucial aspect, from a project success perspective, as an estimation of effort and duration at the initial project phases. Initiative size is one of the key inputs for any estimation models, including data mining ones. Therefore it was decided to use size computed with function points for this purpose, as it is considered to be a very accurate approach. For building data mining models, the International Software Benchmarking Standards Group (ISBSG) database [10] was used, consisting of a large number of high quality data regarding completed projects, and the foremost software size information assessed using function point methods developed by the International Function Point Users Group (IFPUG), the Netherlands Software Metrics Association (NESMA), the Finnish Software Metrics Association (FiSMA), the common software measurement consortium (COSMIC) and also the Mk II method proposed by the United Kingdom Software Metrics Association (UKSMA). Based on the database, two models were built, separately for effort and duration, where each of them consisted of three algorithms: a generalized linear model (GLM), a multilayer artificial neural network (ANN) and CHAID decision trees. The prediction results of the algorithms for each model were combined in order to provide estimations robust to noise within the data, and evaluated using forecast error measures. The empirical part of this article outlined above and presented in Sect. 5 is preceded with an overview of common project estimation approaches (Sect. 2), knowledge discovery in project management (Sect. 3) and a literature review (Sect. 4).

2   Project Estimation

Project success is dependable on delivering a product within a defined timeframe, and with a budget and quality that meets end-user and sponsor expectations [11]. Those attributes are considered as a project's triple constraints or iron triangle, because they are defined during project initiation and planning, and any further alternations to one of them negatively impacts the others.

Duration and budget has the largest impact on the successful completion of a project, since cost or time overrun is usually compensated for by lower quality of the final product. They are defined in a process of estimation that tends to be one of the most crucial and demanding in software project management, due to the complexity of information technology systems that are based on logically connected instructions, modularity and dispersion. Moreover it is conducted at the early stages of the project, and as such, approximation of project cost and duration are based on incomplete information about the functionalities of the final product and the activities that need to be completed in order to deliver it. Therefore this estimation is conducted with high uncertainty and probability of error that may lead to under or overestimation. According to Boehm [12] the uncertainty is the highest at project initiation, and decrease with the passing of time and increase in information availability. Currently it assumes that the error of estimates is on the level of +100/−50 % in a feasibility study, +50/−25 % for requirements and +20/−10 % for design [13].

During the estimation process, duration is usually reflected in months and cost is derived from effort, which is measured in man-days. For this purpose numerous traditional methods are used, that are mostly based on guesstimating, analogy or expert knowledge. The most recognizable ones are considered to be analogy-based estimation, program evaluation and review technique (PERT), Delphi, Planning Poker or bottom and top-down. Due to their simplicity they are highly popular, especially those based on expert knowledge [4], but in the hands of an inexperienced project manager, may generate extremely error prone estimates, mostly due to underestimation. The other approach is to utilize parametric methods like: the constructive cost model II (COCOMO II), the Putnam model (SLIM) and the software evaluation and estimation resources – software estimating model (SEER-SEM), which are derived from mathematics and statistics. For estimation purpose those techniques use source of code lines (SLOC) of the software system, historic databases of completed projects and numerous formulae for project cost and duration calculation. Although parametric methods provide automatic and repeatable methods they tend to be ineffective in terms of modern dispersed and modular systems, and those developed using 4GL programming languages [8], and for projects implemented with agile methodologies.

Due to the abovementioned imperfections of SLOC for measuring the size of software and using it for effort and duration estimation from a project management perspective, organizations apply FPM. It allows measuring the functionalities of a system from an end-user perspective. Moreover, FPM is independent of technology, programming language, and software development methodology used. The functionality of the software system is measured using function points (FP) that are assigned to each system's functions, grouped into components. Function point analysis (FPA) was first introduced in 1979 by Allan Albrecht [14], and in 1986 transformed into IFPUG method. The popularization of function points sparked the development of alternative approaches to IFPUG like NESMA, COSMIC or Mk II that vary to some degree in method of counting the system's functionalities. In practical consideration, the difference between the newest versions of them are inappreciable, especially considering the most popular ones: IFPUG and COSMIC. Over the 30 years of the method's existence more than 20 FPA approaches have been developed. In order to standardize software sizing using function points, a function size measurement working group was established in 1994 that published the ISO/IEC 14143 norm. It consists of set of rules, which FPM methods need to conform to, and additionally provide guidance for its use. As a result only five of the methods have been acknowledged by the ISO/IEC: IFPUG, NESMA, COSMIC, FiSMA and Mk II (UKSMA) [15].

Function point analysis is considered as a very accurate sizing method due to the end-user and product functionality perspective, and its technology independence. Nevertheless it may tend to be subjective with regard to assigning points to a system's features, and in the hands of untrained staff may generate false assessments. Moreover, estimating effort and duration needed to complete a project and develop the final product using methods based on FSM assessment is mostly dependent on formulae that are prone to omit factors that impact project budget and timeframe, like organizational culture, existing project and software development methodology, and the skills of the project staff and its effectiveness. Therefore, although function points measurement methods deliver accurate sizing measures, with respect to estimation of effort and duration, there is a necessity for an additional approach that would deliver accurate predictions and address the abovementioned limitations.

Additionally it needs to be mentioned that software size has a significant impact on the estimation of project constraints [16]. Other factors, like type of the final product, programming language or the system's architecture, have less influence on their assessment. Therefore the proper choice of sizing method is crucial for delivering accurate estimates, and for purpose of this article, function point analysis was selected to be used in conjunction with other project attributes for building data mining models in order to predict project effort and duration.

3   Knowledge Project Management

Knowledge in software project management is a key resource that determines the successful achievement of project goals . According to PMI, project knowledge can be grouped into 10 knowledge areas: integration, scope, time, cost, quality, human resources, communication, risk, procurement and stakeholder management [1]. It is created at every stage of project lifecycle as both the unstructured knowledge of team members, and in the form of documentation, repositories and databases. Proper use of available knowledge impacts not only the development of software and its functionalities within an assumed quality, but also delivering it within defined budget and timeframe.

Project knowledge management compromises two main dimensions. The first, micro-knowledge, is the knowledge needed to perform a particular task, or to solve a given problem. During the process of its acquisition, creation, application, transfer and sharing it becomes macro-knowledge, which is the total knowledge required to conduct the project [17]. It also includes developing organizational ability to conduct initiatives, introduce new products and services to the market, and achieving competitive advantage.

The majority of organizations that conduct software initiatives maintain project databases. They are maintained usually by the project management office (PMO), and contain key project performance metrics gathered during its lifecycle. The following information can be distinguished in project databases [8]:

1. Cost – staff, phase and total effort
2. Schedule – milestones, activities, phases
3. Quality – defects found, effort required
4. Product characteristics – development language, technology, architecture, size
5. Project characteristics – methodology, resources allocated
6. Project progress – budget and schedule performance, effort and schedule changes.

The information gathered is mostly used for project monitoring and reporting. It allows tracking initiative progress, identifying any deviations from baselines and implementing corrective actions. Moreover it is used for reporting purposes in order to keep sponsors, stakeholders and management informed. The project database and the information stored within it allows deriving knowledge (on lessons learnt, best practices) from completed initiatives, that can be used further for conducting new projects, in order to mitigate risks and increase the project success factor within an organization.

In terms of estimation, a project database is commonly used for analogy-based based estimation and as an input for adjusting parametric techniques. Nevertheless it can be also applied in knowledge discovery process in databases, [18] for the prediction of project constraints using data mining techniques. In the last 20 years, data mining has became extremely popular and is used in wide range of disciplines, especially for those where risk and uncertainty is substantial. It relies on the exploration and analysis of large quantities of data in order to discover meaningful patterns and rules [19]. For this purpose interdisciplinary techniques are used that derive from statistics, machine learning, artificial intelligence and pattern recognition. The widespread application of data mining (i.e. credit scoring, customer churn, drug testing) is a result of their outstanding prediction capability, that contributes to decreased operational risks, increased sales, reduced time to market of new products and eventually achieving a competitive advantage.

Depending on the aim of an application and its expected outcome two types of data mining tasks, descriptive and predictive, can be distinguished. The first focuses on finding useful characteristics and human-interpretable patterns describing a given dataset. The second performs inference on the data in order to predict future values [20]. They both require a data set in order to generate an outcome, but in terms of descriptive data-mining is it is unlabeled data set (unsupervised learning), while for predictions, supervised learning algorithms are used to analyze a training dataset and produce an inferred function that can be used for mapping new cases. Within predictive tasks two major groups of techniques can be applied, depending on the type of outcome variable; binary or discrete variables are used for classification algorithms, and numerical ones for regression.

Recent research has been done in terms of applying data mining techniques for project management,the areas of initial estimation, project controlling and monitoring [21, 22], risk and quality management [23, 24] or maintenance cost estimation [25]. Nevertheless the most important of these from the perspective of project success is effort and duration estimation, for which data mining algorithms require good sizing measurement in order to generate accurate predictions.

4 Literature Review

With growing data mining popularity in recent 20 years researchers recognized its potential application for software projects estimation, especially at early project lifecycle. Their motivation was mainly to replace or using in conjunction with traditional error prone and often ineffective techniques with new approaches based on modern machine learning and statistical algorithms in order to boost estimation accuracy and increase project success rate. For this purpose the researchers applied various classification and prediction techniques such as: regression, decision trees, neural networks, case-based reasoning or support vectors machines. The comprehensive literature review of software development cost estimation techniques, including application of data mining algorithms, was conducted by Jorgensen and Sheppard (2007) [26]. Wen et al. (2012) [27] focused their review on machine learning data mining techniques that were utilized for effort estimation in last two decades. Table 1 presents only selected publications from effort and duration estimation area at initial project stages with utilization of data mining techniques in order to indicate the most important findings and research limitations.

Most of the researchers focused on validating various data mining algorithms and comparing their effectiveness in order to determine the most accurate one [23, 27, 29–33]. The results achieved were inconclusive and it hardly can be distinguished the most precise technique in terms of delivered predictions. Although that all publications presented data mining models' outstanding accuracy and prediction capability for effort and duration estimation. The discrepancies in results between used techniques were minor and mostly caused by applying various datasets for training algorithms. This is a consequence of data quality issues and chosen data preparation approach that contributes to models' outcome variations [30]. Therefore the researchers pointed out an importance of data pre-processing that impacts highly models' accuracy [26, 34].

In order to improve prediction accuracy of data mining techniques applied for software effort estimation in recent years researchers explored utilization of ensemble methods. Mittas and Angelis [35] conducted comparison of data mining techniques used for cost estimation across 6 databases and indicated that algorithms deliver different accuracy depending on training dataset, hence they should be applied in groups. Kocaguneli et al. [36] proposed an approach of selecting best performing techniques and using them for building an ensemble model. Although, the outlined by researchers framework of using random sampling for training base models and combining over a dozen data mining algorithms definitely boost outcome model's accuracy but introduces substantial complexity and increase of computational time, that may exclude the framework from practical use. Due to mentioned limitations ensemble methods, like bagging and boosting, are rarely deployed by practitioners for real life scenarios and mostly only predictions sourced from up to three techniques are combined using averaging or voting.

Effort and duration estimation data mining techniques require a database of completed projects that consist of numerous observations and attributes describing an initiative. Moreover for research purposes it should be open to public for replication of results. Due to deficiency of databases meeting the above criteria for training algorithms researchers applied databases used widely for validating source of lines of code or function points models. Depending on origin, the most used ones for data mining estimation models are:

- SLOC – COCOMO [37], NASA/Promise [38], SourceForge [39]
- FP – Albrecht [40], ISBSG [41]

The most comprehensive collection of data about historic projects is ISBSG that is constantly updated with software initiatives from numerous industries and countries, validated with data quality criteria and consist up to date with more than 6000 observations.

Table 1. Selected research papers in domain of data mining application for effort and duration estimation

No	Authors	Title	Year	Aim	Algorithms	Database
1	I.Barcelos Tronto, J.Simoes da Silva, N. Sant'Anna	Comparison of Artificial Neural Network and Regression Models in Software Effort Estimation	2006	Effort estimation	Neural networks, linear regression	COCOMO
2	D.Dzega, W.Pietruszkiewicz	Classification and Metaclassification in Large Scale Data Mining Application for Estimation of Software Projects	2009	Duration estimation	Decision trees: C4.5, random tree and CART	SourceForge
3	A.Bakır, B.Turhan, A.Bener	A comparative study for estimating software development effort intervals	2010	Effort estimation	Linear discrimination, k-nearest neighbor and decision tree	Promise and Softlab Data Repository
4	C.Lopez-Martin, C.Isaza, A.Chavoya	Software development effort prediction of industrial projects applying a general regression neural network	2011	Effort estimation	General regression neural network, regression	ISBSG
5	J.Balsera, F.Fernandez, V.Montequin, R.Suarez	Effort Estimation in Information Systems Projects using Data Mining Techniques	2012	Effort and duration estimation	Decision tree MARS	ISBSG
6	K.Dejaeger, W.Verbeke, D.Martens, B.Baesens	Data Mining Techniques for Software Effort Estimation: A Comparative Study	2012	Effort estimation	13 algorithms including: ordinary least squares regression, MARS, CART, neural network, case-based reasoning, support vector machines.	Cocnasa, Maxwell, USP05, COCOMO, Desharnais, the Experience, ESA, ISBSG, and Euroclear

Source: Own elaboration based on [28]

Software size has the most significant influence on effort and duration estimation with use of data mining techniques [42]. Although, as an input variable it could be used size assessed with traditional estimation techniques, most of researchers based their models on databases where software size is calculated using SLOC and FP. Due to deficiency of project databases, mostly not intentionally, they applied sizing approaches that tend to deliver the most precise results, especially in terms of function points. Moreover it was presented that combined approach of FP and data mining techniques could deliver accurate effort and duration predictions.

Despite effectiveness of data exploration techniques in exemplifying project constraints at project early stage, there are hardly known any applications in practice. The reason behind that is lack of comprehensive approach that could be used for models' implementation. The researchers rather focused on comparing accuracy of data mining algorithms applied for software estimation than on applying them in practice. Additionally for building models databases where used that consist of small number of observations (i.e. COCOMO: 63, NASA: 60) that could lead to overfitting and overoptimistic estimations. It can also occur when single algorithm is used, which can preform well on one dataset but when different data is processed it can generate error prone predictions. Moreover applied by researchers databases are often outdated and often sourced in 80 s and 90 s, hence due to technology change may lead to false conclusions [26].

Therefore, in this paper it was proposed an approach that addresses all those limitations. ISBSG dataset is applied for training data mining models that consist of large volume of project data and sizing attribute calculated using function points. Moreover three algorithms are used in combination, separately for effort and duration estimation, in order to prevent overfitting and increase models' robustness to noises within the data.

5   Effort and Duration Estimation Using Function Points and Data Mining Techniques

This section of the article presents a combined approach for effort and duration estimation at project early stage with use of function points for software sizing and data mining techniques for mentioned project constraints prediction. For this purpose CRISP-DM [43] methodology was applied, which provided guidance through the modeling process. Data about completed projects was sourced from ISBSG database that provides the most comprehensive and reliable information about software initiatives conducted in numerous industries across the world. It is constantly updated and validated by ISBSG organization and version R12 used for modeling purposes consist of 6006 observations about projects that were conducted in last two decades. Foremost the database provides information about size of implemented software measured with function points, mostly using IFPUG method, but as well COSMIC, FiSMA and NESMA (see Fig. 1), which was used in this article as an input variable for estimating effort and duration.

As a result of preliminary modeling and by conducting literature review for building data mining models three prediction algorithms were selected from regression and machine learning area: generalized linear model, multilayer artificial neural network and CHAID decision trees. They are considered by practitioners as precise techniques that deliver accurate estimations and are robust to noises within the data that could affect algorithm's prediction capability. GLM is a generalization of ordinary linear regression

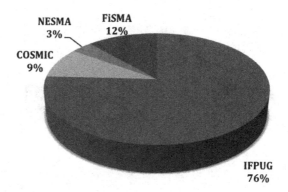

Fig. 1. Breakdown of FSM methods in ISBSG database.
Source: Own elaboration based on [10]

that depending on response variable type, distribution and variance appropriate link function is used to represent relationship between attributes [44]. It has a remarkable ability to analyze large datasets with non-linear variables. Artificial neural networks compute values from inputs using interconnected layers of neurons and non-linear activation function. They are capable of learning through back-propagation process that relies on modifying weights to the expected results, therefore it may adapt to the data and exclude irrelevant information [45]. The last algorithm applied, CHAID, uses non-binary and easy to interpret trees for reflecting relationships within data, and chi-square for significance testing.

GLM, ANN and CHAID techniques were used for both effort and duration. For each dependent variable the predictions delivered by those algorithms were combined using arithmetic mean (see Fig. 2). It was motivated with possibility of overfitting particular model to data that may result in false estimations. Moreover, depending on quality of dataset algorithms may generate diverse predictions. Therefore, averaging the results make them robust to those limitations and increase estimation accuracy. Additionally, due to used large dataset for purposes of this article, that significantly decrease possibility of models' overfitting, both it was decided not utilize ensemble methods based on sampling (boosting or bagging). An application of these aggregation techniques for building models would increase complexity and computational time of models, thus from practitioner point of view could present a major limitation.

In order to build accurate data mining models the ISBSG database was processed through data preparation. Firstly 28 variables were selected based on their potential impact on effort and duration prediction. In terms of sizing it was decided to use *Relative Size* that represents counted software function points grouped into 9 categorical values (ranges). Utilization of categorical independent variables rather than continuous ones tend to boost model's accuracy due to narrowed complexity and segmentation necessity of data required during building models in order to find rules and associations. Next attributes with poor quality and substantial number of missing values were removed. For numeric variables three standard deviations from mean criterion was applied to exclude any potential outliers that could affect models' learning process.

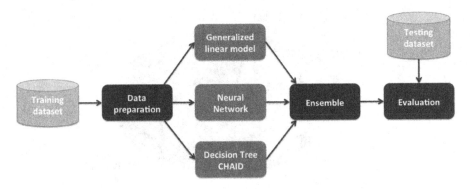

Fig. 2. Effort and duration prediction model process based on function points sizing.
Source: Own elaboration

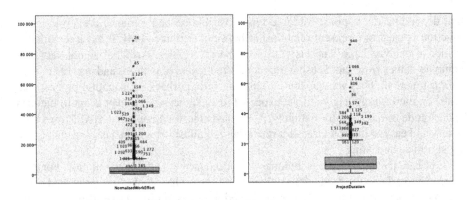

Fig. 3. Box plot for depended variables *Effort* and *Duration*.
Source: Own elaboration based on SPSS Modeler

The depended variable *Effort* (derived from *Normalized Work Effort*) presents total effort required to preform the project reflected in hours, and *Duration* (*Project Elapsed Time*) total project elapsed time in months. In order to use the same units the first one was transformed to work months [46]. Both variables had positive skewness (see Fig. 3) that indicated distribution other than normal. Therefore, two tests were conducted to verify normality of distributions: Kolmogorov-Smirnov and Shapiro-Wilk. Significances of statistics generated by those tests were lower than 0,05 therefore null hypothesis that there is a normal distribution within effort and duration was rejected. Taking into consideration that data mining algorithms including GLM, ANN and CHAID generate more accurate predictions for numeric dependent variables with normal distribution *Effort* and *Duration* were log-transformed.

The above-presented approach for data preparation narrowed dataset to 11 independent, 2 depended variables (Table 2), and 1494 observations (projects). In order to verify dependency between input and output attributes Pearson correlation and stepwise regression was preformed. Both *Effort* and *Duration* had the biggest relationship with sizing variable measured with function points (0,672 and 0,256 respectively).

Table 2. Selected variables for effort and duration estimation

No	Variable	Description	Type	Categories	Role
1	Industry Sector	Organisation type	Nominal	14	Input
2	Application Type	Type of application being addressed	Nominal	16	Input
3	Development Type	New development, enhancement or re-development	Nominal	3	Input
4	Development Platform	PC, Mid Range, Main Frame or Multi platform	Nominal	4	Input
5	Language Type	Programming language (2GL, 3GL, 4GL)	Nominal	3	Input
6	Package customization	Indicates whether the project was a package customisation	Nominal	3	Input
7	Relative Size	Function points grouped into categories	Nominal	7	Input
8	Architecture	System architecture	Nominal	6	Input
9	Agile	Agile used?	Flag	2	Input
10	Used Methodology	Development methodology used?	Nominal	3	Input
11	Resource Level	Development team effort, development team support, computer operations involvement, end users or clients	Nominal	4	Input
12	Effort	Total project effort in work months, log-transformed	Continuous	–	Target
13	Duration	Total project elapsed time in months, log-transformed	Continuous	–	Target

Source: Own elaboration based on [28]

Other independent attributes had lower ability for predicting depended variables (0,1-0,2). In terms of stepwise regression for *Effort* only 5 variables were included into model mostly due to high influence of *Relative Size*. Regarding *Duration* the regression required 9 independent attributes in result of more similar affect on the output. Nevertheless none of input variables were excluded from the dataset because their dependency on *Effort* and *Duration* is on significant level, which may leverage models' estimation accuracy. Correlation between output variables was on level 0,470 that is considered to be strong taking into account large amount of varied observations within the dataset.

For further modeling purposes the dataset of 1494 projects (see Table 2) defined during data preparation process was split into training (80 %) and test (20 %) dataset. The first one was used for building models and the other for validating their effort and duration estimation capability. Due to large set of data used for purposes of this article it was decided not to use sampling methods for building ensemble models (bagging or boosting) and also not to utlilitize k-fold cross validation.

Three data mining prediction algorithms were applied with use of SPSS Modeler software for both depended variables: generalized linear model, multilayered neural network and CHAID decision trees. Achieved estimations from each of them were merged (averaged) separately for effort and duration in order to potentially boost prediction accuracy. For validating models forecast error measures were utilized: mean error (ME), mean absolute error (MAE), mean squared error (MSE) and root mean squared error (RMSE) [45, 47]. Additionally magnitude of relative error (MRE), mean magnitude of relative error (MMRE) and prediction at level k PRED(k) were used that are commonly applied for assessing accuracy of software estimation models. According to Conte, Dunsmore and Shen [48] 'good' estimating model should have MMRE $\leq$ 0,25 and PRED (0,25) $\geq$ 0,75. Nevertheless such criterion is hardly achieved especially when models are trained based on large heterogeneous datasets that consist of mix-sized projects derived from various industries [49].

Table 3 presents prediction accuracy measures for built effort and duration estimation models. Results for individual algorithms GLM, ANN and CHAID are compared with merged models where generated predictions by those three techniques were averaged. As it can be noticed forecast errors across all models are on similar level and differences are almost imperceptible. For effort prediction the best performing algorithm was generalized linear model, where square root of the variance of the residuals (RMSE) that indicates distance between observed and predicted values for testing dataset was 0,402 (ANN 0,418 and CHAID 0,412). Additionally the difference between RMSE and MAE for all effort estimation models is very small therefore it can be stated that large errors did not occur. In terms of duration estimation the lowest generated forecast errors delivered neural network, where RMSE for testing dataset was on level 0,25 (GLM 0,268 and CHAID 0,273). The variance between RMSE and MAE was very small which indicates that, similarly to effort models, large errors did not exist.

Analyzing commonly used measures for assessing software estimation models it can be noticed that for both effort and duration estimation models MMRE was slightly above 20 %. This indicates that predicting with those models effort and timeframe required to complete a project only in 20 % cases error can occur. It is considered to be very good level below 25 % Conte criterion. PRED(0,25) values were averaging around 60 %, which points out that models were within 25 % accuracy in 60 % of time. This is lower than assumed 75 % level that good estimation model should posses but considering large and diverse database used for training and validating it can be accepted as a satisfactory. Additionally, if considered PRED(0,3) indicator the accuracy increase even by 10 %.

For both effort and duration estimation the most accurate models were the merged ones. They outperformed individual algorithms achieving the highest MMRE and PRED based on training and testing dataset. The final model for effort prediction had for testing dataset MMRE of 0,04 and PRED(0,25) of 0,597. In relation to duration estimation the merged model achieved accuracy MMRE of 0,245 and PRED(0,25) of 0,591.

To conclude, all models built based on sizing measured with function points have very good software project effort and duration prediction capability. Forecast errors obtained where small and estimation accuracy was very good especially considering large volume of diverse data used for training purposes. For effort estimation the best performing algorithm was generalized linear model, and for duration artificial neural networks. Nevertheless, the prediction accuracy between algorithms used was almost insignificant and each one of them could be used individually for effort and duration

Table 3. Forecast errors and accuracy measures of built GLM, ANN and CHAID models for effort and duration prediction

	Generalized linear model		Artificial neural network		CHAID Decision tree		Combined model	
	Training	Test	Training	Test	Training	Test	Training	Test
Effort								
ME	0,000	-0,012	0,008	0,002	0,000	-0,008	-0,004	-0,011
MAE	0,288	0,310	0,308	0,331	0,287	0,313	0,288	0,310
MSE	0,139	0,162	0,159	0,175	0,140	0,169	0,139	0,160
RMSE	0,373	0,402	0,398	0,418	0,374	0,412	0,373	0,400
MMRE	0,203	0,053	0,226	0,113	0,225	0,050	0,187	0,040
PRED(0,25)	0,599	0,604	0,571	0,545	0,612	0,607	0,618	0,597
PRED(0,3)	0,680	0,662	0,657	0,623	0,680	0,662	0,685	0,662
Duration								
ME	0,000	0,003	0,000	0,009	0,000	0,012	0,000	0,008
MAE	0,206	0,217	0,188	0,198	0,193	0,212	0,186	0,201
MSE	0,075	0,072	0,065	0,063	0,068	0,074	0,064	0,064
RMSE	0,274	0,268	0,255	0,250	0,261	0,273	0,253	0,252
MMRE	0,228	0,263	0,213	0,259	0,217	0,251	0,205	0,245
PRED(0,25)	0,611	0,558	0,623	0,588	0,654	0,568	0,659	0,591
PRED(0,3)	0,700	0,646	0,706	0,653	0,732	0,653	0,750	0,675

Source: Own elaboration

estimation. The merged approach of combining results of GLM, ANN and CHAID by averaging output estimates delivered even more accurate predictions. Additionally, it overcomes possibility of overfitting and difference in algorithms' performance depending on utilized database and depended variable. Models could be even more accurate if deployed for particular organization and trained based on homogeneous dataset.

6   Conclusions

Effort and duration estimation of software projects at early stage during initiation and planning is considered as one of the most challenging tasks in project management on which project success is dependable. The reason of that is lack of information about the functionalities of the final product and activities necessary to preform in order to develop and implement the software system. Therefore, project managers and other project practitioners during estimation process act on incomplete information where uncertainty and risk occurrence is significant. For estimation purposes they utilize mostly traditional manual techniques that derive from expert knowledge or are based on analogy. These methods tend to be error prone and deliver overoptimistic estimates that result in cost and schedule overrun, which may contribute to project failure. Additionally for estimation purposes researchers and practitioners deployed in last 30 years numerous techniques that are based on sizing assessed with FP. Despite their accuracy in terms of size calculation they lack of ability to estimate effort and duration, especially if considered various project management culture within organizations and large complex projects that are nowadays often conducted.

On the other hand data mining is growing in popularity. Their techniques derived from statistics, artificial intelligence and machine learning poses outstanding prediction capability that can be applied for various purposes especially where uncertainty occurs and may contribute to risk materialization, ultimately financial loses (i.e. credit scoring, customer attrition). Therefore, for last two decades researchers explored deployment of data mining algorithms for software estimation but despite demonstrating their exceptional accuracy for effort and duration prediction there can be found hardly any deployment in practice. The reason of this may be that the proposed approaches focus on performance of individual algorithms and mostly are tailored for particular dataset instead of presenting robust to noise, change and data heterogeneity complex models. Moreover a role of software sizing is omitted that is the most significant input variable for effort and duration estimation and its proper assessment impacts prediction accuracy.

The aim of this paper was to present a combined approach of functional size measurement and data mining techniques for effort and duration estimation. The software size assessed with function points tends to generate the most accurate results. It was utilized as an input variable for three robust data mining prediction algorithms: generalized linear model, artificial neural network and CHAID decision tree. For this purpose ISBSG database was used that provides information about software size calculated using IFPUG, NESMA, COSMIC and FiSMA methods. Based on preprocessed dataset models were built separately for effort and duration estimation. Moreover, merged approach was explored that combines predictions delivered by GLM, ANN and CHAID using arithmetic mean. Obtained results demonstrated a very good capability of used individual data mining algorithms for effort and duration estimation based on software sizing assessed with function points. Nevertheless the proposed merged approach of combining GLM, ANN and CHAID predictions by averaging generated even more accurate predictions and foremost overcome possibility of overfitting and delivering false predictions by individual algorithms depending on quality of data used for training.

The further research should focus on deploying the proposed approach in practice as a decision support tool that could be used for early effort and duration estimation of small to large software projects. It may be integrated with existing project management tools and preferably be maintained by project management office that would ensure proper quality of input data and models' update in order to retain their accuracy in project changing environment. Data mining techniques with use of function points for sizing require historic database of completed projects in order to tailor models for organization's specific project management culture. The proper attention should be given to quality of data since data mining models are sensitive to anomalies and missing values. Therefore, preferably they should be implemented within capability maturity model integration (CMMI) certified organizations where certainly the proposed approach would contribute to increase process success rate.

References

1. Project Management Institute: A Guide to the Project Management Body of Knowledge - PMBOK Guide. Project Management Institute (2013)
2. Marchewka, J.: Information Technology Project Managment - Providing Measurable Organizational Value. Wiley, Hoboken (2003)
3. Standish Group: The CHAOS Manifesto 2011. Standish Gr. Int. EUA. 25 (2011)
4. Czarnacka-Chrobot, B.: Analysis of the functional size measurement methods usage by polish business software systems providers. In: Abran, A., Braungarten, R., Dumke, R.R., Cuadrado-Gallego, J.J., Brunekreef, J. (eds.) IWSM 2009. LNCS, vol. 5891, pp. 17–34. Springer, Heidelberg (2009)
5. Neimat, T.: Al: Why IT projects fail. Proj. perfect white Pap. Collect., pp. 1–8 (2005)
6. Tan, S.: How to Increase Your IT Project Success Rate. Gart. Res. Rep. (2011)
7. Mieritz, L.: Survey Shows Why Projects Fail (2012)
8. Galorath, D., Evans, M.: Software Sizing, Estimation, and Risk Management. Auerbach Publications, Boca Raton (2006)
9. Wells, G.: Why projects fail. Manag. Sci. J. (2001)
10. International Software Benchmarking Standards Group: ISBSG Repository Data Release 12 - Field Descriptions (2013)
11. Schwalbe, K.: Information Technology Project Management. Course Technology, Boston (2014)
12. Boehm, B.W.: Software Engineering Economics. Prentice Hall, Englewood Cliffs (1981). 10, 4–21
13. Laird, L.M., Brennan, M.C.: Software Measurement and Estimation: A Practical Approach. Wiley, Hoboken (2006)
14. Albrecht, A.: Measuring application development productivity. In: IBO Conference on Application Development, pp. 83–92 (1979)
15. Czarnacka-Chrobot, B.: Standardization of software size measurement. In: Tkacz, E., Kapczynski, A. (eds.) Internet – Technical Development and Applications. AISC, vol. 64, pp. 149–156. Springer, Heidelberg (2009)
16. Hill, P.: Practical Software Project Estimation: a Toolkit for Estimating Software Development Effort & Duration. McGraw Hill Professional, New York (2010)
17. Gasik, S.: A model of project knowledge management. Proj. Manag. J. 42, 23–44 (2011)
18. Piatetsky-Shapiro, G., Frawley, W.J.: Knowledge Discovery in Databases (1991)
19. Linoff, G.S., Berry, M.J.A.: Data Mining Techniques: For Marketing, Sales, and Customer Relationship Management. Wiley, New York (2011)
20. International Society of Parametric Analysts: Parametric Estimating Handbook. ISPA (2008)
21. Iranmanesh, S.H., Mokhtari, Z.: Application of data mining tools to predicate completion time of a project. Proc. World Acad. Sci. Eng. Technol. 32, 234–240 (2008)
22. Azzeh, M., Cowling, P.I., Neagu, D.: Software stage-effort estimation based on association rule mining and Fuzzy set theory. In: Proceedings - 10th IEEE International Conference on Computer and Information Technology, CIT-2010, 7th IEEE International Conference on Embedded Software and Systems, ICESS-2010, ScalCom-2010, pp. 249–256 (2010)
23. Balsera, J.V., Montequin, V.R., Fernandez, F.O., González-Fanjul, C.A.: Data Mining Applied to the Improvement of Project Management. InTech. (2012)
24. Nagwani, N.K., Bhansali, A.: A data mining model to predict software bug complexity using bug estimation and clustering. In: ITC 2010 - 2010 International Conference on Recent Trends in Information, Telecommunication, and Computing, pp. 13–17 (2010)

25. Shukla, R., Shukla, M., Misra, A.K., Marwala, T., Clarke, W.A.: Dynamic software maintenance effort estimation modeling using neural network, rule engine and multi-regression approach. In: Murgante, B., Gervasi, O., Misra, S., Nedjah, N., Rocha, A.M.A., Taniar, D., Apduhan, B.O. (eds.) ICCSA 2012, Part IV. LNCS, vol. 7336, pp. 157–169. Springer, Heidelberg (2012)

26. Jorgensen, M., Shepperd, M.: A systematic review of software development cost estimation studies. IEEE Trans. Softw. Eng. **33**, 33–53 (2007)

27. Wen, J., Li, S., Lin, Z., Hu, Y., Huang, C.: Systematic literature review of machine learning based software development effort estimation models. Inf. Softw. Technol. **54**, 41–59 (2012)

28. Kobyliński, A., Pospieszny, P.: Zastosowanie technik eksploracji danych do estymacji pracochłonności projektów informatycznych. Studia i Materiały Polskiego Stowarzyszenia Zarządzania Wiedzą, pp. 67–82, Bydgoszcz (2015)

29. Dzega, D., Pietruszkiewicz, W.: Classification and metaclassification in large scale data mining application for estimation of software projects. In: 2010 IEEE 9th International Conference on Cybernetic Intelligent Systems, CIS 2010 (2010)

30. Dejaeger, K., Verbeke, W., Martens, D., Baesens, B.: Data mining techniques for software effort estimation: A comparative study. IEEE Trans. Softw. Eng. **38**, 375–397 (2012)

31. Brewer, J., Dittman, K.: Methods of IT Project Management. Prentice Hal, New York (2009)

32. Ruchika Malhotra, A.J.: Software effort prediction using statistical and machine learning methods. Int. J. Adv. Comput. Sci. Appl. **2**, 145–152 (2011)

33. Pai, D.R., McFall, K.S., Subramanian, G.H.: Software effort estimation using a neural network ensemble. J. Comput. Inf. Syst. **53**, 49–58 (2013)

34. Lopez-Martin, C., Isaza, C., Chavoya, A.: Software development effort prediction of industrial projects applying a general regression neural network. Empir. Softw. Eng. **17**, 738–756 (2012)

35. Mittas, N., Angelis, L.: Ranking and clustering software cost estimation models through a multiple comparisons algorithm. IEEE Trans. Softw. Eng. **39**, 537–551 (2013)

36. Kocaguneli, E., Menzies, T., Keung, J.W.: On the value of ensemble effort estimation. IEEE Trans. Softw. Eng. **38**, 1403–1416 (2012)

37. Reifer, D.J., Boehm, B.W., Chulani, S.: The Rosetta stone: Making COCOMO 81 Files Work With COCOMO II. Univ. South Calif. 1–10 (1998)

38. PROMISE Software Engineering Repository. http://promise.site.uottawa.ca/SERepository/

39. SourceForge. http://sourceforge.net

40. Albrecht, A.J., Gaffney, J.E.J.: Software function, source lines of code, and development effort prediction: a software science validation. IEEE Trans. Softw. Eng. **SE-9**, 639–648 (1983)

41. International Software Benchmarking Standards Group. http://www.isbsg.org

42. Villanueva-Balsera, J., Ortega-Fernandez, F., Rodríguez-Montequín, V., Concepción-Suárez, R.: Effort estimation in information systems projects using data mining techniques. In: Proceedings of the 13th WSEAS International Conference on Computers - Held as part of the 13th WSEAS CSCC Multiconference, pp. 652–657 (2009)

43. Pete, C., Julian, C., Randy, K., Thomas, K., Thomas, R., Colin, S., Wirth, R.: CRISP-DM 1.0 (2000)

44. Giudici, P., Figini, S.: Applied Data Mining for Business and Industry. Wiley, New York (2009)

45. Larose, D.T.: Data Mining Methods and Models. Wiley, New York (2007)

46. Boehm, B.W., Abts, C., Brown, A.W., Chulani, S., Clark, B.K., Horowitz, E., Madachy, R., Reifer, D.J., Steece, B.: Software Cost Estimation with Cocomo II. Prentice Hall PTR, Upper Saddle River (2000)

47. Han, J., Kamber, M., Pei, J.: Data Mining: Concepts and Techniques. Morgan Kaufmann, San Francisco (2006)
48. Conte, S.D., Dunsmore, H.E., Shen, V.Y.: Software Engineering Metrics and Models. Benjamin/Cummings Pub. Co., Menlo Park (1986)
49. Jorgensen, M.: A critique of how we measure and interpret the accuracy of software development effort estimation. In: 1st International Workshop on Software Productivity Analysis and Cost Estimation. ss. 15–22 (2007)

Functional Size Measurement for Processor Load Estimation in AUTOSAR

Hassan Soubra[1(✉)], Alain Abran[2], and Mehdi Sehit[3]

[1] École Supérieure des Techniques Aéronautiques et de
Construction Automobile – ESTACA, Levallois, France
hassan.soubra@estaca.fr
[2] École de Technologie Supérieure – ETS, Université du Québec,
Montréal, Canada
alain.abran@etsmtl.ca
[3] École Supérieure d'Informatique, Électronique, Automatique – ESIEA,
Laval, France
sehit@et.esiea-ouest.fr

Abstract. Functional size measurement (FSM) gives a measure of a software product and can be used to build objective estimation models for predicting project effort and duration. AUTOSAR is an architecture standard that allows collaboration on basic Electrical and Electronic (E/E) functions while providing a platform to develop new innovative ones. AUTOSAR allows portability and reuse of software functions on different hardware architectures. However, designing software functions in AUTOSAR requires several software allocation decisions which impact on E/E system performance and development costs. In this context, processor load estimation becomes an important task early in software development projects for automotive real-time embedded systems. This paper analyzes the relationship between FSM and ECU processor load in AUTOSAR, and introduces the SYMTA/S tool and an automation prototype tool developed in this study. The findings demonstrate a relationship between FSM and processor load.

Keywords: COSMIC · AUTOSAR · FSM · ECU · Processor load · ISO 19761

1 Introduction

Software functional size is a key input for building software development estimation models, effort models, benchmark models, and quality models [1]. Software measurement is a powerful tool for managing software projects, allowing application of engineering principles to software development, and providing an objective, quantitative base for management decisions. For instance, software size gives a measure of the software product itself, and can be used to obtain development productivity ratios and build objective estimation models for predicting project effort and duration.

Among the many challenges facing the automotive industry today are escalating production costs related to the use of Electrical and Electronic (E/E) systems. E/E systems

© Springer International Publishing Switzerland 2015
A. Kobyliński et al. (Eds.): IWSM-Mensura 2015, LNBIP 230, pp. 114–129, 2015.
DOI: 10.1007/978-3-319-24285-9_8

are composed of Electronic Control Units (ECUs) interconnected by a communication network and relying heavily on software. E/E systems have been known, since their early days, for being complex systems that integrate both software and hardware, creating many challenges [2]. They are designed by Original Equipment Manufacturers (OEMs) to provide specific functionalities, which are described in sometimes quite abstract terms. Moreover, they are implemented at various technological levels and with a number of different interfaces that may themselves be a mix of software and hardware functionalities. These variations in functionality levels across hardware and applications were not easily discernible in early E/E systems design [3]. Today's car prices are highly related to the use of E/E systems, in which software plays an even more important role because of both functionalities and infrastructure. Consequently, software reuse and carryover have become inevitable for OEMs [4, 5].

Moreover, the increasing complexity of E/E architecture requires methods and tools for design automation and synthesis of distributed systems in order to assess alternative solutions for estimated performance and safety indicators [6, 7].

The AUTOSAR (AUTomotive Open System ARchitecture) consortium [8] was formally launched in July 2003 by the automotive industry, including manufacturers, suppliers and tool developers. It has created a basis for collaboration on basic functions while providing a platform which encourages competition for innovative functions. One of AUTOSAR's main objectives is to standardize a large number of ECU software modules to facilitate reuse; it also aims to prepare for the increase in functional scope of E/E systems. AUTOSAR has become an important part of production design criteria for many vehicle manufacturers, especially the automotive electronics industry. Its ECU software design methodology is gradually replacing the earlier version, which was decentralized and OEM specific. AUTOSAR is the new generation of ECU software design architecture, methodology and meta-model [9, 10].

The use of software functional size, measured in function points, goes hand in hand with AUTOSAR objectives in terms of managing automotive software projects [11]. For instance, functional size can be used in AUTOSAR to estimate ECU software development cost and duration. It can also be used for purposes such as processor load estimation, network traffic estimation and acceptance condition estimation [7].

COSMIC [12] provides a standardized method for measuring the functional size of software from both Management Information Systems and real-time domains. COSMIC is considered a second-generation FSM and has been accepted as an International Standard (ISO/IEC 19761, Software Engineering – COSMIC – A functional size measurement method). Version 4.0.1 of the COSMIC manual is available on the COSMIC website [13]. While this release includes a number of refinements, the original principles of COSMIC have remained unchanged since first published in 1999. Functional sizes measured by COSMIC are designed to be independent of any implementation decisions embedded in the operational artifacts of the software. This means that the functional user requirements (FUR) can be extracted not only from software already developed but also from the software model before implementation.

This paper presents a study of the relationship between processor load and functional size based on the COSMIC ISO 19761 standard for ECU software designed in AUTOSAR. The aim is to provide a basis for building objective estimation models to predict processor load. The COSMIC-based FSM procedure used in this work is described in detail in [14].

The paper is organized as follows. Section 2 presents a literature review of processor load estimation and FSM in automotive real-time embedded systems. Section 3 presents overviews of COSMIC, AUTOSAR and SYMTA/S. Section 4 presents our proposed COSMIC-based FSM procedure in the AUTOSAR architecture. Section 5 presents a study of the relationship between processor load and functional size on a set of over 150 input models on multiple ECUs. Section 6 presents our conclusions and a discussion of future work.

2   Related Work

This section presents related work, first on methods or processes tackling real-time related performance constraints in AUTOSAR and, second, on COSMIC-based FSM procedures for automotive real-time embedded systems (RTES) with a focus on measurement purposes and context for proposed procedures.

2.1   Related Work on Processor Load Estimation

In [15] a timing tool was proposed for different phases of the development process based on ARTOP and AUTOSAR's timing extensions: this tool provided prediction and verification of timing constraints of embedded software.

In [16] the importance and application of timing interfaces were discussed suggesting that AUTOSAR requires a basic timing model to allow application of such timing interfaces.

In [17] an algorithm was presented for optimizing implementation of AUTOSAR runnables in a concurrent program executing a set of tasks. The authors showed that there is an opportunity for optimizing memory requirements when implementing a system. Their plan proposed a solution with minimal memory usage that respects real-time schedulability constraints.

In [18] Hegde et al. demonstrated that, because there can be as many as 75 to 80 ECUs in some vehicles, load balancing mechanisms are needed to ease ECU integration and for efficient utilization of CPU power in ECUs.

2.2   Related Work on Using COSMIC-Based FSM Procedures

This sub-section presents work on COSMIC-based FSM procedures in the context of real-time embedded systems (RTES) with particular emphasis on measurement purposes.

In [11] a guideline was presented for measuring functional size in accordance with COSMIC ISO 19761 for ECU Application Software designed following AUTOSAR architecture: in this case, the measurement was performed manually. In [14] an FSM procedure based on this guideline [11] was presented and used to illustrate the application of a proposed automation verification protocol.

In [19] a software development effort estimation process was presented using the COSMIC functional size method. The FSM results were summarized in a classic file containing COSMIC Functional size of the specifications. Renault decided to develop an estimation process to predict its software development effort early in the project specification requirements phase.

In [20] a functional size measurement (FSM) procedure was proposed for real time embedded software requirements documented using the Simulink modeling tool. The procedure proposed in this study is for development effort estimation.

In [21] a tool was proposed for estimating code size, but was not evaluated in detail.

In [22] a tool based on COSMIC was presented for measuring the functional size of embedded automotive software early on, using a UML profile that captured all the information needed for functional size measurement according to COSMIC. The case study was conducted at Saab using requirement specifications and software implementations developed by Saab and GM.

In summary, related works on COSMIC-based FSM procedures for automotive real-time embedded systems focused on software development effort estimation or code size estimation. No research reports on processor load estimation in AUTOSAR were found.

3   Overviews of COSMIC, AUTOSAR and SYMTA/S

This section presents overviews of COSMIC, AUTOSAR and SYMTA/S.

3.1   COSMIC Overview

COSMIC measures the Functional User Requirements (FUR) of software. The result obtained is a numerical 'value of a quantity' (as defined by the ISO) representing the functional size of the software.

Functional size measured by COSMIC is designed to be independent of any implementation decisions embedded in the operational artifacts of the software. This means that FUR can be extracted not only from software already developed but also from the software model before it is implemented.

Version 4.0.1 of COSMIC consists of three phases:

1. In the Measurement Strategy Phase the COSMIC Software Context Model is applied.
2. The COSMIC Generic Software Model is applied in the Mapping Phase.
3. In the Measurement Phase, the actual measurement results are obtained.

The measurement result corresponds to the functional size of FUR, and is expressed in COSMIC Function Points (CFP).

In COSMIC, a functional process is a set of data movements representing an elementary part of FUR for the software being measured. The set is unique within the FUR and is defined independently of any other functional process. A functional process may have only one triggering Entry. Each functional process begins processing on receipt of a data group moved by the triggering Entry data movement of the functional process. The set of all data movements of a functional process is the set needed to meet its FUR for all possible responses to the triggering Entry. According to COSMIC, software functionality is embedded within the functional flows of data groups. Data flows can be characterized by four distinct types of movement. Two types (Entries (E) and Exits X)) between the functional user FU and a COSMIC functional process allow the exchange of data with a functional user across a boundary. Two other types (Reads (R) and Writes (W)) between a COSMIC functional process and the persistent storage allow exchange of data with the persistent storage hardware. The measurement result corresponds to the functional size of the FUR of the software measured, and is expressed in COSMIC Function Points (or CFP).

3.2   AUTOSAR Overview

AUTOSAR provides a set of concepts and a methodology for design and implementation of automotive E/E systems. AUTOSAR methodology follows a model-driven approach where software and hardware architectures are designed using an AUTOSAR meta-model. The layered architecture of AUTOSAR methodology is illustrated in Fig. 1. The virtual functional bus (VFB) view (1) presents AUTOSAR Application Software as a set of software components (SWC 1, SWC 2, SWC 3 and SWC 4) communicating through the VFB (2) via communication ports. The main objective of the VFB view is to abstract high level software functionalities, rendering them independent of low level hardware/software implementation, and allowing designers to validate the interactions between SWCs before implementation.

Using the ECU description (3) and the system constraint description (4), SWCs are then mapped to ECUs available in the hardware architecture (5). The Run Time Environment RTE (6) provides the necessary environment for interactions between SWCs implemented on one ECU (intra-ECUs) or on several (inter-ECUs). RTE may be considered as an instance of VFB per ECU.

SWCs, the main elements of Application Software in AUTOSAR, contain the functional description of the Software. There are two types of SWC: Sensor/Actuator SWC and Application SWC. While Application SWCs are defined regardless of hardware architecture and ECU location, Sensor/Actuator SWCs are bound to the ECU to which the sensor/actuator is physically connected. The internal behavior of an SWC is defined as a set of Runnable entities (Runnables) executed at runtime. A Runnable represents a portion of the code that will be executed on the target ECU. A Runnable is mapped to an Operation System (OS) task. Runnables exchange information using inter-Runnable variables, as the use of global variables is not permitted in AUTOSAR.

3.3   SYMTA/S Overview

The SYMTA/S tool models and analyzes real-time embedded systems in order to measure system performance (e.g. Worst Case Execution time -WCET, CPU load, end to end latencies, etc.) while taking into account various scheduling constraints and

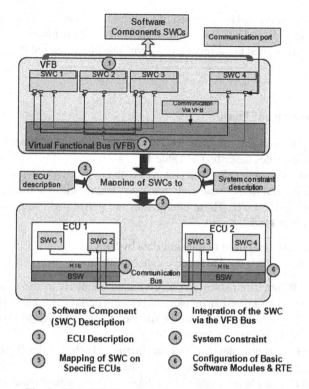

Fig. 1. AUTOSAR methodology as presented in [11].

differing execution scenarios. SYMTA/S is suitable for several system architectures including AUTOSAR.

SYMTA/S's graphical interface allows users to model both hardware and software layers of a system, visualize the models created, run simulations and visualize analysis results in the form of graphs.

Analysis and measurement procedures applied to a modeled system are implemented in Python. SYMTA/S provides a complete library allowing manipulation of all elements of the system modeled.

Results of applied procedures are saved in XML files containing the complete description of the systems modeled.

4 An FSM Procedure for ECU Software Designed Following AUTOSAR

To correctly measure the functional size of ECU application software designed following AUTOSAR, the measurement objective, scope and other elements must be identified and well defined. The proposed procedure is based on the measurement guideline presented in [11] and the procedure in [14]. To obtain functional size a set of mapping rules was applied to the modeled system. The Measurement Phase is presented below.

4.1   The Measurement Phase

The data group movements of each AUTOSAR Runnable (Functional Process) are identified using the rules described in Table 1.

A Software Component (SWC) can interact with another SWC, with an AUTOSAR service module located in the basic software layer, and/or with a sensor/actuator physically connected to the ECU. These interactions are performed using communication ports. There are two kinds of ports:

A. Provide Ports (PPort) used to transmit data by SWCs.
B. Require Ports (RPort) used to receive data by SWCs.

Through an RPort, Runnables can receive data elements in the Sender-Receiver communication mode, or they can invoke an operation or require access to the persistent storage in the Client-Server communication mode. Thus an RPort is mapped to a COSMIC Entry data group movement (rule 2).

Through a PPort, Runnables can send data elements in the Sender-Receiver communication mode, and can execute an operation in the Client-Server communication mode. Thus a PPort is mapped to a COSMIC Exit data group movement (rule 3).

AUTOSAR InterRunnablesVariables are typed data elements shared between Runnables belonging to the same SWC. An AUTOSAR Read InterRunnablesVariable is mapped to a COSMIC Entry data group movement (rule 4). An AUTOSAR Write InterRunnablesVariable is mapped to a COSMIC Exit data group movement (rule 5).

Runnables can be activated by a DataReceivedEvent which corresponds to a data reception via an RPort. However, they also can be activated by an AUTOSAR TimingEvent, which is mapped to a COSMIC Triggering Entry data group movement (rule 1).

In the FSM procedure proposed in this paper, only communication ports with a Sender-Receiver or a Client-Server interface are taken into account. There are no AUTOSAR elements that can be mapped to COSMIC Read/Write data group movements, as Runnables do not have direct access to the persistent storage: this access is provided by the NVRAM manager module located in the basic Software layer.

Table 1 presents the rules for identifying the data group movements. The rules for obtaining the functional size of each functional process and the whole software are presented in Table 2.

Table 1. Rules to identify data group movements in the context of AUTOSAR.

Rule N°	AUTOSAR element	Cosmic data group movement
1	RTE TimingEvent	Entry data group movement (E)
2	Require Port (RPort) connected to the Runnable	Entry data group movement (E)
3	Read InterRunnables Variable	Entry data group movement (E)
4	Provide Port (PPort) connected to the Runnable	Exit data group movement (X)
5	Write InterRunnables Variable	Exit data group movement (X)

Once all the data movements in a Runnable have been identified, the standard size value of one CFP is assigned to each data movement. The final step consists of aggregating the results to obtain the functional size of each Runnable (rule 6). The functional size of the Runnables are next aggregated to obtain the functional size of the ECU application software being measured (rule 7).

Table 2. Rules for obtaining the functional sizes of the Runnables and the whole Software.

Rule N°	AUTOSAR element	Cosmic data group movement
6	*Runnable*	Aggregate the identified data group movements to obtain the functional size of the *Runnable*
7	ECU Application Software	Aggregate the functional sizes of the identified *Runnables* to obtain the functional size of the software

5   ECU Load and Functional Size

This section investigates the relationship between ECU Load and functional size measured using the proposed COSMIC-based FSM procedure. In our work, we used SYMTA/S to create different AUTOSAR models and obtain the ECU processor load required by the models. The Measurement Phase is presented below.

5.1 Experimental Set-up

A set of 164 distinct input models (Table 3) generated using SYMTA/S, were used to measure system performance including WCET, CPU load, end to end latencies, etc., taking into account various scheduling constraints and different systems architectures (e.g. number of ECUs used). Each AUTOSAR model was composed of one or more SWC (Software components) which, in turn, were composed of one or more Runnables. Table 3 presents seven different architectures created using various numbers of ECUs, the total number of AUTOSAR models created within these different architectures and the total number of Runnables per architecture. For example, for architecture A, 107 models were created composed of one ECU; for architecture B, 12 models were created composed of two ECUs. The experiment consisted of four steps:

1. We measured the functional size of an input AUTOSAR model after its allocation to one of the seven architectures. To speed up the measurement process and reduce the possibility of human error, we used an automated prototype tool developed in our study.
2. We observed the processor load, in the AUTOSAR model developed using SYMTA/S, run from 0 % (free) to 100 % (fully occupied).
3. We correlated the relation between ECU processor load (from step 2) and COSMIC functional size (from step 1).
4. We used linear regression analysis to build estimation models of ECU processor load for AUTOSAR models.

Table 3. Number of ECUs within an Architecture, and Corresponding number of Models.

Architecture	Number of ECUs in the architecture	Total number of AUTOSAR models used in the architecture	Total number of Runnables used in the architecture
A	1	107	107
B	2	12	24
C	3	5	15
D	4	21	84
E	5	7	35
F	6	11	66
G	7	1	7
Total number in all architectures		**164**	**338**

5.2 The Automation Tool

An automation prototype tool in JAVA was developed at ESTACA [24]. The inputs are SYMTA/S simulation files that include both AUTOSAR models and ECU processor load information. This tool makes it possible to measure automatically software functional size, in CFP, designed following AUTOSAR methodology and meta-model. This tool is also capable of measuring, simultaneously, a group of input specifications. The prototype tool's primary functionalities:

A. Automatically measures COSMIC functional sizes of the input models.
B. Determines ECU processor load for each input model using processor load information in SYMTA/S simulation files.
C. Yields ECU load vs COSMIC functional size graphs using input files.
D. Estimates processor load for additional models using previously generated graphs by using ECU load vs COSMIC functional size graphs from step A to estimate ECU processor load for new input models.

The tool outputs the functional sizes, ECU Load, and curves plotting the relationship between Functional size and ECU Load. Figures 2, 3, 4 and 5 illustrate examples of outputs using the automation tool. Regression models developed from a set of models can then be used to estimate the processor load of other models which did not contribute to the initial regression model.

5.3 Analyzing the Data

In statistics, correlation quantifies the degree to which two variables are related. The Bravais-Pearson product-moment correlation coefficient (r) [23] is a measure of the linear correlation between two variables X and Y. The correlation coefficient shows the degree Y tends to change as X changes. When r is 0.0, there is no relationship. When r is positive, Y increases as X increases. When r is negative, Y increases as X decreases. It is widely used in the sciences as a measure of the degree of linear dependence between two variables. While correlation is used to determine the existence of a relationship between two variables X and Y, linear regression finds the best line that predicts Y from X.

Using the Bravais-Pearson linear correlation coefficient to calculate the relation between ECU load and COSMIC functional size on 21 different AUTOSAR models from architecture A, we obtained a correlation coefficient of 0.93 (1). We concluded that the two variables are strongly dependent indicating a positive correlation between COSMIC Functional Size and CPU processor load: when the functional size of AUTOSAR models increases, the ECU processor load of the host ECU increases.

$$r_p = \frac{\sum\limits_{i=1}^{N} (x_i - \bar{x}) \cdot (y_i - \bar{y})}{\sqrt{\sum\limits_{i=1}^{N} (x_i - \bar{x})^2} \cdot \sqrt{\sum\limits_{i=1}^{N} (y_i - \bar{y})^2}} \tag{1}$$

Figure 2 shows the functional size (x coordinate) of 107 AUTOSAR models embedded in one ECU (Architecture A), and the corresponding ECU processor load (y coordinate).

To verify the correlation is also valid for an architecture composed of multiple ECUs, we applied the same approach to AUTOSAR models distributed respectively on: Architecture B, Architecture C, Architecture D (Fig. 3), Architecture E (Fig. 4), Architecture F (Fig. 5) and Architecture G. The ECUs have the same simulated characteristics. The figures show ECU processor load (y coordinate) and COSMIC functional size (x coordinate) in the different architectures.

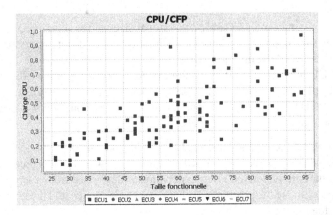

Fig. 2. Functional Size and processor load of Architecture A (1 ECU and N = 107).

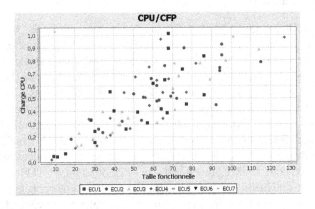

Fig. 3. Functional Size and processor load of Architecture D (4 ECUs and N = 84).

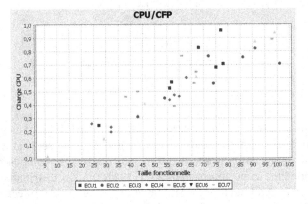

Fig. 4. Functional Size and processor load of Architecture E (5 ECUs and N = 35).

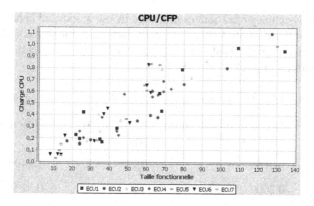

Fig. 5. Functional Size and processor load of Architecture F (6 ECUs and N = 66).

Figures 2, 3, 4 and 5 show a strong correlation between COSMIC functional size of an AUTOSAR model and ECU processor load, independently of the number of ECUs used in the E/E architecture and how the models are embedded in the ECUs.

5.4   Using Linear Regression Models to Estimate Processor Load of Other Input Models

The fourth step consists in the design of an estimation model of processor load for other AUTOSAR models using linear regression. Linear regression finds the best line that predicts ECU processor load from COSMIC functional size.

A linear regression model graph for each ECU of each architecture was built using the 164 models from Table 3. The regression model ($R^2 = 0.546$) of Architecture A with 107 models on a single ECU (Fig. 6) was then used to estimate ECU processor loads of 24 "new" AUTOSAR models ("new" in the sense that they were not in the initial set of ten models of Architecture A used to build the regression model of Fig. 6).

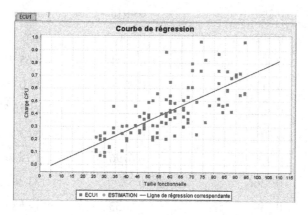

Fig. 6. Regression model for ECU1 from Architecture A ($R^2 = 0.546$).

To verify the accuracy of estimates produced by our automated approach, the ECU processor load of these 24 models were directly simulated, measured with SYMTA/S, and then compared with the load estimates produced with the regression models built from the 107 models of Architecture A (Table 4).

Table 4. Number of ECUs within an Architecture, and Corresponding number of Models.

Model N°	Actual data load from SYMTA/S	Estimates from regression model	Difference (%)
1	0.066	0.21	14.40 %
2	0.2009	0.21	0.91 %
3	0.143	0.2256	8.26 %
4	0.32	0.3509	3.09 %
5	0.2009	0.4291	22.82 %
6	0.0975	0.21	11.25 %
7	0.2817	0.3509	6.92 %
8	0.2044	0.2882	8.38 %
9	0.2511	0.3978	14.67 %
10	0.4287	0.4448	1.61 %
11	0.3335	0.4135	8,00 %
12	0.1957	0.3822	18,65 %
13	0.3783	0.4918	11,35 %
14	0.6091	0,5074	10,17 %
15	0.299	0,4918	19,28 %
16	0.3724	0,3665	0.59 %
17	0.6096	0.5231	8.65 %
18	0.2171	0.3978	18.07 %
19	0.4682	0.5857	11.75 %
20	0.59	0.6483	5.83 %
21	0.6968	0.6796	1.72 %
22	0.3366	0.57	23.34 %
23	0.5495	0.6953	14.58 %
24	0.4076	0.5074	9.98 %

Results of the comparison showed twelve estimates with a disparity less than 10 % and ten estimates with a disparity between 10 % and 20 %. Finally, only two estimates had a disparity higher than 20 %.

Table 4 presents 24 models with actual ECU processor load data obtained using SYMTA/S and estimates obtained using the automation tool. The results of the comparison made per model are also presented. Figure 7 shows ECU processor load estimates produced by our automated approach in blue and actual ECU processor load data measured with SYMTA/S in red, for the 24 models used in this step.

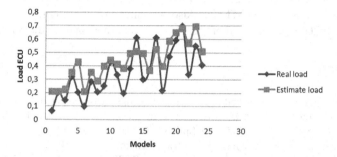

Fig. 7. Processor load: Estimates VS SYMTA/S processor load data

The mean difference between the actual data and the estimated data for the 24 models is 10.59 %. The accuracy of the estimates is approximately 90 %.

In our study, we observed a dependence of ECU processor load on COSMIC functional size. Estimates produced by our approach can be used to determine ECU processor load with fair accuracy. These results need to be verified using the data of other architectures and, as a next step, real-life AUTOSAR models. Finally, using linear regression models, one can use the automated approach to estimate processor load for one specific ECU or a set of ECUs.

6   Conclusion

FSM is traditionally used to estimate development effort, manage project scope changes, measure productivity, benchmark, and normalize quality and maintenance ratios. FSM goes hand in hand with AUTOSAR objectives for managing automotive software projects.

Designing software functions in AUTOSAR requires several software allocation decisions. For example, an important task in software development projects for automotive real-time embedded systems is estimating processor load, which in turn impacts E/E systems performance and development costs.

This paper presented a study of the relationship between FSM and processor load, in AUTOSAR. The findings have demonstrated the dependence of ECU processor load on COSMIC functional size. A proposed prototype tool allowed estimate of ECU processor load for a model using its functional size for a specific ECU.

To verify the accuracy of the estimates produced by our automated approach, the ECU processor load of 24 models were directly simulated and measured with SYMTA/S, and then compared with load estimates produced with regression models built from an architecture composed of a single ECU.

The proposed automation tool can be adapted to different design rules (naming rules, specific memory blocks, etc.). A video demonstrating the automation prototype tool presented in this section, in addition to the tool itself, are freely available as downloads on ESTACA's website [24]. In future studies, additional estimates from different architectures will be produced and compared with the ECU processor load of directly simulated and measured with SYMTA/S. Also, we intend to apply our prototype tool to estimate the ECU processor load of "real life" systems and analyze the related data.

References

1. Marín, B., Pastor, Ó., Giachetti, G.: Automating the measurement of functional size of conceptual models in an MDA environment. In: Jedlitschka, A., Salo, O. (eds.) PROFES 2008. LNCS, vol. 5089, pp. 215–229. Springer, Heidelberg (2008)
2. Broy, M.: Challenges in automotive software engineering. In: Proceedings of the 28th International Conference on Software Engineering (ICSE 2006). ACM Press (2006). Keynote
3. Bischof, H., Donhauser, B., Meder, K.: The ECU of a rear wheel steering system. In: 8th International Conference on Automotive Electronics (ICAE 1991), London, pp. 208–213, October 1991
4. Heinecke, H., et al.: AUTomotive Open System ARchitecture – an industry-wide initiative to manage the complexity of emerging automotive E/E-architectures. In: Convergence 2004, International Congress on Transportation Electronics, Detroit (2004)
5. Fürst, S., et al.: AUTOSAR – a Worldwide Standard is on the Road. In: 14th International VDI Congress Electronic Systems for Vehicles, BadenBade (2009)
6. Daghsen, A., Chaaban, K., Saudrais, S.: Software function allocation and configuration of an AUTOSAR-compliant system. In: SAE 2012 World Congress & Exhibition, Detroit, Michigan, USA, April 2012
7. Soubra, H.: The use and benefits of Functional Size Measurement in the context of AUTOSAR. In: 23rd UKSMA – UK Software Metrics Association Annual Conference, London, UK (2012)
8. http://www.autosar.org
9. Heinecke, H., et al.: AUTOSAR – Current results and preparations for exploitation. In: Euroforum Conference, 3 May 2006
10. Fennel, H., et al.: Achievements and exploitation of the AUTOSAR development partnership. In: SAE Convergence Congress, Detroit (2006)
11. Soubra, H., Chaaban, K.: Functional size measurement of electronic control units software designed following the AUTOSAR standard. In: 22nd International Workshop on Software Measurement & 7th International Conference on Software Process and Product Measurement - IWSM-MENSURA, Assisi, Italy, 17–19 October 2012. IEEE Computer Society Press (2012)
12. Lesterhuis, A., Symons, C.: The COSMIC Measurement Manual, version 4.0.1 (2014). http://www.cosmic-sizing.org/publications/measurement-manual-401/
13. http://cosmic-sizing.org

14. Soubra, H., Alain A., Ramdane-Cherif, A.: Verifying the accuracy of automation tools for the measurement of software with COSMIC--ISO 19761 including an AUTOSAR-based example and a case study. In: Joint Conference of the International Workshop on Software Measurement and the International Conference on Software Process and Product Measurement (IWSM-MENSURA), Rotterdam (The Netherlands), Nov. 2014, pp. 23–31. IEEE CS Press (2014)

15. Scheickl, O., Ainhauser, C., Gliwa, P.: Tool support for seamless system development based on AUTOSAR timing extensions. In: Embedded Real-Time Software Congress (ERTS) (2012)

16. Scheickl, O., et al.: How timing interfaces in AUTOSAR can improve distributed development of real-time software. In: GI Jahrestagung (2), pp. 662–667 (2008)

17. Zeng, H., Di Natale, M.: Efficient implementation of AUTOSAR components with minimal memory usage. In: 2012 7th IEEE International Symposium on Industrial Embedded Systems (SIES). IEEE (2012)

18. Hegde, R., Gurumurthy, K.S.: Load balancing across ECUs in automotives. In: 2009 International Conference on Communication Software and Networks (ICCSN 2009). IEEE (2009)

19. Stern, S., Guetta, O.: Manage the automotive embedded software development cost by using a Functional Size Measurement Method (COSMIC). In: ERTS^2 2010, 5th International Congress & Exhibition, Toulouse (2010)

20. Soubra, H., Abran, A., Stern, S., Ramdan-Cherif, A.: Design of a functional size measurement procedure for real-time embedded software requirements expressed using the Simulink model. In: IWSM-MENSURA, Nara, Japan, pp. 76–85. IEEE CS Press (2011)

21. Lind, K. Heldal, R.: Estimation of real-time software code size using COSMIC FSM. In: The IEEE International Symposium on Object/Component/Service-Oriented Real-Time Distributed Computing (ISORC 2009), pp. 244–248 (2009)

22. Lind, K., Heldal, R.: A model-based and automated approach to size estimation of embedded software components. In: Whittle, J., Clark, T., Kühne, T. (eds.) MODELS 2011. LNCS, vol. 6981, pp. 334–348. Springer, Heidelberg (2011)

23. Artusi, R., Verderio, P., Marubini, E.: Bravais-Pearson and Spearman correlation coefficients: meaning, test of hypothesis and confidence interval. Int. J. Biol. Markers 17(2), 148–151 (2002)

24. http://www.estaca.fr/hassan-soubra/

Selecting the Right Visualization of Indicators and Measures – Dashboard Selection Model

Miroslaw Staron[1](✉), Kent Niesel[2], and Wilhelm Meding[3]

[1] Computer Science and Engineering, University of Gothenburg, Gothenburg, Sweden
miroslaw.staron@gu.se
[2] Volvo Car Group, Gothenburg, Sweden
kent.niesel@volvocars.com
[3] Ericsson AB, Gothenburg, Sweden
wilhelm.meding@ericsson.com

Abstract. Background: Contemporary software development organizations utilize multiple channels to disseminate information about their indicators, measures, trends and predictions. Selecting these channels is usually done based on the availability of the visualization technology and a set of requirements elicited from stakeholders at the company. Eliciting these kind of requirements can be labor-intensive and time-consuming. **Goal:** The objective of this research is to develop a method for selecting which dashboard should be used. As the set of dissemination patterns of measures in modern organizations is limited, this method should be able to identify the needs of visualizations at the company and match them to the dissemination patterns and their supporting technology. **Method:** The research method applied is action research conducted at Volvo Car Group. The action research is conducted as part of a project redesigning a large project status reporting tool and has been designed to quantify the requirements elicited from the stakeholders of the system. **Results:** The results is the dashboard selection model which consists of seven dimensions – type of reporting, data acquisition method, type of stakeholders, method of delivery, frequency of updates, aim of the information, and length of data processing (flow). **Conclusions:** The conclusions show that using this model leads to a rapid identification of the best visualization method for measurement data, which has a cost-saving impact on measurement programs and effect-maximizing impact on the companies.

1 Introduction

Contemporary medium-to-large software development organizations often rely on quantitative information in monitoring their products and processes [Sta12]. These kind of companies use measures and indicators to both monitor the status and to plan long-term evolution of their business [Par10]. In order to effectively trigger decisions, support evolutions and prevent problems, the ways in which the measures are visualized and communicated have to vary.

In this paper we recognize the need for variability of information visualization types in modern software companies based on how information should

© Springer International Publishing Switzerland 2015
A. Kobyliński et al. (Eds.): IWSM-Mensura 2015, LNBIP 230, pp. 130–143, 2015.
DOI: 10.1007/978-3-319-24285-9_9

be disseminated and how it is supposed to be used. Normally, this variability is designed when developing measurement systems or dashboards and is constant over time. Therefore it is a prerequisite of success that the elicitation of the requirements for these dashboards is correct and efficient. However, there exists only a limited set of technologies for storing, processing and visualizing the results of measurement processes.

Therefore in this paper we address the following research question – *How to efficiently map stakeholders' requirements to indicator dissemination patterns including the supporting visualization?*

The result of addressing this question is the dashboard selection model – a method for quantifying the requirements for dashboards and matching them to dissemination patterns. The model has been developed as part of an action research project at Volvo Car Group. The goal of the project was to support the company's transformation of project status reporting by studying and evolving project reporting practices and eliciting future requirements for the reporting processes.

The remaining of the paper is structure as follows. Section 2 presents the most relevant related work in literature regarding the experiences of selecting dashboards. Section 3 describes the design of the action research project where the model was developed.

2   Related Work

We review work in three areas – standardization in the area of measurement in software engineering (which is an important input to the creating measures and KPIs), measurement theory (in general and its applications in software engineering) and visualization of metrics in software engineering.

2.1   Dashboards and Visualization

In our previous work we identified the need for building dashboards at different levels of the organization by studying team decision meetings at RUAG Space [FSHL13]. The results from the evaluation showed that one should combine different views and information in one dashboard, but the visualization of the data is the most crucial aspect for the success dashboard's adoption.

In our later studies we expanded the evaluation of dashboards to more companies – SAAB Electronic Defense Systems, Ericsson and Volvo Cars [SMH+13]. During the study one of the observations was that the standard visualizations of data available from measurement instruments (aka metric tools) focus on the data rather than the information need, which requires a more thorough design.

Telea [Tel14] described a set of modern data visualization principles which we used when developing examples of how a dashboard should visually be designed.

Staron and Meding [SM09a] designed a set of principles of for assessing the reliability of information, which was the base for constructing one of the dimensions of the dashboard selection model – delivery method. This method was proven to be useful when designing industrial measurement systems, e.g. for monitoring bottlenecks [SM11].

In our previous work we also studied how information visualization in form of models helps decision making in large companies – [MS10]. The results showed that the alignment of the type of model and the decision is one of the prerequisites for efficient software development and prevents waste.

2.2   Standardization

Measurement theory has been used as a basis for the main international standard in measurement on common vocabulary in metrology – VIM [oWM93]. The standard defines such concepts as measurement uncertainty, measurand and quantification. These definitions capture the meaning of the concepts from the measurement theory in engineering. These concepts are important when setting up the measurement program and its visualization – in particular when considering the assessment of how the data should support the decisions at the company (e.g. whether the product is ready to be releases w.r.t. its quality, [SMP12]).

VIM standardizes the most important concepts which influence measurement processes, for example:

- Measuring instrument: device used for making measurements, alone or in conjunction with supplementary device(s).
- Measuring system: set of one or more measuring instruments and often other devices, including any reagent and supply, assembled and adapted to give measured quantity values within specified intervals for quantities of specified kinds.

The standard specifies the concepts, but does not prescribe any specific means for visualization of use of these concepts in practice. In this paper we set off to address the need for such a linkage.

2.3   Measurement Theory

Kitchenhamn [KPF95] presented a framework for software measurement validation which focused on the need for linking the empirical properties of metrics to their corresponding empirical entities. This kind of link is important when selecting measures and their visualizations, which impacts the data-flow dimension of the dashboard selection model.

Briand et al. [BEEM96] presented the concepts from the measurement theory in the context of software engineering. In addition to the theoretical illustration of units, scales, admissible transformations and other related concepts, the authors illustrated the implications of applying them in software engineering – e.g. by discussing the property of additivity for complexity measures. This paper has also influenced the design of the data-flow dimension in the dashboard selection model.

3   Research Design – Action Research

In this study we applied the principle of action research as advocated by Susman and Evered [SE78] and used in our previous studies with the same company [RSB+13, RSM+13, RSB+14]. The action research set-up provided us with a unique opportunity to be part of a project at Volvo Car Group (VCC) which aimed at a redesign of a large program status reporting tool. The tool was used to monitor the progress of car development projects and was divided into three parts – Key Performance Indicators, Milestone reporting and Risk monitoring. In our work we focused only on the Key Performance Indicators part as it was aligned with the researcher's competence and the company's interest.

The research was organized in action research cycles, which is shown in Table 1.

Table 1. Action research cycles

Cycle	Goal	Outcomes
Project initialization	Understand the practices of using the tool	Plan for assessing the KPIs
Development of tools	Prepare research instruments	KPI quality model, dashboard selection model
Interviews	Collect the data	A set of dashboard selection models

In the first cycle we focused on refining the initial problem formulation – how to effectively elicit requirements for a new dashboard.

In the second cycle we prepared research instruments for defining the dashboard selection model – preparing the dissemination patterns based on literature studies and discussions with focus group at the company. The result of this cycle was the dashboard selection model presented in this paper.

In the third cycle we focused on applying the dashboard selection model and on understanding its advantages and shortcomings.

4   Dashboard Selection Model

4.1   Dissemination Patterns in Modern Companies

During the first cycle of our action research project we observed the dissemination patterns of metrics in large software development companies. These patterns are presented in Fig. 1.

The classical dissemination pattern is the top-down communication from managers to employees and the bottom-up reporting of status from employees to management. This communication is based on pre-defined templates created by management or process methodologists which intend to unify the ways of working across the company.

Fig. 1. Metrics dissemination patterns in large software development companies

The new pattern is the communication from teams to management. The teams define themselves which kind of information they want to communicate and which information is important for the team, the product and at that particular time.

Finally, there is also the new pattern of facilitated knowledge-sharing between the teams. There are usually no indicators or measures defined when this type of knowledge-sharing takes place, but the teams organize knowledge-sharing sessions in order to spread good practices and warnings about pitfalls.

Given these dissemination patterns, in the first action research cycle we identified a set of characteristics of measurement systems and dashboards. These characteristics form a model which is presented in Fig. 2.

The characteristics shown in Fig. 2 capture the way in which dashboards and measurement systems are used (report vs. dashboard), who the stakeholders are or how the dashboards are distributed to their stakeholders. These characteristics evolved during the next action research cycle into the dashboard selection model.

Fig. 2. Initial model for diversity of measurement systems

4.2   Dashboard Selection Model

Dashboard selection model is a graphical way of choosing properties of a dashboard, based on the information needs of stakeholders. It is divided into seven dimensions with each dimension defined by two alternatives – from full focus on one alternative, through equal focus on both, to the full focus on the other alternative.

The seven dimensions of the dashboard selection model are:

- **Type of Dashboard** – defining what kind of visualization is needed. Many dashboards are used as reports where the stakeholders input the data and require the flexibility of the format – the alternative is named *report* whereas some require a strictly pre-defined visualization with the same structure for every update – the alternative designated as *dashboard*. There is naturally a number of possibilities of combining the flexibility and the strict format, which is denoted by the scale between fully flexible and fully strict.
- **Data Acquisition** – defining how the data is input into the tool. In general the stakeholders/employees can enter the data into the tool – e.g. making an assessment – the alternative is named *manual* or they can have the data being imported from other systems – this alternative is named *automated*. The previous selection of a dashboard for visualization quite often correlates to the selection of the automated data provisioning.
- **Stakeholders** – defining the type of the stakeholder for the dashboard. The dashboards which are used as so-called information radiators often have an entire *group* as a stakeholder, for example a project team. However, many dashboards which are designed to support decisions often have an *individual* stakeholder who can represent a group.
- **Delivery** – defining how the data is provided to the stakeholders. On the one hand the information can be delivered to a stakeholder in such forms as e-mails or MS Sidebar gadgets – the alternative is *delivered* to the stakeholders and *fetched*, which requires the stakeholder to actively seek the information in form of opening a dedicated link and searching for the information.
- **Update** – defining how often the data is updated. One alternative is to update the data *periodically*, for example every night with the advantage of the data being synchronized but with the disadvantage that it is not up-to-date. The other alternative is the *continuous* update which has the opposite effects on the timeliness and synchronization.
- **Aim** – defining what kind of aim the dashboard should fulfill. One of the alternatives is to use the dashboard as an information radiator – to spread the *information* to a broad audience. The other option is to design the dashboard for a specific type of *decision* in mind, for example release readiness [SMP12].
- **Data Flow** – defining how much processing of the data is done in the dashboard. One of the alternatives is to visualize the *raw data* which means that no additional interpretation is done and the other is to add the interpretations by applying analysis models and thus to visualize *indicators*.

The graphical representation of the dashboard selection model is presented in Fig. 3. Each line represents one dimension and each dot can be moved to one of the positions – e.g. fully towards report for the type of dashboard.

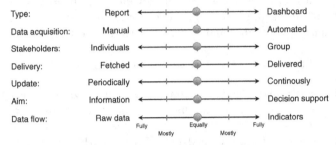

Fig. 3. Dashboard selection model – visualization

Each selection of one of the dimensions is captured by a short, natural language, sentence describing why and how the stakeholder reasons about his need.

4.3   Examples

The dashboard selection model can be applied to a set of existing tools and classify them based on the dashboard model which they represent. For example, MS Excel can be used to visualize the data, but it primarily is dedicated to other purposes. If MS Excel is used to visualize measurement systems and contains a dedicated visualization of indicators, its classification could be done as presented in Fig. 4. This example comes from our previous work on the frameworks for developing measurement systems [SMN08].

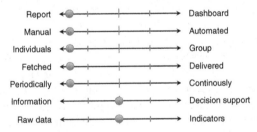

Fig. 4. Dashboard selection model – classification of MS Excel with indicators

An example of such a measurement system is shown in Fig. 5. The colored cells present the indicators and the measures, trends and raw data are available in other worksheets in the same workbook.

The evaluation of the MS Sidebar gadgets as a means of visualization of measures and indicators is classified as shown in Fig. 6. An example gadget from our previous works is also shown in Fig. 7.

In such a gadget, the data is pre-processed in form of indicators, fetched from core product development systems, wide spread, used both for radiation and for decision support [SMN08, SMP12, SMH+13, SM09b].

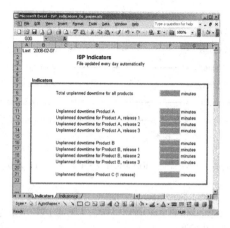

Fig. 5. Example of a visualization using MS Excel.

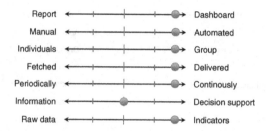

Fig. 6. Dashboard selection model – classification of gadget

Another example of a tool used for similar purposes is Tableu, which has been evaluated in our previous studies [PSSM10] and is presented in Fig. 8. The tool provides a number of pre-defined visualizations and analysis recipes, but is interactive and therefore not fully suited as an information radiator [Coc06]. However it is important that the presentation can be understandable [KS02, SKT05].

Yet another example is a class of tools referred to as information radiators, i.e. dashboards dedicated to spread the information to a broad audience. Their classification is presented in Fig. 9. These tools are designed with one purpose

Fig. 7. Example of a gadget

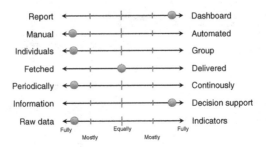

Fig. 8. Dashboard selection model – classification of Tableu

in mind and are meant to be non-interactive. Their primary use is in landscapes and during decision meetings.

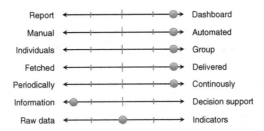

Fig. 9. Dashboard selection model – classification of information radiators

An example of an information radiation from Ericsson is presented in Fig. 10. It shows the usage of a network in a laboratory environment and is dedicated for the project team to observe the status of their test network. For the confidentiality reasons the names of the tested products are covered with greyed boxes.

The last example is a typical Business Intelligence tool (not a specific product, but a class of products) with the possibility to create reports and to work with the data, but at the same time with the possibility to create dashboards as presented in Fig. 11.

5   Evaluation

In the last action research cycle we used the dashboard selection model when eliciting a possible next generation of the project reporting tool at the company. Using the dashboard selection model for the elicitation of requirements for a future tool was a good candidate for the evaluation. Since we had the opportunity to work with users of the project reporting tool, we could verify that the requirements captured by the dashboard selection model were consistent

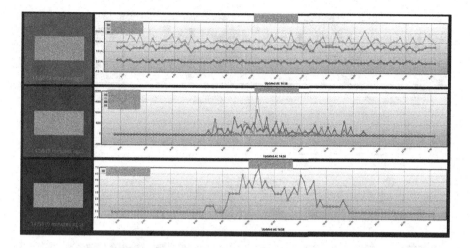

Fig. 10. An example of information radiator

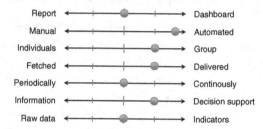

Fig. 11. Dashboard selection model – classification of Business Intelligence tools

with their envisioned new version of the tool. The current version of the tool is presented in Fig. 12 and shows one of the forms for reporting the KPIs (Key Performance Indicators) for one of the areas.

In this cycle we interviewed nine stakeholders from different parts of VCC – from software development (and electrical systems development), through mechanical engineering, manufacturing engineering to purchasing organization. All of the interviewees had a role in the project leadership – from the main project manager, through sub-project managers to sub-sub-project managers. We included also the project quality managers (two persons) who were in charge of monitoring the KPIs in the tool and controlling the quality of the projects. The project quality managers had a more holistic view on the product while the project management had more focus on the project progress and quality. All stakeholders had a significant number of years of experience with projects at VCC and worked with previous version of the project status reporting tools.

The result from the evaluation is presented in Fig. 13. Each dot represents one stakeholder.

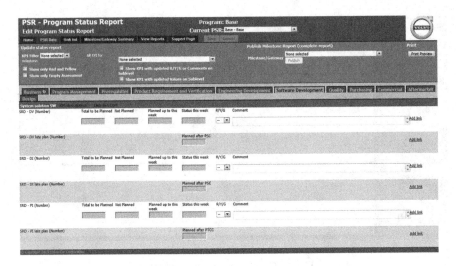

Fig. 12. Project status reporting tool – a screenshot

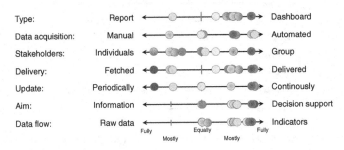

Fig. 13. Result from using the dashboard selection model for designing the future project reporting tool

The dots representing the answers of each interviewee in Fig. 13 are spread over the entire model, which is a result of different views on the needs for such a tool. Since the tool is used at a large organization, this is quite a normal situation and the dashboard selection model helped to compactly visualize this diversity.

We analyzed each of the characteristics separately to elicit the potential next evolution step. We summarize them in Table 2 per dimension of the dashboard selection model.

One of the conclusions based on the interviews was to evolve the project reporting tool's presentation possibilities to support wider spread of the status – i.e. to introduce a dashboard to the entire project team. By using this model a more particular set of requirements was collected and stakeholders' relation between different elements (e.g. what should be manual and what should be automatic) were elicited.

Another significant finding was that by using this model we could link the set of answers which differed from the rest (e.g. the yellow dot in the type dimension)

Table 2. Summary of qualitative data for each dimension

Dimension	Summary
Type	The tool should provide a possibility to show per default the status of the project in a simple form, addressing such questions as *Which areas are green ?*, *How up-to-date is the information?*, *When is the next deadline?*, and *What is the trend towards the deadline?*
Data acquisition	Importing of data from source systems should be fully automated (e.g. importing diagrams, numbers), but the status assessment of KPIs should be manual in order to give the stakeholders the possibility to valuate the numbers
Stakeholders	The view/presentation should be divided into "classes of users" – individual with interactive features as possibility of drill-down, and groups with static informative screens like information radiators
Delivery	Most of the interviewees would like to see easier/simpler way of finding the relevant information – delivered, e.g. links to specific information which has been updated, periodical reports, e.g. in e-mails; however, some sub-project managers (mid level of the project management hierarchy) prefer the information be fetched to prevent e-mail overflow
Update	The data could be updated periodically but it should be synchronized – when indicators are calculated they should be calculated in such a way that the information quality properties are retained
Aim	Most of the interviewees would like to see more decisions to be based on the data available in this tool – it would be clearer who should make the decisions, what the decisions have been made and it could serve as a basic communication to everyone about the status
Data flow	The tool should contain more KPIs/indicators (majority of indicators/data), but these should be complemented with raw data as in source systems (e.g. project planning) – to support KPI assessment; KPIs should be treated as the primary means of communicating the status, not as a complement to the qualitative assessment

to a specific type of functionality envisioned by the interviewee. Without this model there was a risk that this answer would be considered as insignificant.

6 Conclusions

Developing dashboards for monitoring of product quality, project progress or customer satisfaction are popular in modern software development companies.

The dashboards present quantitative data in a visually appealing manner and help to spread the information to broad population and to support designated stakeholders in making decisions. Depending on the purpose of the dashboard, its elements can vary in terms of applied technology, visualization or interactivity with users.

In this paper we address the problem of choosing the right dashboard for the right purpose by presenting a dashboard selection model and evaluating it at Volvo Car Group in an action research project.

The dashboard selection model is based on the patterns of dissemination of information in modern software development companies and allows to choose between dashboards for visualizing project status in large office landscapes and stakeholder specific MS Sidebar gadgets dedicated to provide pre-selected information for stakeholders in order to make decisions. The use of the dashboard selection model allows to quantify requirements for metrics information visualization from a number of stakeholders. It can be applied both as a tool for requirement elicitation and as a tool for market survey at the company.

Using the dashboard selection models allow metrics teams to focus on their core business – designing metrics and supporting measurement processes – and therefore in the future we intend to expand it to support automated selection of the right visualization based on the stakeholders' needs (e.g. by linking the model to pre-defined set of visualizations).

Acknowledgment. This work has been partially supported by the Swedish Strategic Research Foundation under the grant number SM13-0007.

References

[BEEM96] Briand, L., Emam, K.E., Morasca, S.: On the application of measurement theory in software engineering. Empirical Softw. Eng. **1**(1), 61–88 (1996)

[FSHL13] Feldt, R., Staron, M., Hult, E., Liljegren, T.: Supporting software decision meetings: Heatmaps for visualising test and code measurements. In: 2013 39th EUROMICRO Conference on Software Engineering and Advanced Applications (SEAA), pp. 62–69. IEEE (2013)

[KPF95] Kitchenham, B., Pfleeger, S.L., Fenton, N.: Towards a framework for software measurement validation. IEEE Trans. Softw. Eng. **21**(12), 929–944 (1995)

[KS02] Kuzniarz, L., Staron, M.: On practical usage of stereotypes in uml-based software development. In: Forum on Design and Specification Languages (2002)

[MS10] Mellegård, N., Staron, M.: Characterizing model usage in embedded software engineering: a case study. In: Proceedings of the Fourth European Conference on Software Architecture: Companion Volume, pp. 245–252. ACM (2010)

[oWM93] International Bureau of Weights and Measures: International vocabulary of basic and general terms in metrology, 2nd edn. International Organization for Standardization, Genve, Switzerland (1993)

[Par10] Parmenter, D.: Key performance indicators (KPI): Developing, Implementing, and Using Winning KPIs. John Wiley & Sons, Hoboken (2010)

[PSSM10] Pandazo, K., Shollo, A., Staron, M., Meding, W.: Presenting software metrics indicators: a case study. In: Proceedings of the 20th International Conference on Software Product and Process Measurement (MENSURA), vol. 20 (2010)

[RSB+13] Rana, R., Staron, M., Berger, C., Hansson, J., Nilsson, M., Torner, F.: Evaluating long-term predictive power of standard reliability growth models on automotive systems. In: 2013 IEEE 24th International Symposium on Software Reliability Engineering (ISSRE), pp. 228–237. IEEE (2013)

[RSB+14] Rana, R., Staron, M., Berger, C., Hansson, J., Nilsson, M., Törner, F., Meding, W., Höglund, C.: Selecting software reliability growth models and improving their predictive accuracy using historical projects data. J. Syst. Softw. **98**, 59–78 (2014)

[RSM+13] Rana, R., Staron, M., Mellegård, N., Berger, C., Hansson, J., Nilsson, M., Törner, F.: Evaluation of standard reliability growth models in the context of automotive software systems. In: Heidrich, J., Oivo, M., Jedlitschka, A., Baldassarre, M.T. (eds.) PROFES 2013. LNCS, vol. 7983, pp. 324–329. Springer, Heidelberg (2013)

[SE78] Susman, G.I., Evered, R.D.: An assessment of the scientific merits of action research. Adm. Sci. Q. **23**, 582–603 (1978)

[SKT05] Staron, M., Kuzniarz, L., Thurn, C.: An empirical assessment of using stereotypes to improve reading techniques in software inspections. ACM SIGSOFT Softw. Eng. Notes **30**, 1–7 (2005). ACM

[SM09a] Staron, M., Meding, W.: Ensuring reliability of information provided by measurement systems. In: Abran, A., Braungarten, R., Dumke, R.R., Cuadrado-Gallego, J.J., Brunekreef, J. (eds.) IWSM 2009. LNCS, vol. 5891, pp. 1–16. Springer, Heidelberg (2009)

[SM09b] Staron, M., Meding, W.: Using models to develop measurement systems: a method and its industrial use. In: Abran, A., Braungarten, R., Dumke, R.R., Cuadrado-Gallego, J.J., Brunekreef, J. (eds.) IWSM 2009. LNCS, vol. 5891, pp. 212–226. Springer, Heidelberg (2009)

[SM11] Staron, M., Meding, W.: Monitoring bottlenecks in agile and lean software development projects – a method and its industrial use. In: Caivano, D., Oivo, M., Baldassarre, M.T., Visaggio, G. (eds.) PROFES 2011. LNCS, vol. 6759, pp. 3–16. Springer, Heidelberg (2011)

[SMH+13] Staron, M., Meding, W., Hansson, J., Höglund, C., Niesel, K., Bergmann, V.: Dashboards for continuous monitoring of quality for software product under development. In: System Qualities and Software Architecture (SQSA) (2013)

[SMN08] Staron, M., Meding, W., Nilsson, C.: A framework for developing measurement systems and its industrial evaluation. Inf. Softw. Technol. **51**(4), 721–737 (2008)

[SMP12] Staron, M., Meding, W., Palm, K.: Release readiness indicator for mature agile and lean software development projects. In: Wohlin, C. (ed.) XP 2012. LNBIP, vol. 111, pp. 93–107. Springer, Heidelberg (2012)

[Sta12] Staron, M.: Critical role of measures in decision processes: managerial and technical measures in the context of large software development organizations. Inf. Softw. Technol. **54**(8), 887–899 (2012)

[Tel14] Telea, A.C.: Data Visualization: Principles and Practice. CRC Press, Boca Raton (2014)

[Coc06] Cockburn, A.: Agile software development: the cooperative game. Pearson Education (2006)

Measurement-as-a-Service – A New Way of Organizing Measurement Programs in Large Software Development Companies

Miroslaw Staron[1]([envelope]) and Wilhelm Meding[2]

[1] Computer Science and Engineering, University of Gothenburg, Gothenburg, Sweden
miroslaw.staron@gu.se
[2] Ericsson AB, Gothenburg, Sweden
wilhelm.meding@ericsson.com

Abstract. Modern software development companies focus on their primary business objectives, delivering customer value and customer satisfaction which often leads to prioritization of core business areas over such areas as measurement. Although the companies recognize the need and importance of software measurement, they often do not have the competence and/or time to focus on software measurement. In this paper we address the challenge of optimizing the measurement processes in modern companies by using cloud computing and by providing measurement (process) as a service for core business of the companies. Similar to the concept of Software-as-a-Service we define the concept Measurement-as-a-Service and describe how to organize a measurement program according to this definition. The Measurement-as-a-Service concept is well-aligned with measurement programs developed according to ISO/IEC 15939 and can help the companies to increase the benefits obtained from the efficient use of metrics.

Keywords: Cloud · Measurement systems · Measurement program

1 Introduction

Modern software development companies focus on their core businesses and on delivering customer value and aligning their processes towards that. Measurement programs in such companies are often designed to support these goals, but they do not form the core business areas and as such can be optimized in a different manner [JA97,SMKN10]. Instead of focusing directly on the customers, the measurement programs are focused on internal stakeholders – which represent either the external customers or internal roles in the company (e.g. quality management) [SM09b].

This kind of evolution of the software business model creates new opportunities for the evolution of the measurement programs at the software development companies – centralizing the development and delivery of the measurement programs in companies. As prescribed by the ISO/IEC 15939 (Systems and

© Springer International Publishing Switzerland 2015
A. Kobyliński et al. (Eds.): IWSM-Mensura 2015, LNBIP 230, pp. 144–159, 2015.
DOI: 10.1007/978-3-319-24285-9_10

Software Engineering – Measurement Processes) standard [OC07, SMN08] the measurement programs should include the set of measurement systems and the infrastructure supporting building and disseminating the knowledge base of software measurement.

In this paper we address the following research problem – *How to support the company's core business processes by optimizing the sharing of measurement competence across different units?* To address this research question we introduce the term *Measurement-as-a-Service, MaaS*. MaaS is a measurement licensing and delivery model in which metrics are licensed on a subscription basis, centrally hosted, collected and delivered on demand. This concept is similar to the concept of Software-as-a-Service and Platform-as-a-Service. As the definition of Software-as-a-Service describes the licensing, delivery model and value proposition for centrally hosted software available on the web, we propose to use measurement in the same way thus achieving such benefits as:

- higher quality of metrics – since the knowledge base (including good and bad practices) are shared easier and faster through the centralized metrics storage/team
- lower maintenance costs – since the centralized storage of metrics is optimized towards handling large quantities of data
- faster adoption of new metrics – since the metric team has the possibility to quickly assess the quality of metrics, has access to the relevant data sources and can reuse measurement systems between different parts of the company.

The method used in this paper is a case study where we define the theoretical framework – MaaS – a priori and use it to describe the measurement program at Ericsson (which is the unit of analysis). Our preposition is that by describing the measurement program using the MaaS conceptual framework we can identify new improvement areas – e.g. how to define value propositions for metrics.

The paper is structured as follows. Section 2 explains the main concepts and elements used in measurement-as-a-service. In Sect. 3 we describe how we used MaaS to describe the measurement program at Ericsson. In Sect. 4 we describe the main related work to our study and finally in Sect. 5 we summarize the main message of the paper and outline the current research directions in this area.

2 Measurement-as-a-Service

MaaS is a measurement licensing and delivery model in which metrics are licensed on a subscription basis, centrally hosted, collected and delivered on demand. This concept is similar to the concept of Software-as-a-Service and Platform-as-a-Service. Figure 1 shows what MaaS consists of and how it relates to the core business processes (e.g. software development).

The main two types of actors in this context are the *Metrics team* and the *Stakeholder*. The metric team is responsible for the measurements – both process-wise (eliciting metrics, developing measurement systems, deploying information products) and competence-wise (assessing the quality of metrics and indicators,

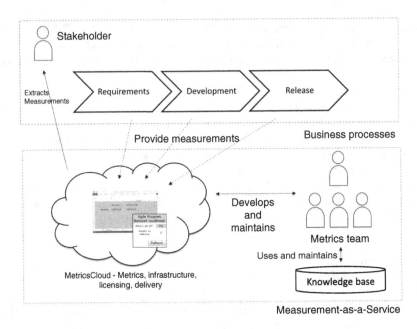

Fig. 1. Conceptual model of a measurement program

optimizing the number of metrics collected). The stakeholders are responsible for their business processes and/or products and use the measures to make decisions in their work [Sta12].

The metrics team is responsible for the development of measures and indicators based on the discussions with the stakeholders. The team has the responsibility for the long-term maintenance of the measurement knowledge base. The measurement knowledge base is the set of documented experiences and artifacts which have been proven to be useful for the organization, the set of best practices and the set of common pitfalls (e.g. measures which were found to be incorrect or leading to negative effects).

The metrics are naturally delivered as a product – *information product* according to ISO/IEC 15939. Examples of the information products can be MS Excel files, web pages with dashboards or MS Sidebar Gadgets. The delivery method for the information products can vary, but is usually similar to the SaaS – using the concept of cloud computing – e.g. [SM14].

The main benefit from organizing the measurement program as MaaS is the clear separation of competence in the organization – stakeholders focus on their business processes whereas the metrics team is the main point-of-contact for the measurement competence.

2.1   Central Hosting

One of the key challenges in managing the measurement program is the ability to deliver the right metrics for the right stakeholders at the right time.

The variability of stakeholders and their goals usually causes the number of measurement systems in the measurement program to grow over time. As the number of measurement systems grew in our collaborating organization and different dissemination patterns appeared (e.g. the distinction between public and local metrics), the company started to introduce an internal, cloud-based metrics dissemination system.

2.2 Collection and Licensing

Although the majority of measurement systems within one organization can be available for all stakeholders, it is often practical to maintain a control over who uses which measurement system – license them. Since (according to ISO/IEC 15939) the measurement systems are dedicated for specific stakeholders, it is natural that the stakeholder's role in the company and the sensitivity of the information dictates the availability of the measurement system. The stakeholder can "license" the measurement system to be: (i) public (everyone can have access to the measurement system with read access right), (ii) local (private, only selected stakeholders can have access to the measurement system with read/write access), and (iii) shared (selected stakeholder can have access to the measurement system with read access). The metrics team manages the licensing – it could be a dedicated measurement support team or a set of roles spread across the company.

In MaaS, licensing is done per subscription. Stakeholders can subscribe to a specific kind of metric or indicator which they need for a particular purpose. The licensing should be time-limited in order to limit the number of unused metrics. It also allows the metric team to focus on the most important tasks at the moment and do not maintain unused metrics.

Collection, however, has a different pattern. Metrics should be collected (especially the base measures) even if they are not used by any stakeholders. The collected metrics can be used for visualizing trends for the stakeholders when they subscribe to the metrics and indicators. In this way the stakeholders have the incentive to use the MaaS supplier rather than to spend time on collecting the data themselves (in periods of time when the metrics is seemingly not useful).

The infrastructure and the automated execution environment form a measurement program together with the measurement systems, source files, raw data, databases and stakeholders. The measurement program is maintained by a measurement team which consists of designers and measurement agents. The metric team consists of the following roles: (i) designers – responsible for design, implementation and maintenance of the measurement systems, (ii) measurement agents – responsible for contacts with stakeholders to elicit information needs in the organization and keep the design of the existing indicators up-to-date, and (iii) metric champions – responsible for identifying and introducing new metrics into the organization.

2.3 Delivered on Demand

The delivery of the metrics should be done on demand – i.e. when the stakeholders who subscribe to a particular metric want to access the data. They could also be delivered automatically when new measurements are available (e.g. nightly after the automated measurement process has been executed).

The on-demand delivery does not require extra storage from the stakeholders' side, but utilizes the central storage. However, it makes the subscribed metrics available when needed (through the use of underlying cloud technologies such as MetricCloud).

2.4 Role of the Metrics Team

The supplier of MaaS is usually the metrics team at the company. The role of the team is then to identify the information needs of the organizations, identify measurements of importance, develop and provision measurement systems and manage the licensing of measurements in the organization. The metrics team realizes such tasks as the quality assurance of the measurement program, the functional development of the measurement program, operational and corrective maintenance and supporting the company with measurement competence.

This new responsibility of the metrics team extends the set of roles identified in the standard for measurement processes – ISO/IEC 15939 – by such roles as: measurement architect (responsible for the overall structure of the measurements, e.g. dependencies, links between information needs), measurement team leader (responsible for the coordination of efforts in the team, e.g. prioritizing assignments) and measurement account manager (responsible for contacts with specific unit, e.g. one product development unit). These roles, in particular the role of measurement account manager, are important for the continuity of the measurement program and its effectiveness in decision processes.

One of the main challenges for the metric team when operating in the MaaS context is the need to develop a *business model for measurement*. The team needs to describe metrics in terms of their value for the customers – *value proposition of the metric* which helps the team to "sell" the metrics to the stakeholders. Since the stakeholder's main focus in the main business of the company, this value propositions should link to the customer value that the company itself delivers.

2.5 Value Propositions

The value proposition for each metric in the measurement program needs to include the goals which are important for the stakeholders, but it can contain common elements depending on the type of the stakeholder. The value proposition for a measurement should address such aspects as:

– Who should be the stakeholder for the measurement?
– How is the measurement linked to the goals of the stakeholder?

Table 1. Measurement value proposition for MaaS

Element	Characteristics	Purpose
Headline	Brief statement of the purpose of the measurement	Grabs attention
Sub-healine	A specific explanation of the measurement – what, for whom and why it is useful	Lists key benefits
Example	A simple example of what the measurement shows	Explains the context
Stakeholder	Role and mandate of the stakeholder	Links the measurement to the stakeholder
Value	Benefits from conducting the measurement	Value of the measurement
Risks	A list of risks of conducting the measurement, e.g. sub-optimizations	Describes the potential problems

- Which information need of the stakeholder is fulfilled by the measurement?
- What value will the measurement bring if conducted?
- Which risks are related to conducting the measurement?

The template for a value proposition for a measurement should contain the elements described in Table 1.

An example of a value proposition for a release readiness indicator [SMP12] is presented in Table 2.

Table 2. Measurement value proposition for MaaS

Element	Characteristics
Headline	Release readiness indicator
Sub-healine	Shows project managers how many weeks are needed to finish the product with a given quality
Example	When the project is finished with new feature development it shows how many weeks the testing and bug-fixing will take
Stakeholder	Release project manager
Value	Can decrease the cost of re-planning by as much as 30 %
Risks	Releasing the product with minimum viable functionality

The value proposition provides a support for stakeholders in adopting the new measurement and allows to make a decision whether to buy a license for this type of service from the MaaS supplier.

3 Case Study – Using MaaS to Describe the Measurement Program at Ericsson

In this paper we introduce the term MaaS, and in this section we use it to describe the way in which the measurement program at one of the units of Ericsson is organized. Ericsson AB (Ericsson) develops large software products for the mobile telecommunication network. The size of the organization during the study is several hundred engineers and the size of the projects is up to a few hundreds. Projects are increasingly often executed according to the principles of Agile software development and Lean production system. In this environment, various teams are responsible for larger parts of the process compared to traditional processes: design teams (cross-functional teams responsible for complete analysis, design, implementation, and testing of particular features of the product), network verification and integration testing, etc. The organization uses a number of measurement systems for controlling the software development project (per project) described above, a number of measurement systems to control the quality of products in field (per product) and a measurement system for monitoring the status of the organization at the top level. All measurement systems are developed using the in-house methods described in [SMN08], with the particular emphasis on models for design and deployment of measurement systems presented in [SM09c]. The needs of the organization evolved from metrics calculations and presentations (ca. 9 years before the writing of this paper), to using predictions, simulations, early warning systems and handling of vast quantities of data to steer organizations at different levels, and providing information from project and line. These needs are addressed by the action research projects conducted in the organization, since the 2006.

3.1 Measurement Program at Ericsson

Measurement programs in industry are socio-technical systems where the technology interacts with stakeholders in order to support certain goals. Even though the term *measurement program* is defined in literature, the international standard ISO/IEC 15939:2007 (Systems and Software Engineering: Measurement process) introduces the concept of *measurement management system* which comprises both the measuring systems (e.g. instruments for data collection and visualization), the infrastructure where these operate, the knowledge bases on the use of measures and the stakeholders involved in the measurement process as conceptually shown in Fig. 2.

The central element of the measurement program is the set of measurement systems and information products. The *measurement systems* are dedicated software applications, designed for measuring quantities, addressing the stakeholder's information needs. The quantities are assembled (or combined) together in order to form indicators which, together with the analysis models, are packaged into information products.

There are multiple solutions about how to realize measurement systems – for example using business intelligence tools and their reporting functionalities or using simplistic MS Excel files (which is shown in Fig. 2). The measurement systems combine the inputs from multiple measurement instruments (either directly of by querying databases) in order to calculate the indicators. The process is specified in the hierarchical measurement information model of the ISO/IEC 15939 standard.

The input to the measurement program is obtained by measuring properties of products, organizations (people) and processes. The measurement is often done by using measurement instruments (e.g. metrics tools) which quantify properties of one entity (e.g. source code of a program) into numbers (e.g. McCabe complexity number). These measurement instruments are often specialized for measuring properties of single entities of single types (e.g. complexity of the C code).

The output of the measurement program is a set of decisions taken in the organizations, the insights into the organizations' processes, products and projects and the early warnings of the coming problems and challenges. These are usually interconnected – e.g. insights can trigger decisions, decisions can require new insights when being implemented [Sta12].

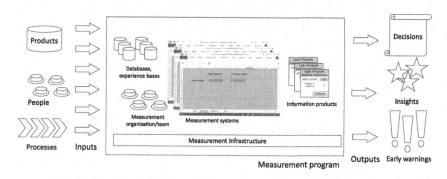

Fig. 2. Conceptual model of a measurement program

3.2   Information Products

Delivering measurement information across organizations can be done in multiple ways. The concepts of information radiators [RS05], metric tools [FP98], business intelligence [EW07] or visual analytics [TC06] were coined for this purpose and each concept describes a specific kind of a measurement system. The work presented in this paper is compatible with these concepts as self-healing is important for all of them – the analyses can be reliable if the right data is available. In order to standardize the discussions and put self-healing in the context, we use the internationally adopted standard for developing measurement programs ISO/IEC 15939 (Software and Systems Engineering measurement processes) [OC07]. An alternative to ISO/IEC 15939 method for defining measures was presented by Chirinos et al. [CLB05], which is based on a metamodel for measures proposed by authors created by combining certain aspects of GQM (Goal Question Metric, [VSBCR02]) into ISO/IEC 15939. In the case of Ericsson the information product is a measurement system.

A typical measurement system at Ericsson is built based on MS Excel and its scripting language VBA (Visual Basic for Applications) as presented in Fig. 3. The main worksheet of the MS Excel file (the grayed page at the top of the figure) contains indicators (green cells in the grayed page) if they are defined by the stakeholders, otherwise it contains values of measures. The indicators worksheet has the associated base and derived measures in other worksheets of the MS Excel file. These measures and indicators are calculated using VBA scripts (VBA for calculating measures and indicators) and VBA scripts for accessing the raw data from other measurement systems.

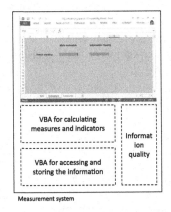

Fig. 3. Example of a measurement system (Color figure online)

The basic control of the quality of the information is done by a separate set of VBA scripts (Information quality) and the result of the control is visualized as one of the indicators on the main page.

Such an architecture of measurement systems is aligned with the prescriptions of the standard [OC07] with the separation between base/derived measures and indicators, associated decision criteria and algorithms for data processing. This architecture is also scalable as it allows developing new measurement systems based on the existing ones (e.g. allowing to reuse existing derived measures in other measurement systems) yet providing the measurement systems towards dedicated stakeholders. Each stakeholder has his/her own measurement system fulfilling his/her information needs.

Another example of an information product at Ericsson is a dashboard presented in Fig. 4. It shows the usage of a network in a laboratory environment and is dedicated for the project team to observe the status of their test network. For confidentiality reasons the names of the tested products are covered with greyed boxes.

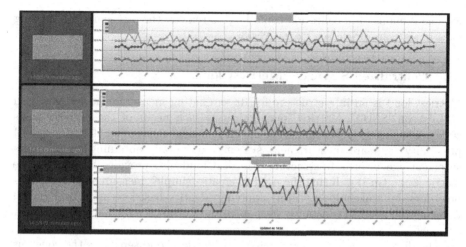

Fig. 4. An example of information radiator

The use of both types of information products differs as the first one is dedicated for decision support for particular stakeholders, is interactive and provides the possibility to access detailed data like trends. The dashboards are dedicated for spreading the information to larger populations (e.g. a project team) and is supposed to contain succinct information that provides enough details so that the users do not need to interact with the dashboard.

3.3   On-Demand Delivery – MS Sidebar Gadgets

An example of the on-demand delivery is the use of MS Sidebar gadgets. A gadget is used as a placeholder for the content on the stakeholders' computer, but the information itself is served through the metric infrastructure [SMN09]. An example of such a gadget is presented in Fig. 5.

Fig. 5. MS Sidebar gadget – an example of on-demand delivery

The gadget presents the number of weeks to release as defined in our earlier work [SMP12] and presents the indicator only. Once clicked the entire measurement system in MS Excel is fetched from the server and is presented to the stakeholder (on-demand delivery). This kind of on-demand delivery combined with continuous data collection could help to remedy the problems with missing data in software processes – e.g. [AN93].

3.4   Centralized Storage – MetricsCloud

MetricsCloud is an infrastructure for disseminating measurement systems used at Ericsson [SM14]. MetricsCloud addresses such needs of the organization's stakeholders as (s-i) dissemination of self-managed measurement systems,(s-ii) possibility to share measurement systems, and (s-iii) obtaining simple measurement execution infrastructure. MetricsCloud also provides benefits to the metric team: (m-i) reducing the need to create "simple" measurement systems - now done by stakeholders, (m-ii) applying identity-based security, and (m-iii) reducing the need to constantly keep-alive the web-server with all measurement systems.

The dissemination of metrics based on MetricsCloud separates the concerns of information delivery and execution/storage of information. This separation of concerns is done by designing cloud systems based on layers according to the principles defined by Pallis et al. [PAL10]. Pallis et al. identifies such layers in a cloud-based system in general – e.g. platform, infrastructure. In this paper we instantiate three of these layers based on the division of responsibility (in the organization): (i) Information product delivery, (ii) Execution and information quality, and (iii) Storage and access as presented in Fig. 6.

Fig. 6. Layers in cloud infrastructure

The top layer contains measurement systems managed individually by stakeholders of measurement systems who need access to information (addressing the needs of s-i, s-ii and m-i). The mid-layer is the layer of execution and update of measurement systems and is managed by the dedicated metric team. The stakeholders of the measurement systems do not need to be concerned about the execution of public measurement systems, but are notified if the measurement systems are not updated (e.g. by information quality indicators [SM09a]). Finally the lowest layer is the standard IT infrastructure of the company with network file servers, web servers and client programs which is managed by the IT department of the company.

3.5   Evolution

The existing measurement program at the studied unit evolved from their decentralized set-up to MaaS measurement programs in a number of steps summarized in Table 3.

This evolution helped the organization to centralize the measurements and "outsource" them internally or externally to the metric team. The metric team has the opportunity to develop a business model where the value of the metrics for the stakeholders is the main interest. This focus on the value helps to emphasize the metrics which bring more value to the company and de-prioritize the metrics which are not that important.

Table 3. Evolution of measurement programs to MaaS

Step	Characteristics
Standardization of measurement systems	Standardized measurement systems based on common tools – e.g. MS Excel, Tableau, QlikView
Common support	Established metric team with the dedicated roles to support the organization
Centralized distribution	Centralization of the distribution of the metrics – e.g. MetricCloud
Licensing	Development of a business model for "selling" metrics to different stakeholders and organizations within the company
Research	Identification and development of new metrics, combined with the business model for "selling" measurements

4   Related Work

One of the aspects important in the use of MaaS internally at companies is the understanding how information product spread – i.e. the internal communication channels and the reusability of metric. One of the works in this area is the work of Atkins et al. [AMVP03] which presents the models for reusability of metrics. Our work complements the reusability aspects by providing the value proposition.

Another work in this area is the work of Jorgensen et al. [Jor99]. As their work shows, this is not an easy task due to the potential different definitions of measures. Jorgensen shows contrasting definitions of measures if quality is defined as "a set of quality factors", "user satisfaction", and "software quality related to errors". Our research recognizes the needs for viewing the same aspects (e.g. quality) from different perspectives - depending on the stakeholder. These needs are also recognized by the measurement team which we collaborated with.

The delivery method for metrics – MetricCloud – have been validated at Ericsson in our previous work. This validation is aligned with the work of

Pawluk et al. [PSS+12] who described the process of introducing a new cloud solution to a large enterprise. The purpose of the cloud is similar to ours and we use their work when designing our cloud system. The current cloud system is an evolution of the previous work on ensuring information reliability done together with Ericsson [SM09a]. In this work we address the problems of ensuring that information is available throughout the enterprise and its understanding [KS02, SKT05, MS10, MST12].

Yoon et al. [YOL13] showed how to establish security into cloud computing. The security of MetricsCloud is based on similar principles but is a simplification of the security policies. All security is based on the enterprise log-in. The licensing model of the measurements, important for MaaS, need the kind of security described by Yoon et al.

Another approach was presented by Zhang et al. [ZZ09] and their CCOA framework. Although a very elaborate framework could be used in our solution we preferred to use a simple approach and focus on the ease-of-use. It is the ease-of-use and performance which are important for similar cloud systems as described by Gong et al. [GLZ+10].

Farooq et al. [FKDW06] presented an approach for structuring the measurement process (ISO/IEC 15939 based) using web services in order to increase scaleability and reuse of metrics. We complement their approach by adding the explicit role of the metrics team, licensing and value propositions for software metrics.

Sakamoto et al. [SMSN13] have developed a tool for mining software metrics and storing them in a web service environment. Their study is a good complement to our work as it addresses the question of metrics acquisition from large software repositories.

5   Conclusions

Modern large software development organizations focus on delivering customer value and often adopt decentralized software development models such as Agile. In these models various units of the organizations can work independently and communicate often. Measures, indicators and Key Performance Indicators are examples of communication means. However, the challenge in such organizations is to manage these means – e.g. keeping them consistent, secure and available on-demand. In this paper we addressed the problem of how to manage this in an efficient way by using a newly introduced concept – Measurement-as-a-Service, MaaS.

MaaS is a measurement licensing and delivery model in which metrics are licensed on a subscription basis, centrally hosted, collected and delivered on demand. This concept is similar to the concept of Software-as-a-Service and Platform-as-a-Service. We introduced this term in this paper and we used it to describe the measurement program at Ericsson – one of our industrial partners. We have shown that Measurement-as-a-Service is targeted towards improving the internal and external management of measurement programs. We showed that using modern, yet simplistic, cloud-based dissemination systems allows to develop new business models for measurement distribution. This new business model allows the stakeholders for measurement systems to focus on their core business activities while leaving the core metric competence to a dedicated entity.

The benefits of using Measurement-as-a-Service help the company to become more effective in their decision processes and allows them to focus on delivering customer value, at the same time having fact-based decisions. The benefits from using MaaS include such aspects as:

- higher quality of metrics – since the knowledge base (including good and bad practices) are shared easier and faster through the centralized metrics storage/team
- lower maintenance costs – since the centralized storage of metrics is optimized towards handling large quantities of data
- faster adoption of new metrics – since the metric team has the possibility to quickly assess the quality of metrics, has access to the relevant data sources and can reuse measurement systems between different parts of the company.

In our further work we intend to explore the notion of value proposition of metrics by studying the value propositions used in our industrial partner. We plan to develop a generic model for describing metrics and indicators in a business-like manner in order to reduce the number of "wrong" metrics collected in industry today.

Acknowledgements. This work has been partially supported by the Swedish Strategic Research Foundation under the grant number SM13-0007.

References

[AMVP03] Atkins, K.L., Martin, B.D., Vellinga, J.M., Price, R.A.: Stardust: implementing a new manage-to-budget paradigm. Acta Astronaut. **52**(2–6), 87–97 (2003). TY - JOUR

[AN93] Abran, A., Nguyenkim, H.: Measurement of the maintenance process from a demand-based perspective. J. Softw. Maintenance Res. Pract. **5**(2), 63–90 (1993)

[CLB05] Chirinos, L., Losavio, F., Bøegh, J.: Characterizing a data model for software measurement. J. Syst. Softw. **74**(2), 207–226 (2005)

[EW07] Elbashir, M., Williams, S.: Bi impact: the assimilation of business intelligence into core business processes. Bus. Intell. J. **12**(4), 45 (2007)

[FKDW06] Farooq, A., Kernchen, S., Dumke, R.R., Wille, C.: Web services based measurement for it quality assurance. In: Proceedings of the International Conference on Software Process and Product Measurement (MENSURA 2006), pp. 241–251 (2006)

[FP98] Fenton, N.E., Pfleeger, S.L.: Software Metrics: A Rigorous and Practical Approach. PWS Publishing Co., Boston (1998)

[GLZ+10] Gong, C., Liu, J., Zhang, Q., Chen, H., Gong, Z.: The characteristics of cloud computing. In: 2010 39th International Conference on Parallel Processing Workshops (ICPPW), pp. 275–279. IEEE (2010)

[JA97] Jacquet, J.-P., Abran, A.: From software metrics to software measurement methods: a process model. In: Third IEEE International Software Engineering Standards Symposium and Forum, pp. 128–135. IEEE (1997)

[Jor99] Jorgensen, M.: Software quality measurement. Adv. Eng. Softw. **30**(12), 907–912 (1999)

[KS02] Kuzniarz, L., Staron, M.: On practical usage of stereotypes in uml-based software development. In: Proceedings of Forum on Design and Specification Languages (2002)

[MS10] Mellegård, N., Staron, M.: Characterizing model usage in embedded software engineering: a case study. In: Proceedings of the Fourth European Conference on Software Architecture: Companion Volume, pp. 245–252. ACM (2010)

[MST12] Mellegard, N., Staron, M., Torner, F.: A light-weight defect classification scheme for embedded automotive software and its initial evaluation. In: 2012 IEEE 23rd International Symposium on Software Reliability Engineering (ISSRE), pp. 261–270. IEEE (2012)

[OC07] International Standard Organization and International Electrotechnical Commission: Software and systems engineering, software measurement process. Technical report, ISO/IEC (2007)

[PAL10] Pallis, G.: Cloud computing: the new frontier of internet computing. IEEE Internet Comput. **14**(5), 70–73 (2010)

[PSS+12] Pawluk, P., Simmons, B., Smit, M., Litoiu, M., Mankovski, S.: Introducing STRATOS: a cloud broker service. In: IEEE CLOUD, pp. 891–898 (2012)

[RS05] Robinson, H., Sharp, H.: Organisational culture and xp: three case studies (2005)

[SKT05] Staron, M., Kuzniarz, L., Thurn, C.: An empirical assessment of using stereotypes to improve reading techniques in software inspections. In: ACM SIGSOFT Software Engineering Notes, vol. 30, pp. 1–7. ACM (2005)

[SM09a] Staron, M., Meding, W.: Ensuring reliability of information provided by measurement systems. In: Abran, A., Braungarten, R., Dumke, R.R., Cuadrado-Gallego, J.J., Brunekreef, J. (eds.) IWSM 2009. LNCS, vol. 5891, pp. 1–16. Springer, Heidelberg (2009)

[SM09b] Staron, M., Meding, W.: Transparent measures: cost-efficient measurement processes in SE. Int. Workshop Softw. Technol. Transf. **1**, 1–10 (2009)

[SM09c] Staron, M., Meding, W.: Using models to develop measurement systems: a method and its industrial use. In: Abran, A., Braungarten, R., Dumke, R.R., Cuadrado-Gallego, J.J., Brunekreef, J. (eds.) IWSM 2009. LNCS, vol. 5891, pp. 212–226. Springer, Heidelberg (2009)

[SM14] Staron, M., Meding, W.: Metricscloud: scaling-up metrics dissemination in large organizations. Adv. Softw. Eng. **2014** (2014)

[SMKN10] Staron, M., Meding, W., Karlsson, G., Nilsson, C.: Developing measurement systems: an industrial case study. J. Softw. Maintenance Evol. Res. Pract. **23**, 89–107 (2010)

[SMN08] Staron, M., Meding, W., Nilsson, C.: A framework for developing measurement systems and its industrial evaluation. Inf. Softw. Technol. **51**(4), 721–737 (2008)

[SMN09] Staron, M., Meding, W., Nilsson, C.: A framework for developing measurement systems and its industrial evaluation. Inf. Softw. Technol. **51**(4), 721–737 (2009)

[SMP12] Staron, M., Meding, W., Palm, K.: Release readiness indicator for mature agile and lean software development projects. In: Wohlin, C. (ed.) XP 2012. LNBIP, vol. 111, pp. 93–107. Springer, Heidelberg (2012)

[SMSN13] Sakamoto, Y., Matsumoto, S., Saiki, S., Nakamura, M.: Visualizing software metrics with service-oriented mining software repository for reviewing personal process. In: 2013 14th ACIS International Conference on Software Engineering, Artificial Intelligence, Networking and Parallel/Distributed Computing (SNPD), pp. 549–554. IEEE (2013)

[Sta12] Staron, M.: Critical role of measures in decision processes: managerial and technical measures in the context of large software development organizations. Inf. Softw. Technol. **54**(8), 887–899 (2012)

[TC06] Thomas, J.J., Cook, K.A.: A visual analytics agenda. IEEE Comput. Graph. Appl. **26**(1), 10–13 (2006)

[VSBCR02] Van Solingen, R., Basili, V., Caldiera, G., Rombach, H.D.: Goal question metric (gqm) approach. In: Marciniak, J. (ed.) Encyclopedia of Software Engineering, pp. 578–583. Wiley, New York (2002)

[YOL13] Yoon, Y.B., Oh, J., Lee, B.G.: The establishment of security strategies for introducing cloud computing. KSII Trans. Internet Inf. Syst. (TIIS) **7**(4), 860–877 (2013)

[ZZ09] Zhang, L.-J., Zhou, Q.: CCOA: cloud computing open architecture. In: IEEE International Conference on Web Services, 2009. ICWS 2009, pp. 607–616. IEEE (2009)

Designing an Unobtrusive Analytics Framework for Monitoring Java Applications

Sampo Suonsyrjä[✉] and Tommi Mikkonen

Department of Pervasive Computing, Tampere University of Technology,
Korkeakoulunkatu 10, 33720 Tampere, Finland
{sampo.suonsyrja,tommi.mikkonen}@tut.fi

Abstract. In software development, attention has recently been placed on understanding users and their interactions with systems. User studies, practices such as A/B testing, and frameworks such as Google Analytics that gather data on production use have become common approaches in particular in the context of the Web, where it is easy to perform frequent updates as new needs emerge. However, when considering installable desktop applications, the situation gets more complex. While analytics facilities are still needed, they should address business logic, not generic traffic as is the case with many web sites. Moreover, analytics should be unobtrusive, and not have a high impact on the evolution of the actual application; thus, analytics should be treated as an add-on, as the target system may already exist. Finally, the instrumentation of features that are observed should be easy and flexible, but the provided mechanisms should be expressive enough for many use cases. In this paper, we examine different alternatives for implementing such monitoring mechanisms, and report results from an experiment with Vaadin, a web framework based on Java and Google Web Toolkit, GWT.

1 Introduction

The introduction of Agile methods [6] caused a paradigm shift in the development of software systems: instead of starting with a set of requirements that are all of the same value, software developers began to embrace a model where systems are first built with only a set of key features to be later extended into a more complete form. As more and more experience regarding the use of the system is gathered, developers write new versions of the system which satisfy user needs better. In fact, one can even claim that the core of iterative development is the ability to learn in each increment, which leads to improved products.

In the process of creating the software in the above fashion, input from users of the system can play a crucial role, given that adequate mechanisms for collecting the input are available. The most traditional way is to design questionnaires or other studies that the end users answer to guide the development, but in particular in the field of web systems, also more sophisticated forms of gathering information exist regarding users and the way the system is being used. For instance A/B testing, where different sets of users use a slightly different version of the software, helps in deciding between two ways to provide similar or the

© Springer International Publishing Switzerland 2015
A. Kobyliński et al. (Eds.): IWSM-Mensura 2015, LNBIP 230, pp. 160–175, 2015.
DOI: 10.1007/978-3-319-24285-9_11

same features. Moreover, analytics frameworks such as Google Analytics provide detailed understanding regarding how users interact with the system to perform more complicated tasks. In general, the ability to gather all this information is opening new possibilities for developers, because even the slightest deviations in user behavior can be tracked and reacted upon.

Although the field of web systems can nowadays be seen to have an edge in collecting post-deployment data, the same need is increasing in other contexts as well, as evidenced by [8]. In this paper, we investigate techniques for monitoring application-level user activity, as well as an option to extend the techniques to cover installable desktop applications, too.

The goal is to track actions at the level of user interface widgets, such as buttons, sliders, and text fields for instance. The work is based on using Java web framework Vaadin [5], where applications are first composed with Java, and then compiled into a form that can be deployed to the web, with the parts of the application that form the user interface being compiled with Google Web Toolkit [12]. As the concrete implementation mechanism for introducing analytics facilities, we experiment using aspect-oriented techniques [4] to bind an existing design to an external data analytics framework.

The rest of this paper is structured as follows. In Sect. 2, we introduce motivation and background of the study. In Sect. 3, we introduce our research questions. In Sect. 4, we describe our demonstrator application and how it has been constructed. In Sect. 5, we provide details of our implementation: showing how data is gathered in an unobtrusive fashion and describing the design of our analytics framework. In Sect. 6, we provide an extended discussion regarding our findings. Finally, in Sect. 7, we draw final conclusions.

2   Background

Analytics is used by businesses of all type to better understand customers. During the recent years, also software engineers and software engineering organizations have understood the opportunity to use more data for making constantly better decisions, but as even sporting teams have improved their performance with the help of analytics, the uses for analytics seem to be fairly general [1].

2.1   Software Analytics

Pachidi et al. [11] have developed the Usage Mining Method that enables conducting classification analyses, user profilings and clickstream analyses on logged operation data. Such data is beneficial for program understanding and reengineering [3]. In addition, as the size and complexity of software systems continue to grow, decision making is becoming even more difficult in the future and thus new solutions such as the use of analytics data are needed [2].

Kristjansson and van der Schuur have formulated the concept Software Operation Knowledge [9]. They describe that to consist of knowledge of in-the-field performance, quality and usage of software, and knowledge of end-user experience and end-user feedback. The researchers continue with stating how software vendors have a great interest in acquiring such knowledge, but that the systematic practice of gathering, analyzing and acting on such knowledge is still limited. Correspondingly, this kind of in-the-field knowledge could benefit usability studies as the lack of long-term data collection is considered as one of the challenges in measuring usability [7].

In general, it is possible to collect usage metrics by executing software applications, but this usually requires some sort of modifications to the source code of the target application. There are a few exceptions however. For example, the Patina system [10] uses Microsoft Active Accessibility API to collect accessibility data, and thus no altering of the source code is needed. The system creates a so-called heatmap, which visualizes the content and location of the user interface controls visible in the application. As a drawback, supporting the accessibility API usually requires some extra work from the application developers and so the coverage of the accessibility API can vary.

As for concrete implementations, one of the most commonly used analysis frameworks is Google Analytics (http://www.google.com/analytics/), which is presently being used by an increasing number of web sites. With it, the developers of a web site can track traffic of a monitored web site and view it in a form that is easy to interpret. The data provides information regarding visitors, their geographical locations, the time they remain on the site, what is the path that users take on the web site, and so on. Since the system operates in the Web, its operation can rely on web protocols that reveal these properties. For a generic desktop application, however, these facilities are not immediately available. Moreover, when considering installable applications, data to be collected is often application specific, not web traffic related as is the case with Google Analytics. However, the popularity of Google Analytics demonstrates that there is an increasing interest regarding user data, which can be made available in an unobtrusive fashion.

2.2 Aspect-Oriented Programming

Aspect-oriented software development provides means for capturing cross-cutting concerns and modularizing them as manageable units [4]. Tackling the issue of tangled code, aspect-oriented programming languages such as AspectJ provide means to insert additional operations to a target program in an unobtrusive fashion with a new construct, so-called *aspect*. Aspects in turn provide increased opportunities for advanced modularity.

At the implementation level, an AspectJ aspect always includes at least two parts: a pointcut and an advice, both of which are code snippets. The pointcut is used to describe the point where the execution of the target program is paused for inserting the additional code programmed in the advice part. Figure 1 provides a simple aspect code that introduces a simple logging facility that records the parameters and the return value of a method call. In this aspect, the pointcut is defined to take effect around the defined function of our example class,

`MyClass::MyFunc`. The `Logger` aspect takes effect as the function is called, and the aspect code is executed both before and after actually executing the original method in a fashion where its execution is not affected. The operations that are being executed before and after running the method can be arbitrary; however for the purposes of software analytics, these include data collection operations.

```
aspect Logger {
pointcut loggedFunction = call("void MyClass::MyFunc(...)");
advice loggedFunction:around() {
   // Log call and method parameters
   tjp->Proceed(); // Run MyClass::MyFunc
   // Log results
   }
}
```

Fig. 1. A sample aspect.

3   Research Questions

The research questions we formed to evaluate our usage data collection and analysis framework are the following.

RQ1: To What Extent can a Data Collecting Feature be Implemented Without Compromising the Evolution of the Target Program? As a starting point for our research, we have taken a view where the design and evolution of the target system, in other words the program from which usage data is to be collected, must remain as independent from data collection and analysis as possible. High priority of this independence is motivated by the fact that in the end analytics data leads to changes in the target program. Therefore, it is crucial that the target program can be under constant change and these data can still be collected from it. This leads to the selection of implementation techniques that are as unobtrusive as possible.

As the evolution of the target program results in data being collected from different versions of the target program, the approach used for collecting data has to ensure that these data are still comparable between the different versions. Thus, not only do we want to find out specific types of data that can be collected with our framework, but also if the data is adequate enough to be compared between different versions of the target program. Finally, as we aim at designing a data collection framework that is independent of the underlying target program, we also introduce an option to reuse the development effort invested in the framework in different setups, including desktop applications as well as web systems built using Java.

RQ2: What Types of Data can be Collected with the Given Approach?
As with any technology, there are restrictions regarding the data that can be collected. In this paper, we are interested in interactions between the user and the application, and therefore we focus on data that is associated with user interactions only. Thus, interactions with e.g. external actors or machines are beyond our scope in this paper.

RQ3: How to Connect the Data Collecting Feature with an Analysis Framework? Being able to record data from a user interface is only a beginning in the way towards understanding how an application is being used. Therefore, it is necessary to load the resulting usage data to an analysis system, which can then be used to further process the data into a meaningful form.

4   Demonstrator Application

To answer the above research questions, we next describe a demonstrator application. First, we introduce the platform on top of which the system is built. Then, we describe the application. Finally, we show how manual instrumentation could be carried out for this application.

4.1   Vaadin Web Framework

Vaadin [5] is an open source framework that is used for developing Rich Internet Applications (RIA). Vaadin applications are written using Java, and they are transformed into AJAX applications with the facilities of Google Web Toolkit (GWT) [12]. The architecture of the system is illustrated in Fig. 2.

Vaadin applications are implemented similarly to Java Standard Edition desktop applications, with all the functionality written using Java. However, instead of using the usual Java UI libraries like AWT, SWT, or Swing, a specific set of Vaadin UI components is used. These components can be compiled into a form that is runnable inside the browser, following the development process of GWT. This process is illustrated in Fig. 3. In addition, new custom made UI components can be implemented when needed to create systems with different kinds of look-and-feel.

4.2   Demonstration Application

To evaluate the designed framework for usage data collection, we selected a Vaadin application, which is fully functional and already developed yet simple enough to be the first test application. The source code is available for download at https://github.com/vaadin/dashboard-demo, and a working demo is located at http://demo.vaadin.com/dashboard.

The target application, called *QuickTickets Dashboard Demo*, demonstrates how the Vaadin framework can be used to create a simple dashboard web application. The main dashboard view is initialized as an object of DashboardView class.

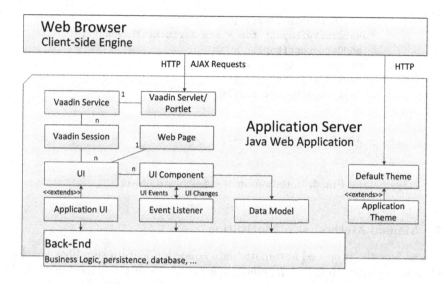

Fig. 2. Vaadin architecture. Image adapted from [5]

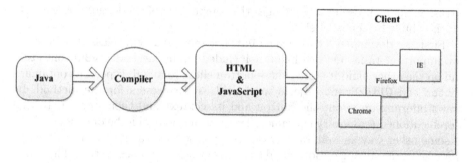

Fig. 3. GWT process of compiling Java to HTML and JavaScript [12]

During the initialization, several objects of HorizontalLayout class are instantiated and pushed to the view with an addComponent method. These include components such as a toolbar and several rows. Buttons are added correspondingly to these layout components in the same manner. In Fig. 4, we demonstrate the initialization of a dashboard object on code level along with a toolbar (a `horizontalLayout` object) and a notify button.

In the following, we demonstrate how collecting usage data works by focusing on buttons that can be pressed by users. While this obviously does not cover all the dimensions of software operation knowledge, this restriction simplifies the presentation to a form that is concrete enough to demonstrate at a detailed level how data collection works.

```
public DashboardView() {
    HorizontalLayout top = new HorizontalLayout();
    addComponent(top);
    Button notify = new Button('2');
    Notify.addClickListener(
        new ClickListener(){
            ...
        });
    top.addComponent(notify);
};
```

Fig. 4. Initialization of a dashboard object.

4.3   Manual Method as a Motivation

To show how the proposed automatic data collection feature simplifies developers' tasks, we first provide a manual implementation of the same function. To this end, we inserted data collecting features manually ourselves to specific places in the original source code of the target application. Thus, this approach is an intrusive one as it essentially changes the source code of the target application, which is built by someone else.

First, we developed a class called DataLogger.java. This class was used for two important tasks. On one hand, it included public method logButtonClick and on the other hand it stored these button clicks to a SQL type of a container. Button and ClickEvent objects were used as parameters for the method. It draws information about the button and its context and then stores it to the aforementioned temporary container. This information could be of course stored in some other way as well, but for our study case this was not seen important. However, some storing options are discussed in the future work section. This class itself was then included in the same java package with the target applications source code files. Up until this point the target applications source code was not altered.

In the unobtrusive part, the whole source code of the target application was then searched through to find each and every place where a new button was instantiated and added to the UI as seen in Fig. 4. As with every button there was also an instantiation of its ClickListener, we always inserted a call to our logEvent method within this instantiation. In Fig. 5, we provide a code snippet that elaborates how this implementation was done.

Clearly, we only used one intrusive insertion to the application, the call to method Logger.logEvent. However, even with this simple application, there were a total of 33 of this kind of button instantiations in the target application, all of which had to be extended with a similar call to our data logging method. While 33 insertions can be implemented once quite fast, the devil is in the complexity that most likely starts to build up when such implementation process is repeated for a while. Especially in a case where the target application is developed by a different person than the one implementing the usage data logging features, there

```
final Button signin = new Button("Sign In");
signin.addClickListener(
   new ClickListener() {
      public void buttonClick(ClickEvent e) {
         Logger.logEvent(signinEvent, e);
         ...
      }
   }
);
```

Fig. 5. Manual implementation of data collection.

is always the risk of forgetting to add these logging features to all the necessary places. Furthermore, even if a special script was developed to insert the logging features automatically to specific places, one would have to be very careful in developing such a script. Although this should reduce the risk of forgetting to log a button at all, any possible extra calls to the data logging methods would then again distort the data and its reliability as button clicks could be recorded not just once but twice or trice and so on.

In the regard of data comparability the manual approach, qualities depend greatly on the specific implementation. In this case study, our implementation gathered data only straight from the context of the target application. This included data types such as buttons caption, session id, and URI fragment. Although having all the data coming from the Vaadin frameworks context creates quite a reliable starting point for a further usage data analysis, target application evolution and changes in for example buttons captions might lead to inconsistencies in collected usage data.

In what comes to the flexibility of the manual approach and usefulness of the data it collects, we saw this approach performing understandably well. Making the application log new kinds of data types was as easy as making it log the first types of data. Of course in a case with a larger-scale application this might take more than a blink of an eye. However, the point in the flexibility criterion is to evaluate if the approach is able to collect also new kinds of data and the manual approach certainly has that as an advantage. Similarly, it collects just the types of data one wants and thus these data should be as useful as any.

5   Data Collection and Analysis Framework

To support usage data collection, we designed a framework where several already existing techniques and tools are used (Fig. 6). These key components are:

- AspectJ is used for creating an unobtrusive monitoring mechanism for the target application.
- Fluentd (www.fluentd.org) is used as the mechanism for unified data collection.

– Elasticsearch (www.elasticsearch.org/overview/elasticsearch) is used as a real-time storage for flexible searches.
– Kibana (www.elasticsearch.org/overview/kibana) is used for creating real-time visualizations and analytics.

This stack that combines Fluentd, Elasticsearch, and Kibana can be considered as an open source alternative to Splunk (www.splunk.com) log management software.

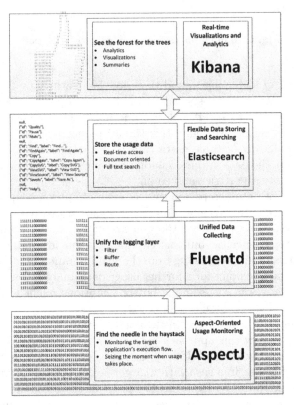

Fig. 6. The designed framework for unobtrusive analytics.

5.1   Aspect-Oriented Usage Monitoring

The aspect-oriented approach to inserting additional features into existing applications is unobtrusive by nature. As already mentioned, we demonstrate this facility by focusing on buttons. To this end, we wish to intervene in the execution every time a button is being added to a UI component (see Fig. 4 in Subsect. 4.2). To attach a pointcut and a logging advice to such call, aspect `AddComponentListener` was created as shown in Fig. 7.

In this aspect, pointcut called `addComponentCall` defines that each time method `addComponent` is called with a button as its parameter, the execution

```
public aspect AddComponentListener {
    // Button clicks are stored in this container.
    DataLogger dataCollector = new DataLogger();
    // To be executed when a button is added to the layout.
    pointcut addComponentCall(Button b):
        call(* *.addComponent(*)) && args(bb);
    // To be executed after a button has been added to layout.
    after(final Button b):
        addComponentCall(b) {
        // Clicks are listened to with a basic Vaadin ClickListener.
        b.addClickListener(
            new Button.ClickListener() {
            public void click(ClickEvent e) {
                dataCollector.logEvent(b, e);
            }
        });
    }
}
```

Fig. 7. Data collector aspect, its pointcut and advice.

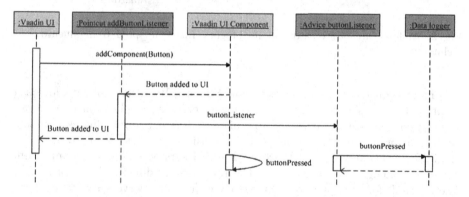

Fig. 8. Insertion of an additional click listener with an aspect.

can be cut for the corresponding advice part. This part will then define an additional click listener. This is shown in Fig. 8.

Finally, a remark must be made regarding the degree of unobtrusiveness of the approach. While the effect of AspectJ code is unobtrusive to the underlying target program, tooling is affected by AspectJ. To begin with, for the build process, a dependency to AspectJ must be inserted to the target application's project file. Additionally, the AspectJ tools must be included in the used IDE, in our case Eclipse.

5.2   Collecting Data with Fluentd

Fluentd was implemented in quite a similar fashion as the AspectJ for monitoring features. However, wherein AspectJ was used for unobtrusively monitoring the usage, Fluentd was used for collecting usage data from the usage points defined with AspectJ. Thus, the core idea of Fluentd is to be the unifying layer between different types of log inputs and outputs. This is illustrated in Fig. 9, in which a box is a component and the arrows describe the data flow.

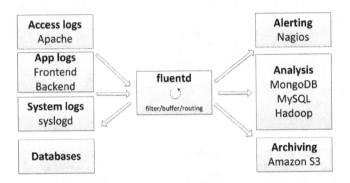

Fig. 9. Architecture of Fluentd and its plugins. Image adapted from [fluentd.org/architecture]

Figure 9 illustrates the architecture of Fluentd. Its various plugins for data input make it easier to unify the logging layer of an application or even an application ecosystem. There are a number of different input plugins available for several programming languages. In this study, we obviously used an input plugin for Java applications. However, Fluentd supports inputs not only from different language applications but also from entirely different kinds of inputs. These include for example access and error logs from web servers and system logs.

The concrete implementation of Fluentd into the target application required that a Fluentd dependency was inserted into the source code of the target application. This was done similarly as with the AspectJ facilities. Additionally, we installed and ran Fluentd on the same machine with the target application. As these requirements are met, the Fluentd process is able to receive the inputs described in Fig. 10. As described with the usage monitoring aspect in Fig. 7, `logButtonClick` method is called whenever a button is clicked.

Similar to the input plugins of Fluentd, its plugins for storing data standardize that front. Depending on the use case, data can be stored in different formats for archiving and analysis, for example. In this study, we used Fluentd for parsing the usage data into JSON and then forwarding them for analysis in Elasticsearch. As seen in Fig. 10, there were different types of usage data related to a button click, its context, and the button itself. These data were first stored in a temporary Java Hashmap object but then forwarded to Fluentd for its filtering, buffering, and rerouting processes.

```
public class DataLogger {
    private static FluentLogger LOG =
        FluentLogger.getLogger("button.click");
    public void logButtonClick(Button b, ClickEvent event){
        Map<String, Object> data = new HashMap<String, Object>();
        data.put("Uri Fragment", Page.getCurrent().getUriFragment());
        data.put("Page", Page.getCurrent().toString());
        data.put("Button Caption", b.getCaption());
        data.put("Button ID", b.getId());
        ...
        data.put("Click X", event.getClientX());
        data.put("Click Y", event.getClientY());
        LOG.log("click", data);
    }
}
```

Fig. 10. Collecting data from a Java application with Fluentd.

5.3 Elasticsearch and Kibana

In our study setup, we used Fluentd and Elasticsearch on the same localhost. Fluentd sent the collected usage data to Elasticsearch, which stored them into its document oriented database without any pre-configurations. As the data was already formatted in JSON, the field names were already there. This in combination with the full-text search abilities made analyzing facilities easily accessible. In addition, Elasticsearch supports real-time access to exploring the stored data.

However, Elasticsearch is only storing the data and making it searchable. Therefore, Kibana was used as a dashboard for displaying the data from Elasticsearch. Through this dashboard, one can make queries and then visualize the results in various different forms. An example visualization is shown in Fig. 11. In the visualization there is a pie chart illustrating how many times a specific button has been clicked.

6   Discussion

To discuss our findings, we next revisit our research questions one by one. In addition, we will also provide some directions for future research.

6.1   Research Questions Revisited

Based on our experiences with the proposed framework, we revisit the paper's questions as follows.

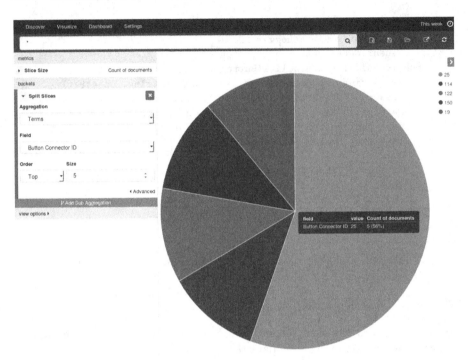

Fig. 11. Screenshot of a Kibana visualization.

RQ1: To What Extent can a Data Collecting Feature be Implemented Without Compromising the Evolution of the Target Program? Aspect-oriented approach to inserting additional features is quite unobtrusive by nature, which is supported by the code snippets. Also in this case, the usage monitoring facilities were inserted without changing the source code of the target application. The only parts which needed some modifications were the dependency addition to a build file and an insertion of an AspectJ file.

As these modifications were not altering the source code itself, the target application's evolution was not compromised nearly as much as with the manual approach. In this sense, if the target application's next version was to include new buttons, the aspect-oriented monitoring would notice them just as they did with all the rest. Therefore, the approach allows the target application to scale in that way without any additional efforts needed to include to the additional buttons as new data collecting points.

However, if the target application was to be changed in the way its buttons are instantiated, the aspect-oriented monitoring needs to be changed correspondingly. Even in this kind of a case though, the modification to the monitoring pointcut would most likely have to be done only once.

RQ2: What Types of Data can be Collected with the Given Approach?
With an aspect-oriented monitoring approach, pointcuts could be made on a vast variety of different points in the execution flow. For instance, we could have associated the pointcuts with the initialization of objects of a particular class, as well as any other public method. The same goes for advices, which can contain almost arbitrary code that is needed for monitoring.

Additionally, aspect-oriented techniques support various different types of data that can be collected. Software operation knowledge in general includes information such as in-the-field performance, quality and usage of software, and knowledge of end-user experience, and end-user feedback, and to some extent this is necessarily platform-specific. In our case, the Vaadin framework provides an API to get such data directly from the platform. For instance, there are straightforward methods to get information on timestamps, URI fragments, button captions, and so on. With such information, it is possible to gain knowledge for example about the clickstream a user leaves behind, the average time they spent on a specific page, or what kind of errors are logged the most.

All in all, the aspect-oriented approach provides us with the same flexibility in gathering different types of data as the manual approach did. With such arbitrary data types, the problems of analytics are more about asking the right questions than getting enough data.

RQ3: How to Connect the Data Collecting Feature with an Analysis Framework? Although collecting data can be done in most cases in a various ways, further exploring and analyzing of data might turn out more difficult. The use of a standardized analysis framework might require the data to be in a specific format. In this regard, the data logging tool's ability to unify the data it collects becomes important. In this study, Fluentd was used for collecting data, and it also performed the unifying by turning the data into the JSON format. This again was a format that the data storing solution supported and the visualization tool had an access to. Thus, the data collection tool's unifying feature enabled us to form an end-to-end analytics framework starting from the usage monitoring and peaking in the visualizations.

In circumstances such as these, general collection frameworks can provide a way to standardize parts of the logging even if data inputs and outputs varied from time to time. This becomes especially important when the aim is to combine data from different kinds of sources such as access, error and application logs.

6.2   Future Work

The work reported in this paper is only the very beginning of research regarding using aspects as a tool for analyzing user interactions. As already pointed out, at present we have a mechanism for collecting the data, and next challenge is to figure out which part of the data is truly meaningful, and how should the gathered data be used. Some of the directions for future work are listed below.

Extending the Measurement Point Set. In addition to collecting straightforward data on user actions, broadening the focus to cover attributes such as in-the-field performance or end-user feedback can turn out as helpful opportunities for various different fields. For instance, a short user experience survey could be injected as an aspect into a specific point of execution flow, an error log could be sent to developers when a system crashes, or a sorry-note could be shown to the user in case of system performing under a specified level. Being able to perform this in a non-intrusive fashion could improve user experience considerably, with no risk to the future evolution of the system.

Experimenting with Real-Life Apps. Obviously, the feasibility of the above data collection approaches is domain dependent, and the type of the application as well as the setup created for testing has an impact on whether or not operations are offline or real time. Therefore, experimenting the different approaches with real-life applications and developer needs forms an important part of future work. Our present strategy is to execute these experiments together with Vaadin and the associated developer community. In addition, once we reach a maturity level where the analysis framework can be used in production use, we wish to study how interaction data that has been automatically collected relates to user studies executed in more conventional fashion.

7   Conclusions

Fueled by the opportunities provided by the web and associated tools, analytics regarding the use of software applications have become a central aspect in software development. The rationale is that data regarding the fashion a software system is used helps in understanding the true needs of end users. This in turn enables the design of more satisfying software applications, with improved performance, simplified interactions, and superior user experience. However, gathering data on real-life use of applications is sometimes difficult, in particular when considering installable applications that cannot be easily updated remotely. Moreover, creating practical tools for analysis commonly requires application specific attention.

In this paper, we are experimenting how analytics facilities similar to web applications can be introduced to desktop and Rich Internet Applications written in Java. To keep the application intact from analytics facilities, we are using AspectJ as the implementation technique for introducing application-level monitoring, which allows us to hook analytics facilities to user interface events in a non-intrusive fashion. As for analysis, we are using an already existing tool set, where open source systems play a key role. The implementation we have created is concise, and it can be easily generalized to other applications if needed.

Based on our experiences reported in this paper, we find aspects a technique that is well-suited for creating data extraction features for already existing applications. In particular, given that the applications follow certain conventions, it appears to be relatively straightforward to create join points that are easily repeatable. Since we wish to track user actions, starting with user interface widgets is the natural starting point and almost all user interaction mechanisms in modern programs follow certain patterns, we believe that the results we have obtained can be generalized to many other environments, too. Moreover, already existing analysis tools provide support for filtering, analysing and visualizing data at real-time.

Acknowledgment. The authors wish to thank Digile Need4Speed program (http://www.n4s.fi/) for its support for this research.

References

1. Begel, A., Zimmermann, T.: Analyze this! 145 questions for data scientists in software engineering. In: Proceedings of the 36th International Conference on Software Engineering, pp. 12–23. ACM (2014)
2. Buse, R.P., Zimmermann, T.: Information needs for software development analytics. In: Proceedings of the 34th International Conference on Software Engineering, pp. 987–996. IEEE Press (2012)
3. El-Ramly, M., Stroulia, E.: Mining software usage data. In: Proceedings of 1st International Workshop on Mining Software Repositories (MSR 2004), pp. 64–68 (2004)
4. Filman, R., Elrad, T., Clarke, S.: Aspect-Oriented Software Development. Addison-Wesley Professional, Reading (2004)
5. Grönroos, M.: Book of Vaadin. Uniprint, Turku (2011)
6. Highsmith, J.: Agile Software Development Ecosystems. Addison-Wesley Longman Publishing Co. Inc., Boston (2002)
7. Hornbaek, K.: Current practice in measuring usability: challenges to usability studies and research. Int. J. Hum. Comput. Stud. **64**, 79–102 (2006)
8. Juergens, E., Feilkas, M., Herrmannsdoerfer, M., Deissenboeck, F., Vaas, R., Prommer, K.: Feature profiling for evolving systems. In: Proceedings of the 19th International Conference on Program Comprehension, pp. 171–180. IEEE (2011)
9. Kristjánsson, B., van der Schuur, H.: A Survey of Tools for Software Operation Knowledge Acquisition. Department of Information and Computing Sciences, Utrecht University, Technical report UU-CS-2009-028 (2009)
10. Matejka, J., Grossman, T., Fitzmaurice, G.: Patina: dynamic heatmaps for visualizing application usage. In: Proceedings of the SIGCHI Conference on Human Factors in Computing Systems, pp. 3227–3236. ACM, April 2013
11. Pachidi, S., Spruit, M., van de Weerd, I.: Understanding users behavior with software operation data mining. Comput. Hum. Behav. **30**, 583–594 (2014)
12. Perry, B.W.: Google Web Toolkit for Ajax. OReilly Short Cuts. OReilly (2007)

A Functional Software Measurement Approach to Bridge the Gap Between Problem and Solution Domains

Erdir Ungan[✉] and Onur Demirörs

Graduate School of Informatics,
Middle East Technical University, Ankara, Turkey
{erdir,demirors}@metu.edu.tr

Abstract. There are various software size measurement methods that are used in various stages of a software project lifecycle. Although functional size measurement methods and lines of code measurements are widely practiced, none of these methods explicitly position themselves in problem or solution domain. This results in unreliable measurement results as abstraction levels of the measured artifacts vary greatly. Unreliable measurement results hinder usage of size data in effort estimation and benchmarking studies. Furthermore, there exists no widely accepted measurement method for solution domain concepts other than lines of code, such as software design. In this study, an approach is defined to distinguish problem and solution domains for a software project and a software size measurement methodology for solution domain is proposed based on software design sizes.

1 Introduction

Software projects are conducted to solve a problem in the real life. Similar to the case in other engineering disciplines, it is possible to develop multiple solutions to a problem. As these solutions may differ greatly, their size and the effort required to realize them also vary significantly.

This fact, makes it difficult to establish a direct relationship between the product and the process to develop that product. As there is no one-to-one relationship between a problem and its possible solutions, it is difficult to define a relation between the size of the problem and the solution.

Within the discipline of software measurement, there exists methods that measure both problem and solution domains. Problem domain measurements came a long way since their initiation and can quantify problem definitions and specifications. Solution domain measurements are more formal and more precise as they are based on physical constructs and models.

However, problem domain measures fall short in accuracy as inputs to prediction models, and solution domain measures emerge too late in a project lifecycle to be used in predictions. We believe this is one of the main problems in software measurement (and estimation) as a discipline.

· The main reason for problem domain measurement's failure in representing the development effort lies in the ambiguity of the process of developing a solution to a

A. Kobyliński et al. (Eds.): IWSM-Mensura 2015, LNBIP 230, pp. 176–191, 2015.
DOI: 10.1007/978-3-319-24285-9_12

problem at hand. Developing a solution to a problem is a "soft" area. Therefore problem domain concepts fail to predict solution domain concepts on their own.

Most of the measurement and estimation methods assume that there is a continuity in the development lifecycle, which begins with the problem statement and ends with development and testing of the software product.

However, there is an inherent discontinuity between the concepts of problem and solution. There is a gap between these two domains which the actual engineering or "art" as some would call traverses.

Jackson states that, the solution is an answer from the machine domain to the problem [29]. Therefore the relation between these two domains is not straightforward. It is affected by the designer's skills, imagination, and experience. Certain factors such as use of design patterns, similarities between problem-solution tuples in an organization's historical data and traditions of an organization tend to help making this problem to solution transformation formal and algebraic. Most of the estimation methods in the literature exploit these factors and try to calculate solution domain concepts such as development effort using certain multipliers for external factors and/or curve fitting algorithms.

Measurements in problem domain are good for representing problem domain concepts and measurements in solution domain are good for representing solution domain concepts. Problem domain concepts such as price, features, can be represented by problem domain measurements such as function points, feature points, use case points. Solution domain concepts such as development effort, physical size, and developer performance can be represented in solution domain sizes such as LOC and design based sizes.

In this context, software size measurement plays an important role. It is widely accepted that software size is one of the key factors that potentially affect the cost and time of the software projects [17, 21, 22, 27, 41].

1.1 Problem Statement

In software project management it is crucial to be able to accurately quantify the size of software as the size information is utilized as an input in most of the management activities such as developing project estimates (e.g., effort, cost), risk assessment, productivity measurement, performance management, benchmarking, quality management.

Problems of Granularity: Most, if not all, measurement methods in problem domain does not incorporate a definition for abstraction and/or granularity level of the system being measured. FSM methods such as COSMIC do define the granularity level of functionality to be measured but they don't define the granularity level of the system itself.

Today, software systems can be so large that it became virtually impossible to define and communicate a whole system within a single analysis. This applies to both functional and structural aspects of the definition of a system. Big software systems are now defined in various levels of decomposition. Correspondingly, their functionality is defined in various levels. Their architecture is vertically decomposed in many layers as well as horizontally into components.

Development of subsystems resulting from the decomposition of a bigger system can be delegated to separate development teams, departments or even companies. Software projects are defined for intermediate software products such as services, layers and components. These projects can be defined so disjointed that there may be no information available to identify the decomposition level of the software product. The end product can be a subsystem of a bigger system which is in turn a subsystem of a bigger system. Similarly, the software product can be utilizing smaller systems which in turn utilize further smaller systems themselves.

As problem domain software measures, that is predominantly FSM methods, lack the information about the granularity level of the system being measured, size of a super system, sub system or a component are all represented in a single level. Making, measurements non additive, non-homomorphic and non-transitive. This violates the metrological requirements for a measurement. With existing measurement methods, size of an overall system will be different from their total size and cannot be calculated from the size of its subordinates.

The level of granularity and hence, the number of Objects of Interest directly affect the measurement result.

Functional process is not a universal or absolute definition for level of abstraction/granularity. It is a relative definition for granularity as system functionality definitions can be broken down into sub system functionality definitions and one may start to define functional processes with a functionality definition which is either higher or lower in level of abstraction in the continuum of problem-solution domain chain.

Defining functional process in each level of structural abstraction is possible. Rules for defining functional processes can be applied to any level of system definition and therefore the granularity level for the functionality definition will be consistent within the level in which the measurement is performed. However, there will be functional processes defined in different system decomposition levels, making the granularity level defined by function process neither universal nor absolute.

Moreover, as far as software maintenance is concerned, changes request can be in any level of decomposition. That is, changes in a requirement can be measured by FSM methods, however a change request only causing a change in the implementation is hard to measure by using artifacts in higher levels. Similarly, two low level changes would be represented by the same measurement in higher levels. Based on this resolution problem, FSM methods may prove to be inaccurate while to measure lesser than functional user requirement level changes.

Problems in Effort Estimation: During the last thirty years, numerous estimation models for software projects were developed. Besides these generic models, organizations also developed their own, specific estimation models. However, effort estimation models still far from the required accuracy.

Parametric effort estimation methods in the literature take three main aspects into consideration. Software Size, external factors and subjective assessments.

Most of the methods in the literature utilize functional size measurement methods such as Function Points, IFPUG, COSMIC, NESMA and similar methods [6]. These methods measure software size based on requirements and specifications, which is ready at the beginning of the project lifecycle.

On the other hand measurement methods in solution domain, based on source code, design constructs and algorithms generally correlate better with development effort data than those in problem domain [34, 43]. However, solution domain sizes cannot be obtained early in the project lifecycle which is the time estimations are actually needed.

In order to overcome this, estimation methods suggest either predicting software size and use those approximate values for estimation or measure domain size and convert it to solution domain size based on some historical data [24, 45]. Both these approaches again, introduce errors in estimation.

Problems in Benchmarking: The above mentioned problems in measurement results and granularity also affects the quality of data in benchmarking data sets. Özcan Top and Yilmaz [37] conducted a study in our research group on benchmarking data sets such as ISBSG, and concluded that, those sets lack structural information about the projects. We cannot deduct information about the abstraction level of measurements in those data sets. Comparing data from varying abstraction levels will result in erroneous benchmarking. With existing measurement methods, size of an overall system will be different from their total size and cannot be calculated from the size of its subordinates. And one cannot get the information about how total size for a project is calculated. Similarly, studies also shown that the quality of the measurement in public data sets is questionable and reliability of any size information is disputed.

1.2 Solution Approach

In this study, we recognize the separation of problem and solution domains. We relate activities, artifacts and their corresponding size measurements to these domains.

While separating the problem and solution domains, we also suggest that problem and solution domain definitions shift as problems are decomposed into smaller problems. System decomposition and abstraction techniques guide this shift through the engineering process.

Similar to the most common FSM methods, we consider data movements as the base functional component for measurement. Data movement is an abstract, domain independent concept. It is atomic as far as a decomposition level is concerned and can be well defined for a given measurement view.

Abran [8] states this as: "The key concept of functionality at the highest level of commonality that is present in all software was identified as the data movement. This data movement concept was then assigned to the metrology concept of a size unit".

Considering that data movements is a common feature of many FSM methods there is a quite broad consensus that data movement is a good representation of the concept of the functional size of software [23].

We believe definition of functionality is traversable through decomposition levels. Therefore, we perceive the functional requirements as definitions of functionality which can be defined in various abstraction levels. Hence, different levels of functional processes can be defined in corresponding decomposition levels. Functionality allocated to a structural entity in a decomposition level can be broken down into smaller functional processes defined in a lower decomposition level.

We suggest that the definition of functionality is defined in a chain of alternating problem and solution domains. That is, a solution (function) poses as a problem for lower levels of decomposition and a problem (expected outcome) will be attained through solutions (functions) in a further lower level of decomposition.

This leads us to the notion that a Base Functional Component for functionality, may exist in both problem and solution domains based on the perspective therefore posing as a common concept in both domains.

The Base Functional Component for Data Movement Point (DMP) measurement method is based on the data movement concept which is commonly present in both domains. We suggest that, through such a method, size information obtained in one domain will be usable in other.

We propose that a measurement framework which incorporates decomposition levels into measurement will mitigate the problems defined above.

Estimation of concepts in the problem domain and solution domain will be more accurate if they are based on concepts residing in their respective domains. However, as mentioned before, existing measurement methods are confined in one domain and utilized for normalizing or estimating concepts in the other domain.

We propose a measurement framework consisting of a functional size measurement method and an approach for approximating functional size. Our functional size measurement approach is based on the approach introduced by the COSMIC method. Size approximation is based on structural decomposition considerations.

It is possible to measure software size using the lowest level of decomposition for data movement, automatically. Then, it is possible to scale up the measurement by mapping lower decomposition level objects to objects in higher levels.

We also present a software tool to perform the measurement method defined.

2   Previous Studies on Measuring Functional Software Size Based on Software Design Models

Bévo et al. [8] associates the concepts of UML version 1.0 and COSMIC-FFP version 2.0. Their approach is based on use cases and class diagrams. Each use case maps to a functional process in COSMIC notation. Actors of a use case are considered as functional users. Scenarios of a use case are transformed into data movements and each class of a class diagram is mapped with a data group. However, triggering events and measurement layers in COSMIC notation are not mapped to any UML concept. Proposed approach was verified with five case studies in [9]. The procedure is applied in a measurement tool named, Metric Xpert.

Jenner [25] evaluates the model of Bévo et al. and improves the model by mapping additional UML concepts to COSMIC concepts. Unlike Bévo et al. he (she) maps each functional process to a sequence diagram. Interaction messages in each sequence diagram are mapped to data movements. She suggests usage of swim lanes to represent measurement layers. This procedure is also supported by a measurement tool [24].

Poels's [39] model which was developed by associating the concepts of COSMIC and the concepts of the business model and the services model of MERODE [28] allows measurement of multilayered applications. The model is proposed for the measurement of management information systems applications. Based on the business model and

COSMIC mapping; functional processes corresponds to a set of class methods and data movements are mapped to each of these class methods. Classes of the business model corresponds to data groups.

Unlike Bévo et al. [8], Nagano et al.'s proposal [35] allows measurement of real time applications from xUML [32] concepts. The model utilizes Class, state transition, and collaboration diagrams. The attributes of the class diagrams, message parameters and control signals are considered as candidate data groups. Collaboration diagrams are utilized for the identification of triggering events. Finally, set of data movements in collaboration diagrams correspond to functional processes.

Azzouz et al. [4] presents a proposal based on the fundamentals of Bévo's [8] and Jenner's [24] models and develops a tool to automate the functional size measurement process of management information systems projects developed with Rational Unifies Process (RUP) methodology. The model utilizes use cases and use case scenarios in three phases of the development methodology. These phases are business modelling, requirements analysis and design. One advantage of this proposal is that the tool had integration with Rational Rose tool.

Condori-Fernández et al. [33] presents a proposal to measure the functional size of object oriented systems. The proposal works based on the OO-Method requirements model including functions refinement tree, use case diagrams and sequence diagrams. Use cases and functions of the refinement tree correspond to functional processes. Sequence diagrams' elements corresponds to data groups and data movements. The model does not explain triggering events. Although the model does not have a tool support, it has been verified in [14–16].

Habela et al. [18] presents a mapping of UML version 1.5 and COSMIC FFP version 2.2 in the use case context. The proposal depends on detailed use case definitions and use case diagrams. Use cases are mapped with functional processes and scenario descriptions are mapped with data movements. In the literature there is no such study to describe the verification of the proposal.

Levesque et al. [19] develops a model for the measurement of management information systems from use cases and sequence diagrams. In the model, each use case corresponds to functional process and each actor of the use case corresponds to functional user. Sequence diagram elements are mapped to data groups and data movements. In this model data manipulations are also taken into account. Error messages in the sequence diagrams correspond to data manipulations. Levesque's proposal does not supported with a measurement tool. In addition, it was mentioned that the result of the case study conducted with Rice Cooker case [17] displayed %8 difference from the original measurement result.

Marín et al.'s [36] proposal allows measurement of object oriented systems developed using OO-Method. OO-Method, being a Model Driven Architecture approach, has a three tier architecture: presentation tier, logic tier, and database tier. Layer concept of COSMIC measurement method is associated with these tiers. Interaction units in presentation tier are associated with functional processes.

On the other hand, the proposal involves three models: the requirements model, the conceptual model and the execution model. The conceptual model is composed of four models: the object model, the functional model, the dynamic model and the presentation model. Classes in the object model are associated with data groups, whereas attributes of the classes are associated with data attributes. Finally, the proposal has a well-defined rule structure, tool support and has been verified using various case studies.

3   Problem Domain and Solution Domain Distinction

A real world problem, as humans see it, is a behavior-first domain. Humans perceive a problem or a need by the behavioral aspect first. We first perceive the cause and effect, which are behavioral, then attach those to objects. Solutions however, are object-first, rendering the solution domain an object-first domain.

The procedure of solving a problem is, essentially, devising components to attain the desired behavior. This phenomenon, makes the mapping of problem domain concepts to solution domain concepts arbitrary and non-mathematical.

Similarly in software engineering. The problem is defined as behavior-first and solution as object-first.

A problem can be represented as a hierarchy of sub-problems. A higher level problem can be broken down to lower level problems. This phenomenon is defined as Functional Decomposition in engineering.

Similarly, components can also be represented as a hierarchy of sub-components. A larger component can be broken down to smaller lower level components. This phenomenon is defined as Structural Decomposition in engineering.

However there exists no natural relation between these decompositions in two domains. Any mapping in between items in any decomposition level is problem and solution specific and not straightforward. One "item" in the functional decomposition tree in the problem domain may correspond to several "items" in the structural decomposition tree and vice versa. This is the main factor that there is a gap between problem and solution domain which is crossed through use of engineering problem solving.

Axiom: Software is a systems that consists of data movements in various levels of granularity. Abran elaborates on this on [1, 2].

The question about "how" a problem is solved is essentially the process of breaking down a larger "What" question to smaller "What" to do questions. The question "What?" stands for the description of a need or the aim of the system and the question "How?" stands for the solution devised for this problem.

The decomposition for a system can happen in any level and may be extended vertically to higher and lower levels. Theoretically this extension is infinite. Higher and higher level problems can be defined as well as lower and lower level solutions.

Engineering is about defining the start and end points for a system. Limiting the highest level with system boundary and lower level with system abstraction principles. In our approach, lowest level is the methods of a class, whereas lower levels can be defined for physical bytes in the memory, registers in the memory, bits defining mnemonics of instructions etc.

Figure 1 displays the boundaries of problem and solution domains for software engineering discipline. Positions of work products and software lifecycle activities with respect to these domains are also defined.

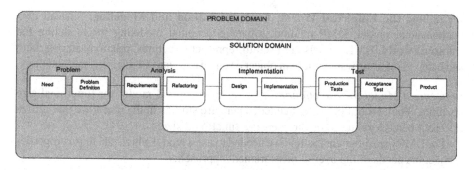

Fig. 1. Problem and solution domain borders in a software project lifecycle

Problem domain, by definition, involves the real life need and problem definition. Activities performed to understand the problem such as requirements elicitation and requirements development also lie in the problem domain. Moreover, the validation of the solution, that is, validating whether the solution meets our needs also lie outside the solution box and in problem domain. High-level requirement based testing and related test case generation activities may fall in this category.

Solution domain, on the other hand, involves the activities performed towards building a solution to the problem. Typically, these activities include detailed analysis, design, implementation and integration. Implementation typically involves coding and unit test activities.

In order to prove our suggestion on the separation of problem and solution from a metrics point of view, we conducted two studies [42, 43] with I.Unal. In the first study we investigated the correlation of problem and solution domain sizes with the problem and solution domain effort. In the second study, we conducted a case study where a single set of requirements were to be developed using two different implementation approaches. Both studies supported our suggestions about problem and solution domain separation. A similar but theoretical study by Lavazza and Bianco [28] also demonstrates the independence of problem and solution domain through the Rice Cooker case originally designed by COSMIC [17].

4   Suggested Measurement Approach

In this study we suggest a functional size measurement approach which is essentially based on COSMIC FSM principles. In essence, it is the measurement of data movements within a defined level of decomposition. It also provides information about level of decomposition in which the functional size is measured. We refer to the method as Data Movement Point (DMP).

Describing the Empirical World: Characterization and Modeling: The method considers characterization and modeling of the software system in two dimensions: Functional size and structural decomposition.

Describing the Empirical World: Characterization and Modeling: Instead of a mathematical model, DMP method utilizes conceptual modeling for modeling the empirical world. UML models are used to represent structures, relations among them and behavior of a software system in object oriented software engineering methodology.

Conceptual Model for Functional Size: As a conceptual model for functional size attribute, a behavioral model is needed. There are studies in the literature that utilize different behavioral diagrams to measure functional size.

For DMP measurement method we needed to use a model which had these properties to meet the needs of the overall measurement approach:

- Enable automated generation of the model by backfiring form the existing software products in the solution domain.
- Can be defined in various decomposition levels.
- Can be used to model concepts both in problem domain and solution domain.
- Give as much information as possible about the software model.

Based on these needs, we chose sequence diagram as the main software model for the empirical world to measure functional size attribute.

Definition of Atomic Level of Decomposition: It is hard to distinguish concepts belonging to different intermediate levels of decomposition from each other. However, lowest level of decomposition (minimum size of granule) can be identified for a measurement objective.

The objective of the DMP measurement method is to measure the functional size of the software to use in project management activities such as effort estimation, performance management, productivity management and benchmarking. Therefore the lowest level of decomposition relevant to this objective would be the lowest level of data movement in which actual effort is put in development. In object oriented software development, this level would be the method level. The lowest level of decomposition for Data Movements in an object oriented system design would be the calls (and methods) of an object. There would be no lower levels of data movement to be developed.

Definition of Tier: Each decomposition of the system will result in a new Tier of system definition. Each increase in the tier number represents one higher level of decomposition traversed in the description of the system.

Each tier consists of objects communicating with same tier level of objects. One set of objects in a tier can be present in a higher level if the entry and exit point of data movements between them and other objects does not change on their end. That is, certain object may belong to more than one tier at the same time.

The method level decomposition is defined as universal Tier 0 for every measurement. Then each consolidated view of decomposition is defined as Tier 1, Tier 2, Tier 3 etc. Tier number is defined based on specific system definition. It is a definitive value and does not infer any ratio in scale, it is a measurement in ordinal scale.

Mapping Phase. Mapping phase in DMP method corresponds to mapping the scenarios to decomposition levels, that is mapping sequence diagrams to tiers.

A specification begins by identifying the entities in the problem domain and their interrelationships and continue further by detailing the functions performed by and the internal state of each object.

The next step would be to identify which objects could allow decomposition and the layers of abstraction in each decomposition level.

A major advantage of object oriented development and UML modeling is that, solution domain entities can be defined in a direct and natural correspondence with the real world, since problem domain entities may be introduced directly into the model.

a. Identifying Scenarios: Based on the decomposition level (Tier Value) for the measurement, definition of the functional processes and their triggering entries change.
   1. The triggering entry of the functional process must be visible in the system model defined at this level.
   2. The structural entity receiving the triggering entry must be visible in the system model defined at this level.
   3. The output of the process (Exit or Write) must be visible in the system model defined at this level.

   Note that, functional process in higher tiers, will also be preset in lower tiers as their triggering entries will also be present in lower tiers. That is, certain functional processes will have different sizes in different tiers. Typically increasing by the decreasing tier number.

b. Identifying Objects: There exist several rules to check whether a structural entity belongs to a Tier.
   • The tier of a structural entity is the level of decomposition it has over the class/method level.
   • If there exists no more super entities for an object, that tier is considered the maximum Tier for that object. For further tiers the object is considered to exist in every higher than its maximum tier level.

c. Identifying Atomic Data Movements: Within atomic level of functional processes, the data movements are represented as method calls between structural entities (objects). This call is not an abstraction or a superstructure but the actual developed method call during the implementation. In other words, this call must be able to be represented as a single code instruction.

d. Identifying Tiers: The lowest tier level in DMP method is 0. Tier 0 corresponds to the decomposition level in which all communication between structural entities (namely objects, in this level) is carried on with atomic data movements, a single method call.

The Measurement Phase. Once the measurement tier, functional process and objects participating in the process is identified. The sequence diagram for the process is drawn. In the sequence diagram of the functional process, these calls between objects correspond to data movements (Synchronous message, Asynchronous message, Creation message, Destruction message, Self message, Found message).

Applying the Measurement Function and Aggregating Measurement Results. The size of a functional process is found by counting the total number of data movements (calls) within its sequence diagram. The size of a software component or a software product for a tier is calculated by summing of all its functional process sizes in that tier. In order to calculate the size of developed software (with the purpose of effort estimation), re-used or COTS components should be identified as a single structural entity in the models.

4.1 Measurement Tool – SDMC

We have developed a measurement tool specifically designed to perform this task. The tool was developed as a graduate project in METU Informatics Institute, Software Management graduate program by Yalın Meriç with the co-supervision of Erdir Ungan and Onur Demirörs [46]. The tool was named Sequence Diagram Metric Collector (SDMC).

In order to automate and communicate UML diagrams, Object Management Group (OMG) has developed XMI which is an XML standard to formalize UML data and provide a method to exchange metadata information between different systems. SDMC tool generates and interprets XMI files defining sequence diagrams.

SDMC gets folders with source code files in it so that, the measurement can be performed independent of the framework or IDE utilized. SDMC can interpret most popular object oriented programming languages such as: Java (versions 1.4, 5, 6), C# (versions 1.2, 2, 3, 4) and Visual Basic (7.1, 8, 9).

SDMC counts data movements in each sequence diagram. In order to obtain a well-structured measurement result, this is consolidated and interpreted. For the base level – Tier 0- measurement, the data should have been queried based on measurement date, project and component. For the component level, data movements between methods should be grouped by the classes in the components. So that, only data movements coming out and in of the components are counted. Similarly, for user defined class clusters, which form the layers, design level components and interfaces the measurer defines, the data movements should be grouped by the groups.

5 Validation

In order to validate our solution to these problems and research goals we set in Sect. 1; we defined these goals for the case study we performed.

1. Verify that it is possible to measure existing software products by backfiring measurable software models from source code.
2. Verify that DMP is a better input for effort estimation than problem domain sizes.
3. Investigate DMP's representation of project effort vs. solution domain sizes'.
4. Verify that DMP method results are reliable and repeatable.
5. Verify that DMP is easier to learn and use than other FSM methods.

In order to increase the number of samples and investigate the performance of DMP in different software development environments, we conducted four case studies in four different environments.

First case study was conducted in a company which maintains a big MIS software framework. The company releases monthly releases. That is, the development timeframe and effort is fixed for each release. They include new features, bugs fixes and changes in existing modules. The second case study was conducted with student projects. Different student groups were required to develop a software product with the same purpose and a common problem definition. The third case study was conducted with an IT department of a governmental institution. The fourth case study was conducted with a single very big simulation project developed for the defense industry.

Case Study Results: Due to limited length of this paper, we cannot present the results of the case study in detail. One can see the details of the validation case study in [44] Results indicated that LOC size correlates better with effort than both COSMIC and DMP within an organization. However, when we look at the overall correlation, that is, cross organization effort correlation, DMP performs better than LOC. This result is expected as changes in development technology and environment impacts the LOC the most. DMP on the other hand, is less prone to this effect as it is more abstract in nature.

In each case DMP's correlation was higher than COSMIC's which also backed up our initial claims.

DMP measurements do have a good correlation with LOC sizes. The correlation of COSMIC size with LOC however is found to be much lower both in our study and other studies in the literature. Based on this, we may say that DMP measurement is a better base for predicting LOC for the purpose of effort estimations.

Measurement Effort with DMP. We have observed that, modeling the source code from the sequence diagram for tier 0 measurements can take time as long as a couple of hours based on the size of the code, number of structural entities, layers and the computation power of the computer the SDMC tool is running on. However, as the measurement was performed automatically, the human effort needed to conduct the measurement was very small.

For higher Tier measurements, the measurement time and effort is less as the size of higher level models and hence their DMP size are lower. However, in the industry companies tend to omit detailed design phases or require design models only for complex elements of the project.

On the other hand, FSM measurement (e.g. COSMIC, IFPUG) takes much more time and human effort. In our previous studies, we had calculated the average effort for COSMIC measurements as 2 min per FP for experts and much higher for inexperienced measurers [45]. DMP is a great improvement on other FSM methods for measurement effort.

Learning Curve for DMP. We had the chance to let software engineers perform the measurement in Cases 1 and 3. As far as Tier 0 measurements are concerned, it took a negligible time for them to learn how to use SDMC and measure DMP from the source code.

We had explained the rationale of the method and told them how to use it for higher tiers in previous phases of a project. Those with experience in software design and development had no difficulties in practicing the method. However, those with experience in only analysis had difficulties on predicting the tier level of a measurement performed in earlier stages.

Nonetheless, compared with our previous experiences in COSMIC training, measurers learned to DMP method in much less time and with higher success. In case 1 they mentioned it was natural for them to predict how deep an entity will go in decomposition as they are accustomed to imagine further levels of development while they are writing requirements or developing pseudo designs for the requirements.

5.1 Validity Threats

Different organizations have different definitions for project effort. The method of collecting the effort data also differs. Cross case evaluations based on effort data may have less accuracy compared to evaluations within a single organization.

In Case 2, student projects were investigated. Being class assignments, the quality of project documents and accuracy of project data may be lower than those collected from actual projects in the industry.

6 Conclusion

We defined a measurement approach based on a concept that is common in both problem and solution domains; data movement. This streamlines measurement of both project and product attributes in two domains. This improves conversion of units, estimations, approximations and normalization of several size definitions and values.

Improvements in Reliability of Measurement Results. We minimize human errors and subjective assessments by basing the Tier 0 measurements to actual constructs, which can be measured by an automated tool.

For higher level measurement results we traverse through higher levels utilizing metadata for the lowest level. Only point of human interpretation is in the generation of this metadata which relates lower level concepts to higher level ones. This mitigates measurement errors as there is less room left for interpretation and renders errors recoverable by fixing the metadata.

Resilient Measurement. Existing FSM methods follow a top down approach in modeling. Functional size measurement methods in the literature first develop an abstract model for a system definition for measurement purposes and then conduct measurement on that model. This abstraction needs to model the whole system correctly to make a successful measurement. Imperfect, partial or incomplete system definitions result in erroneous measurement models and this in turn have a big impact on the measurement results as the measurements use this model as a basis and use in every step of measurement procedure.

However, DMP method have a bottom up modeling approach. The measurement model is based on atomic level of decompositions. This makes the measurement results less susceptible to erroneous and incomplete system definitions. Missing parts of a system will not affect the other parts and aspects of the measurement model. Only error in the measurement results will be missing size for the missing definitions. This makes the DMP model much less susceptible to imperfect, partial or incomplete system definitions.

By DMP method, it is possible to measure specifications defined in levels lower than functional user requirements. This makes measurement of components in highly decomposed systems possible independent of other sub systems and components.

DMP method also makes it possible to size software changes that are defined in lower resolution levels than functional user requirements.

Better Effort Estimations. Most estimation models in the field dictate using several factors and multipliers to convert problem domain sizes to solution domain sizes and utilize historical data to estimate the project effort based on the solution domain size.

Assuming an inherent relation between different size measurements in different domains and predicting one using other actually introduces another level of estimation error. We suggest an estimation approach which rely on the same concepts that the measurement method does will eliminate the gap caused by such conversions and by this approach, estimations will become less prone to gaps between domains and project phases.

Moreover, most FSM methods either does not include data manipulations in measurement or just incorporate the size of manipulations as an order of complexity to the overall measurement. As discussed above, manipulations defined in a level gradually become movements as decomposition levels deepen. By measuring in lower levels of decomposition, DMP method measures data manipulations which would otherwise be left out in higher levels into measurement. This should also increase the accuracy of estimations.

Better Measurement of Software Changes. By DMP method, it is possible to measure specifications defined in levels lower than functional user requirements. This will make measuring software changes that are defined in lower resolution levels than functional user requirements more accurate than existing FSM methods. Identifying the tier level of change requests will also improve the change management processes as the scope and impact of the change can be better analyzed.

Better Benchmarking. Having decomposition level incorporated into measurement results makes the scope and abstraction of the measured software product visible. This is especially crucial in benchmarking studies as current benchmarking datasets either do not include this information or do not have predefined scale for decomposition level. Comparing measurement methods on the same level of decomposition will greatly improve the accuracy of benchmarking studies.

References

1. Abran, A.: Software metrics need to mature into software metrology. Position Paper Prepared by Software Metrics Need to Mature into Software Metrology (Recommendations), pp. 1–18 (1998)
2. Abran, A.: Software Metrics.and Software Metrology. Wiley and IEEE-CS Press, New Jersey (2010)
3. Baker, A.L., Bieman, J.M., Collins, F., Fenton, N., Gustafson, D.A., Melton, A., Whitty, R.: A Philosophy for Software Measurement, pp. 1–9

4. Azzouz, S., Abran, A.: A proposed measurement role in the Rational Unified Process (RUP) and its implementation with ISO 19761: COSMIC FFP. In: Software Measurement European Forum 2004, Rome (2004)
5. Boehm, B.: Software Engineering Economics. Prentice-Hall, Englewood Cliffs (1981)
6. Ozkan, B., Turetken, O., Demirors, O.: Software Functional Size: For Cost Estimation and More, pp. 59–69 (2008)
7. Boehm, B.W.: Estimating Software Costs. Prentice Hall, Englewood Cliffs (1981)
8. Bévo, V., Lévesque, G., Abran, A.: Application de la méthode FFP à partir d'une spécification selon la notation UML: compte rendu des premiers essais d'application et questions. In: 9th International Workshop Software Measurement, Lac Supérieur, Canada, pp. 230–242 (1999)
9. Bevo, V.: Analyse et Formalisation Ontologique des Procédures de Mesure Associées aux Méthodes de Mesure de la Taille Fonctionnelle des Logiciels: de Nouvelles Perspectives Pour la Mesure. Doctoral thesis, Université du Québec à Montréal - UQAM, Montréal (2005)
10. Boehm, B.W.: Software Engineering Economics. Prentice-Hall Inc, Englewood Cliffs (1981)
11. Dekkers, C., Gunter, I.: Using backfiring to accurately size software: more wishful thinking than science? IT Metrics Strat. 6(11), 1–8 (2000)
12. Kemerer, C.F.: An empirical validation of software cost estimation models. Commun. ACM 30(5), 416–429 (1987)
13. Symons, C.: COSMIC GROUP CASE STUDY: RICE COOKER, pp. 1–15 (2010)
14. Condori-Fernández, N., Pastor, O.: An empirical study on the likelihood of adoption in practice of a size measurement procedure for requirements specification. In: 6th International Conference on Quality Software – QSIC, Beijing, pp. 133–140 (2006)
15. Condori-Fernández, N., Pastor, O.: Evaluating the Productivity and Reproducibility of a Measurement Procedure. In: ER Workshops, pp. 352–361 (2006)
16. Condori-Fernández, N.: Un procedimiento de medición de tamaño funcional a partir de especificaciones de requisitos. Doctoral thesis, Universidad Politécnica de Valencia, Valencia (2007)
17. COSMIC Group: Rice Cooker – Cosmic Group Case Study. École de technologie supérieure, Université du Québec à Montréal - UQAM, Mo
18. Glowacki, E., Serafinski, T., Subieta, K., Habela, P.: Adapting Use Case Model for COSMIC-FFP based Measurement
19. Levesque, G., Bevo, V., Cao, D.T.: Estimating software size with UML models. In: Proceedings of the 2008 C3S2E Conference on - C3S2E 2008, p. 81 (2008)
20. Poels, G.: Definition and validation of a COSMIC-FFP Functional Size Measure for Object-Oriented Systems, pp. 1–6 (2003)
21. Zhao, H., Stockman, T.: Software sizing for OO software development - object function point analysis. In: GSE Conference
22. ISBSG Data Collection Questionnaire. http://www.isbsg.org
23. ISO: ISO/IEC 14143-1- Information Technology – Software measurement - Functional Size Measurement. Part 1: Definition of Concept (1998)
24. Jenner, M.S.: Automation of counting of functional size using COSMIC-FFP in UML. In: 12th International Workshop Software Measurement, pp. 43–51 (2002)
25. Jenner, M.S.: COSMIC-FFP and UML: estimation of the size of a system specified in UML – problems of granularity. In: 4th European Conference on Software Measurement and ICT Control, Heidelberg, pp. 173–184 (2001)
26. Laranjeira, L.A.: Software size estimation of object-oriented systems. IEEE Trans. Softw. Eng. 16(5), 510–522 (1990)

27. Lavazza, L., Del Bianco, V.: A case study in COSMIC functional size measurement: the rice cooker revisited. In: Abran, A., Braungarten, R., Dumke, R.R., Cuadrado-Gallego, J.J., Brunekreef, J. (eds.) IWSM 2009. LNCS, vol. 5891, pp. 101–121. Springer, Heidelberg (2009)
28. Jackson, M.: Software Requirements & Specifications: A Lexicon of Practice, Principles and Prejudices. ACM Press/Addison-Wesley Publishing Co., New York (1995)
29. Jenner, M.S.: Automation of counting of functional size using COSMIC FFP in UML functional users requirements use case functional process type sub-process, pp. 43–51
30. Jenner, M.S.: Backfiring COSMIC size from Java and C++ code
31. Mellor, S., Balcer, J.: Executable UML: A Foundation for Model-Driven Architecture. Addison Wesley, Reading (2002)
32. Condori-Fernández, N., Abrahão, S., Pastor, O.: On the estimation of the functional size of software from requirements specifications
33. Habra, N., Abran, A., Lopez, M., Sellami, A.: A framework for the design and verification of software measurement methods. J. Syst. Softw. **81**(5), 633–648 (2008)
34. Nagano, S., Ajisaka, T.: Functional metrics using COSMIC-FFP for object-oriented real-time systems. In: 13th International Workshop on Software Measurement, Montreal (2003)
35. Marín, B., Pastor, O., Giachetti, G.: Automating the Measurement of Functional Size . . .
36. Top, Ö.Ö., Özkan, B., Nabi, M., Demirörs, O.: Internal and external software benchmark repository utilization for effort estimation. In: IWSM/Mensura, pp. 302–307 (2011)
37. Rule, P.G.: The importance of the size software requirements, Software Measurement Services Ltd, p. 18, UK (2001)
38. Poels, G.: A functional size measurement method for event-based object-oriented enterprise models. In: 4th International Conference on Enterprise Information Systems – ICEIS, Ciudad Real, pp. 667–675 (2002)
39. Dumke, R., Abran, A.: COSMIC Function Points: Theory and Advanced Practices (2011)
40. Standish_Group: The 2003 CHAOS Chronicles. The Standish Group International, Inc. (2003)
41. Ünal, I., Ungan, E., Demirörs, O.: The effect of implementation technology on software development effort: an industrial case". In: EPIC Workshop, the Proceedings of International Symposium on Empirical Software Engineering and Measurement, Bolzano, Italy (2010)
42. Ünal, I.: Predicting effort from COSMIC FSM method or design size : a case study. Technical report, Middle East Technical University, Ankara (2010)
43. Ungan, E. Ph.D. thesis. Graduate School of Informatics. Middle East Technical University, Ankara, Turkey (2013)
44. Ungan, E., Demirörs, O., Top, Ö.Ö., Özkan, B.: An experimental study on the reliability of COSMIC measurement results. In: Abran, A., Braungarten, R., Dumke, R.R., Cuadrado-Gallego, J.J., Brunekreef, J. (eds.) IWSM 2009. LNCS, vol. 5891, pp. 321–336. Springer, Heidelberg (2009)
45. Del Bianco, V., Lavazza, L., Politecnico, C.: An Empirical Assessment of Function Point-Like Object-Oriented Metrics. In: no. Metrics (2005)
46. Meriç, Y., Ungan, E.: Automated functional size measurement using sequence diagrams, METU (2013)

Improving the COSMIC Approximate Sizing Using the Fuzzy Logic EPCU Model

Francisco Valdés Souto[✉] and Alain Abran

École de technologie supérieure – Université du Québec,
Montréal, Canada
francisco.valdes@spingere.com.mx,
francisco.valdes.1@ens.etsmtl.ca, Alain.Abran@etsmtl.ca

Abstract. In software engineering, the standards for functional size measurement require, for accurate measurement results, that the functionality to be measured be fully known. Therefore, in the early phases of software development when there is a lack of details, approximate sizing approaches must be used instead of the standards themselves: such approximate sizing techniques are typically based on the analysis of historical data of the functional size of a number of completed projects within an organization. This paper revisits a fuzzy logic size approximation technique – the EPCU model, and presents an improved version, which lifts a number of constraints on its design, considering the Vogelezang dataset used in the literature to define the Equal Size Bands approximation approach.

Keywords: EPCU model · COSMIC ISO 19761 · Approximate sizing · Fuzzy logic · Functional size · FSM

1 Introduction

To date, the ISO has recognized five functional size measurement (FSM) methods for software as compliant with ISO 14143-1:

- Four are considered as 1st generation FSM methods: MKII: ISO 20698, IFPUG: ISO 20926, NESMA: ISO 24570, and FISMA: ISO 29881.
- One is referred to as a 2nd generation FSM method: COSMIC – ISO 19761 [6].

These FSM methods work best when the information to be measured – the functional user requirements – is fully known. However, this is most often not the case in the early phases of software development projects when only the non-detailed information is commonly available [4, 13, 14]: approximation techniques are then necessary to tackle this lack of details and to come up within a relevant range of candidate functional sizes.

Similarly, as pointed out in [8], "a rapid size measurement will be acceptable if it can be produced faster and still can deliver a reliable approximation of the detailed size measurement". As observed by Desharnais et al. [11], when the software documentation is lacking it is not possible to apply all the detailed measurement rules and the measurers must then fall back on approximation techniques for sizing the requirements without

© Springer International Publishing Switzerland 2015
A. Kobyliński et al. (Eds.): IWSM-Mensura 2015, LNBIP 230, pp. 192–208, 2015.
DOI: 10.1007/978-3-319-24285-9_13

enough details. While the Desharnais et al. [11] research work focused on the IFPUG FSM [12] method, their key findings are relevant to all FSM methods. For instance, in [11] a number of contexts were identified where the detailed measurement rules cannot be used, such as:

- The documentation is not precise enough for the application of the detailed measurement rules.
- The amount of work required to apply the detailed measurement rules to obtain precise measures of the software, and the work required subsequently to update the detailed measurement results, is perceived by management as being too expensive.

Santillo [13] further states that the "functional size of software to be developed can be measured precisely [only] after the functional specification stage: this stage is often completed relatively late in the development process."

A few researchers have developed approximation approaches [21] for measuring software functional size by analyzing historical data from completed projects; however, few of them have investigated how the performance of such approximation techniques in contexts with missing information, as encountered in the early phases of software projects.

In previous works, a fuzzy logic-based EPCU approach for approximate functional size in COSMIC was proposed by Valdés et al. using as a reference the Equal Size Bands Approach defined by Vogelezang et al. [8]: to do so did not require access to the details of this dataset. For organizations that do not have historical data, this fuzzy logic-based model could be useful to approximate functional size early in the development process.

This paper aims to improve the EPCU approach for approximate functional size without historical data [21, 24], considering the dataset used by Vogelezang et al. [8] to define the Equal Size Bands Approach. More specifically, this paper is focusing on the output variable domain: indeed, in the previous works, the dataset was not accessible and the assumption about the largest category (Very Large) was that its average value (16.4 CFP) represented adequately the full quartile, which meant that most of the largest sizes were close this average. Later access to the detailed dataset and personal feedback from the author of Vogelezang et al. [8] provided additional insights about the dataset, clarifying in particular that the average value (cutoff) for the largest category did not consider larger functional processes.

The rest of this paper is organized as follows. Section 2 describes the related works. Section 3 presents an analysis from the dataset used to generate the Equal Size Band Approximation Approach, and the validation of using a continuous range of possible values from 2 CFP with a "natural" upper boundary, or cutoff, stated at 16.4 CFP for the output variable in the EPCU model approximation approach. Section 4 describes the improvement applied to the EPCU model approximation approach. Section 5 presents the results gathered from the application of the EPCU model approximation approach using the same input data in the case study defined in [24] and the comparison with the previous work. Section 6 presents the conclusions.

2   Related Works

In 1997, Meli [18] proposed two techniques for two distinct types of size approximation, but did not report on their performance:

- Early Function Points (EFP), a faster version of the IFPUG 4.0 approximation method, and
- Extended Function Points (XFP), derived from the EFP after the application of three correction factors.

In 2003, Desharnais et al. [11] analyzed two approximation techniques used in the industry, Function Points Simplified (FPS) [15] and Backfiring [16], using two verification criteria selected from ISO 14143-3: accuracy and convertibility. They reported that, in the organizational context of their study, the FPS technique performed better with an accuracy range of 5 %.

In 2004, Conte et al. [14] extended the Early & Quick (E&Q) technique to the COSMIC FSM method, and indicated that further tests would be needed to make adjustments to the proposal, or to confirm it. This E&Q technique is based on (direct) analogy and (derived) analysis: it is a human-based size approximation method, and is impacted by the approximator ability to "recognize" the components of the system as belonging to the proposed classes.

In 2007, Vogelezang et al. [8] proposed a size approximation technique based on size bands using the quartile approach and reported on a study of 50 projects for the identification of such size bands. They also investigated the influence of distinct factors in approximate sizing and reported that, within their sample of 50 projects, the only factor that had a substantial influence on the size of an average functional process in each of the quartiles was the number of functional processes [8].

In 2007, the COSMIC Group published the 'Advanced and Related Topics' [5] document which describes two types of sizing approximation:

- Early Sizing: for use early in the life cycle of a project, before the Functional User Requirements (FUR) are detailed and specified.
- Rapid Sizing: for use when there is not enough time to measure using the standard method.

These two types of sizing approximation can be considered in the early phases of a development project. In general, an approach to approximate sizing some scaling factor for the type(s) of artifact(s) of the FUR of the software to be measured must be defined locally [5], requiring, for instance, that an average size of the artifacts to be measured be established locally – see Fig. 1.

This scaling factor represents the size expected to be measured when the functional user requirements are at the level of detail where an accurate measurement can be made because all the necessary details are available [8]. This solution needs historical data in order to produce an adequate scaling factor.

In [5], four approaches to approximate sizing of new 'whole' sets of requirements are presented. Each approach is based on two main assumptions:

Level of granularity of the Functional User Requirements (FUR)	Measurement approach	Measurement standard
FUR derived early in project life from • high-level Statement of Requirements for the software and/or • architecture artifacts • etc expressed in locally-defined measurable artifacts, e.g. 'use cases'	Locally-calibrated, approximate version of the COSMIC measurement method	The average size of the locally-defined measurable artifact, expressed in CFP
		↑ 'scaling factor' ↓
The 'functional process level of granularity' (see definition)	COSMIC measurement method	1 x CFP

Fig. 1. Scaling of sizes between different levels of granularity [5]

- There exist historical data to determine the scaling factor (average, or size bands).
- The whole set of requirements is described, or at least there is a commitment, defined by the requirements, about the scope of the software to be developed.

The four approaches described in [5] are:

(1) The Average Functional Process approach. The approximate size of the new piece of software is estimated to be equal to (Number of Functional Processes x Average Size from historical data).

(2) The Fixed Size Classification approach. A statement of requirements is analyzed to identify the functional processes and to classify each of them into one of three or more size classes, called, for instance: Small, Medium, and Large. A corresponding scaling factor is next assigned to each functional process, from historical data.

(3) The Equal Size Bands Approach. The functional processes are first classified into a small number of size bands. In the next step, the average sizes of each band are calculated (preferably calibrated locally), and then these average functional sizes are multiplied by the number of functional processes of the new piece of software, in each band respectively, to obtain the total approximate size.

(4) The Average Use Case approach. This example extends (1) to a higher level of granularity.

In 2011, Santillo [13] proposed the use of the Analytic Hierarchy Process [17], a technique that provides a means for making choices among sizing alternatives, particularly when a number of concurrent objectives have to be satisfied.

In 2012, Valdés et al. [21] proposed a solution using the fuzzy logic model from [2–4], referred to as the Estimation of Projects in a Context of Uncertainty – the EPCU model. This study, as in [11], analyzed the performance of an approximation technique using fuzzy logic [7, 9, 19 and 20] in an early phase context. For comparison purposes, the experiment was carried out also with the Equal Size Bands approach from Vogelezang et al. [8] which had led to an MMRE[1] = 11 % and SDMRE[2] = 9 %: in their experiment, using a reference software system [10] with a full set of stable requirements and its stated measured functional size, for this case study the Equal size band approach provided better approximation results.

In 2013 Almakadmeh [23] designed a framework to assign scaling factors for identifying the level of granularity of functional requirements specifications of software. In [23] two variants of the criteria to assess the levels of granularity were defined: the first one considers a software functional component and the second considers the elements of the UML use-case model. In order to rank the levels of granularity identified, the scaling factors used in [8] were selected; next, the scaling factor assignation is based on conducting an analogy-based comparison with similar pieces of software in which the functional size of those pieces of software is accurately measured using the COSMIC measurement method.

A workshop on discussion on approximate COSMIC FSM at the IWSM/MENSURA 2013 conference reported that "the approximation methods described in the in-progress COSMIC Guideline on Approximation rely on a common principle, namely that the only precisely defined level of granularity of functional user requirements is the functional process level of granularity" [22]. It also mentioned that the approximation methods were based on two approximation principles or a combination of them: Scaling and Classification, which concepts had been identified first in [23], respectively as scaling factors and levels of granularity.

Also in 2013, De Marco et al. [26] investigated to what extend some COSMIC-based approximate sizing could be useful for project managers for early effort estimation for Web applications: an empirical analysis was reported employing data from 25 Web applications to assess whether the two approximate sizes (number of COSMIC Functional Processes (FP) or the Average Functional Process approach) can be exploited to get accurate effort estimates. The conclusion is that the use of COSMIC-based approximate countings were a suitable approach for early effort estimates, while the estimates obtained with the approximate sizes are worse than those achieved employing the size obtained from the application of the standard COSMIC method.

In 2014, De Vito et al. [27] considered the need of a simplified and rapid COSMIC measurement that should avoid the use of scaling factors since incorrect calibrations of the scaling factors can lead to inaccurate approximations, proposed a simplified measurement process (Quick/Early) that can be applied on the use case models and aims to reduce the measurement time. This Quick/Early Approximation approach precision is directly proportional to the level of granularity of the analyzed use cases model: this means that the use cases have to be at least stable requirements –which does not happen too often in the very early stages; still, they conclude that accuracy of Quick/Early is good.

Also in 2014, Valdés et al. [24] reported on a case study of a simulation of the early approximation step using the EPCU model for an industry project for which only the names of the use cases were made available to the participants, without any additional

---

[1] Mean Magnitude of Relative Error (MMRE).
[2] Standard Deviation of MRE (SDMRE).

documentation. This case study confirmed that the EPCU Size Approximation approach does not require local calibration and is useful when there are no historical data available; in addition it is less expensive than the calibration of the equal size band approach which requires historical data.

For the case study with a real industrial project, the EPCU Size Approximation approach came up with better results with a MMRE of 45 % in comparison an MMRE = 63 % for the Equal Size Bands Approach, while both approaches led to underestimated results.

In order to integrate the highlights of the literature review in [22] and after, Table 1 was adapted from [24]. This table shows that the validity of most approximations techniques is dependent on the representativeness of the samples with respect to the software being approximated: said differently, to date most of the approximation methods need to be calibrated locally and this requires local historical data. However, in practice, most organizations do not have such data: as

Table 1. Approximation techniques analysis highlights

	Needs local calibration	Requirement granularity level	Consideration
Average Functional Process	X	Functional Process	This approximation is valid as long as there is sufficient reason to assume that the sample on which the size of the average functional process is calculated is representative for the software of which the functional size of which size is approximated. [38]
Fixed Size Classification	X	Functional Process	This approximation is valid as long as there is sufficient reason to assume that the assigned size classification is representative for the software of which the functional size of which size is approximated. [38]
Equal Size Bands approximation	X	Functional Process	This method is recommended for the approximate sizing of software where the distribution of the functional process sizes is skewed. For the business application this method has little added value over the average functional process method (1) or the fixed size classification method (2). [38]
Average Use Case approximation	X	Use Case	This approximation is valid as long as there is sufficient reason to assume that the assigned size classification of an average use case is representative for the software of which the functional size of which size is approximated. [38]
Early & Quick COSMIC approximation	X	Multilevel Approach (*)	The precision of the method is strongly dependent on the training and capability of the practitioners who use it to understand the categories at higher levels of granularity. [38], this approximation approach combines scaling and classification approaches.
Quick/Early		Use Cases	The precision is directly proportional to the level of granularity of the analyzed use cases model.
EPCU approximation approach		Functional Process & Use Cases	Does not require local calibration (less expensive) and is useful when there are no historical data available.

previously pointed out by Morgenshtern: "Algorithmic models need historical data, and many organizations do not have this information. Additionally, collecting such data may be both expensive and time consuming" [1] and approximation techniques based on historical data are of little use for organizations without such data. Alternatives must therefore be developed for such contexts of approximation.

3   Analyzing the Functional Process Sizes in the Quartile Analysis from the Equal Size Bands Approximation Approach Dataset

3.1   Data Set Description

The Vogelezang dataset has been used to generate the equal size bands approximation approach [5]: it includes 47 projects related to four sectors (Banking, Government, Insurance, Logistics). See Table 2. More specifically:

- The project size range for the Banking sector goes from 11 CFP to 2743 CFP, with a project average functional size is 476 CFP with 1345 Functional Process (FP), and a total size of 12375 CFP for all projects.
- For the Government sector, the total size of the set of projects is 3845 CFP with 838 FP where the project average functional size is 481 FP and the project size range for the sector is 64 to 2364 CFP.
- For the Insurance sector, the size range is from 84 CFP to 1311 CFP, the project average functional size is 551 CFP with 342 FP with a total size of all projects is 3305 CFP.
- For the Logistics sector, the number of FP considered is 321, with a total size of 3766 CFP, with a project average functional size of 538 CFP, and a project size range from 193 to 1164 CFP. See Table 2.

Table 2.   Dataset characterization

#Projects	Sector	Project Range (CFP)	Project Average Functional Size (CFP)	#FP	Size (CFP)
26	Banking	11-2743	476	1345	12375
8	Government	64-2364	481	838	3845
6	Insurance	84-1311	551	342	3305
7	Logistics	193-1164	538	321	3766

The dataset contains two general analyses labeled Q-Size and Q-Number, and eight specific analyses by sector, labeled Q-Size (sector$_i$) and Q-Number (sector$_i$). For this new study we will consider the integrated analysis, the concept of both is described below.

- For Q-Size the total measured size [CFP] is divided into four quartiles and the average FP size is calculated from there - see Table 3.
- For Q-number the total number of functional processes is divided into four quartiles and the average and the average FP size is calculated from there - see Table 4.

Table 3. Q-Size considering four sectors

Quartile		% FP included	Description	Average Value
Q1	Small FP's	55%	contains FP's in the range up to 6 CFP	3.7
Q2	Medium FP's	26%	contains FP's in the range 6-10 CFP	7.7
Q3	Large FP's	14%	contains FP's in the range 10-25 CFP	14.6
Q4	Very Large FP's	5%	contains FP's of 25 CFP and larger	44.1

Table 4. Q-Number considering four sectors

Quartile		% FP included	Description	Average Value
Q1	Small FP's	25%	contains FP's in the range up to 4 CFP	2.7
Q2	Medium FP's	25%	contains FP's in the range 4-6 CFP	4.3
Q3	Large FP's	25%	contains FP's in the range 6-8 CFP	7.1
Q4	Very Large FP's	25%	contains FP's of 8 CFP and larger	18.6

In Table 3, it can be observed that:

- Q1(Small FP) contains most of the FP (55 %) which sizes is up to 6 CFP with an average of 3.7 CFP.
- Q2 (Medium FP) contains 26 % of the total FP with a range of functional size from 6 to 10 CFP with an average of 7.7 CFP.
- Q3 (Large FP) contains 14 % of FP with an FP average size of 14.6 CFP and the range going from 10 CFP to 25 CFP.
- Q4 (Very Large FP) contains 5 % of the total FP (142 FP with an average of 44.1 CFP) and defines a range larger than 25 CFP.

In Table 4, each quartile contains the 25 % of the FP: the average size for Q1 (Small FP) is 2.7 CFP and the range is up to 4 CFP, the Q2 (Medium FP) defines a range of functional size from 4 to 6 CFP with an average of 4.3 CFP. In the Q3 (Large FP) the average size of FP is 7.1 CFP and the range goes from 6 CFP to 8 CFP. The quartile Q4 (Very Large FP) defines the range from 8 CFP and larger, with an average FP size of 18.6 CFP.

Table 5. Quartiles closeness

Difference	Q-Size	Q-Number
Q2-Q1	4.0	1.7
Q3-Q2	6.9	2.8
Q4-Q3	29.5	11.5

In Table 5, the analysis of the differences of the average size for the Q-Size and the Q-Number shows that for the Q-Number the average sizes for each quartile are closer than in the Q-Size approach.

3.2 Comparison of the 2014 and 2015 Study

In the 2012 and 2014 case study [21, 24], the output variable in the EPCU model was defined using a continuous range of possible values from 2 CFP with a "natural" upper boundary, or cutoff, stated at 16.4 CFP, considering the assumption about the Very Large category is that the average value (16.4) and that it adequately represents the full quartile, which means that most of the sizes are around the average, as is described in [5].

In 2105, using the analyzing the dataset for the Q-Size (Banking), we found that the 16.4 CFP average is for the Q3 (Large FP), including 14 % of the FP and the range goes from 10 to 31 CFP, and that there is another quartile Q4 (Very Large FP) with an average of 51.6 CFP: this means that the average of 16.4 CFP does not represent a relevant value to be used as cutoff for the Banking sector or the sectors described in the dataset used to define equal size bands approximation approach [5].

4   Improving the EPCU Model Approximation Approach

4.1 Redefining the Output Variable

To tackle the lack of historical data issue discussed in the previous studies [21, 24], and considering that there is no universal average functional process from which a scaling factor for early size measurement can be derived [8], the Equal Size Bands Approach, or Quartile, approach (Example 3) defined by Vogelezang et al. [8] was selected in the previous work [21, 24], as the basis for the COSMIC approximate sizing task using the EPCU model approach for business applications.

Vogelezang [8] used measurements on business application development projects, each having a total size greater than 100 CFP. The quartile values from this dataset were as follows: Small = 4.8 CFP, Medium = 7.7 CFP, Large = 10.7, and Very Large = 16.4 CFP [8] – see Fig. 2.

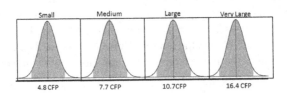

Fig. 2. Quartile size values of Functional Processes (FP)

As discussed in section B, the value 16.4 CFP does not represent a relevant value to be used as cutoff for all the sectors described in the dataset used to define equal size bands approximation approach.

Because this paper is about a functional size not about number of FP's, the Q-Size analysis about the quartiles are used – see Table 3.

Considering this assumption, the average for each quartile is Q1 = 3.7 CFP, Q2 = 7.7 CFP, Q3 = 14.6 CFP, Q4 = 44.1 CFP. Considering the range defined by the quartiles for the Q-Size approach will be [3.7 CFP to 44.1 CFP]. Consequently the range for the output variable is from 2 CFP (minimum functional size using COSMIC for a FP) to 44 CFP, with four linguistic values (fuzzy sets) defined: Low, Average, High, and Very High - see Fig. 3.

In Fig. 3, it can be observed that he range is continuous, but the difference between the quartile averages makes that the Large and Very Large Fuzzy Sets are wider than the Small and Average - see Table 5.

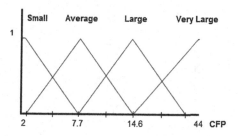

Fig. 3. Output variable schema

5 Application of the EPCU Model Approximation Approach Improved

The 2012 case study used a reference system [21] with its full set of stable requirements and its stated measured functional size, and an industry project [24] for which only the names of the use cases were shared with the participants through a survey form: no other information was shared with the participants who had to determine the size of the project functional requirements through their own evaluation of the input variables.

In order to compare the results about the improvement realized to the EPCU context used to approximate functional size, the same data used in [24] was used, because it is considered as a more realistic simulation of the early approximation step using the EPCU model.

5.1 The Measurement Reference: Software System ALFA[3]

The requirements of the ALFA software system scope were stated in a set of 14 Use Case descriptions. To establish the measurement reference for the comparison of the approximation against measurement results based from the detailed documentation of

---

[3] ALFA project was a project from a Mexican Federal Institution, for confidentiality purposes the Use Cases was are referred by sequential numbers only.

these 14 use cases, the detailed descriptions of the use cases were used by one of the researcher, certified as a COSMIC measurer (CCFL), to obtain the COSMIC measurement size based on the complete detailed documentation.

Table 6 presents, for each use case, the detailed COSMIC measurement results, including the data movement types and their functional size in COSMIC CFP units.

Table 6. COSMIC size of the use cases in the ALFA project

Use case Id	Entry in CFP	Exit in CFP	Read in CFP	Write in CFP	Size in CFP
Use case 1	1	7	6	2	16
Use case 2	5	18	23	9	55
Use case 3	1	12	12	2	27
Use case 4	1	4	2	1	8
Use case 5	1	1	7	0	9
Use case 6	1	2	3	0	6
Use case 7	1	11	11	3	26
Use case 8	1	4	3	0	8
Use case 9	4	3	6	3	16
Use case 10	1	1	1	1	4
Use case 11	5	4	9	5	23
Use case 12	3	3	7	3	16
Use case 13	3	2	5	4	14
Use case 14	1	7	14	0	22
Total size					250

The total functional size for the ALFA software requirements is 250 CFP (bottom line of Table 6), distributed across 14 use cases with a mean of 17.9 CFP per use case, a median of 16 CFP, and a standard deviation of 13 CFP [24].

5.2 Participants Tasks in the Experiment

In the 2014 study the detailed use case information relative to the ALFA project requirements was not made available for the practitioners.

Furthermore, the practitioners participating in the experiment:

- were not familiar with the COSMIC method,
- they had no historical data for approximating the FSM using COSMIC,
- they did not participate in the definition of the EPCU context or know the EPCU model.

The only information the 2014 participants had access to was the list of use cases identified and their own experience with the business process related to the project. Only a form with a list of the 14 use cases identified by the case study (with the real names) was sent by email to 12 practitioners from this organization – see Table 7; only eight set of answers were received.

The participants were asked to perform the following (full data shown in Appendix A):

1. Classify each of the 14 use cases using the linguistic values: Small, Medium, Large and Very Large.
2. Classify the number of objects of interest for each of the fourteen use cases using the linguistic values: Few, Average, and Many.
3. Assign values for the two input variables previously defined from the EPCU context (the functional process size, the quantity of objects of interest related to the functional process [24]) for each of the 14 use cases: considering the subjective classification relative functional size of the use cases and the subjective classification about the number of objects of interest in each use case, each value assigned within the range of 0 to 5 ε **R**.

The Input variables value assignation provided by the practitioners was next fed into the refined EPCU fuzzy logic model.

5.3 Data Analysis

In Table 8, the first column gives the practitioner's ID, the second column gives the 250 CFP reference size for the ALFA system, the third column the functional size calculated using the Equal Size Bands Approach, and the related magnitude of the relative error (MRE) is shown in the fourth column. The columns five and six show the functional size calculated using the EPCU approximation approach using the cutoff in 16.4 CFP (as was established in [24]) and the related MRE respectively. The column seven shows the functional size calculated using the EPCU improved approximation approach developed in this paper (Sect. 4) - i.e., using the cutoff of 44 CFP. The rightmost column indicates the MRE calculated from each size approximated by practitioners.

Comparing results using the Equal Size Bands approach against the reference functional size.

As mentioned in [24], comparing the Equal Size Bands approach, the mean magnitude of the relative error (MMRE) for this dataset is 63 % with respect to the reference size of 250 CFP, and the standard deviation of the MRE (SDMRE) is 5 %. – see Table 8 and Fig. 4.

The maximum MMRE is 67 % (Practitioner 1 and 6) and the minimum is 54 % (Practitioner 8) – see Fig. 4.

Comparing results using an EPCU Size Approximation approach (using a cutoff = 16.4 CFP) against the Equal Size Bands Approach.

In [24] the results show that considering the MMRE the functional size approximated with the EPCU Model (MRE = 45 %) is more accurate than the approximation using the "Equal Size bands Approach" [8] (MMRE = 63 %). The difference between the MMRE obtained using the "Equal Size bands Approach" and the EPCU

Table 7. Experiment information request form

Use cases	Use Case classification (linguistic values)	Use case size (value assignment)	Presence (level, not the number of) of object of interest related to the Use case classification (linguistic values)	Presence (level, not the number of) of object of interest related to the Use case (value assignment)
Use Case 1				
Use Case 2				
Use Case 3				
Use Case 4				
Use Case 5				
Use Case 6				
Use Case 7				
Use Case 8				
Use Case 9				
Use Case 10				
Use Case 11				
Use Case 12				
Use Case 13				
Use Case 14				

Table 8. Experiment results using EPCU size approximation approach

Practitioner	Reference Functional Size in CFP	Estimated Functional Size using the 'Equal Size Bands'	MRE	Estimated Functional Size using EPCU (range from 2 to 16.4)	MRE	Estimated Functional Size using EPCU improved (range from 2 to 44)	MRE
Practitioner 1	250	81.7	67%	186.32	25%	430.76	72%
Practitioner 2	250	93.3	63%	132.76	47%	240.74	4%
Practitioner 3	250	84.6	66%	62.19	75%	81.65	67%
Practitioner 4	250	93.3	63%	114.34	54%	190.33	24%
Practitioner 5	250	105.2	58%	168.13	33%	379.86	52%
Practitioner 6	250	81.7	67%	111.26	55%	183.14	27%
Practitioner 7	250	93.5	63%	130.43	48%	240.91	4%
Practitioner 8	250	114	54%	199.82	20%	493.47	97%
MMRE			63%		45%		43%
SDMRE			5%		18%		34%

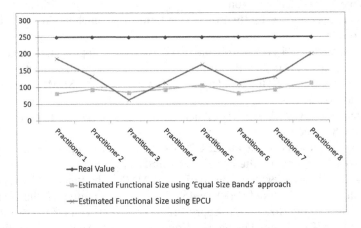

Fig. 4. Case study results for each practitioner

Size Approximation approach is 18 %. In [24] all the practitioners using the both approximation approach obtain estimation results under the reference size 250 CFP-see Table 8 and Fig. 4.

The behavior observed in Table 8 is that the "Equal Size bands Approach" has a smaller SD (SDMRE = 5 %) than the results obtained with the EPCU model approach SDMRE = 18 %: the difference between the SD between the "Equal Size bands Approach" and the EPCU Size Approximation approach is 13 % - see Table 8 and Fig. 4.

Comparing results using an EPCU Improved Size Approximation approach (using a cutoff = 44 CFP) against the reference functional size.

Considering the data in Table 8, the MMRE and SDMRE of the EPCU improved size approximation for all 8 practitioners are presented in the two bottom lines of Table 8 in the columns seven and eight:

- the MMRE with the EPCU model is 43 %,
- the SDMRE is 34 %.
- the maximum MMRE value with the EPCU model is 97 % (Practitioner 8) and the minimum value is 4 % (Practitioners 7 and 2) – see Fig. 5.

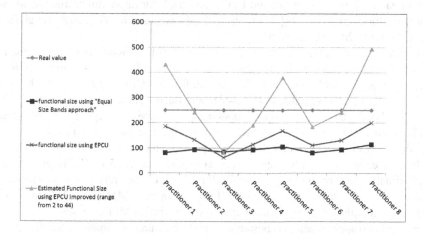

Fig. 5. EPCU improved apprximation approach results for each practitioner

Comparing results using an EPCU Size Approximation approach (using a cutoff = 16.4 CFP) against EPCU Improved Size Approximation approach (using a cutoff = 44 CFP).

In Table 8 in the bottom lines, it can be observed that the MMRE for EPCU Size Approximation approach (using a cutoff = 16.4 CFP) is 45 % with a SDMRE about 18 %. For the EPCU Improved Size Approximation approach (using a cutoff = 44 CFP), the MMRE is 43 % and the SDMRE is 34 %.

The EPCU Size Approximation approach (using a cutoff = 16.4 CFP) shows less dispersion and the EPCU Improved Size Approximation approach (using a cutoff = 44 CFP) shows better results because the MMRE is low.

From the data in Table 8 and Fig. 4, it can be seen that the use of EPCU Size Approximation approach in the early phases, considering the kind of information that is usually available at this phase, presents better results than the use of the un-calibrated "Equal Size Bands Approach".

Figure 5 shows that using a cutoff about 16.4 CFP the approximation of functional size is underestimating; using the cutoff about 44 CFP, the results are above and below from the real value, as discussed by De Marco "An estimation is a prediction that is equally likely to be above or below the actual result" [25].

An important feature of the EPCU Size Approximation approach is that the context does not have to be calibrated: it does not use bands, but rather a continuous range in ε R, which is represented by a membership function up to the upper boundary defined.

In summary, this 2015 case study reports a better performance with respect to the equal size band approach than reported in the earlier 2012 and 2014 case study [21, 24].

6   Conclusions

This research aimed to improve the EPCU approach for approximate functional size without historical data [21, 24], considering the dataset used by Vogelezang et al. [8] to define the Equal Size Bands Approach.

In this paper, the improvement made to the EPCU Functional Size Approximation Approach consisted in defining for the output variable, a continuous range of possible values with a "natural" upper boundary, or cutoff, at 44 CFP, the average of the functional size for FP in Q4 related to the Q-Size approach - Table 3.

As in [24], the EPCU Size Approximation approach does not require local calibration and is useful when there are no historical data available; in addition it is less expensive than the calibration of the equal size band approach which requires historical data.

For the experiment with a real industrial project, the 2015 EPCU Improved Size Approximation approach (cutoff in 44 CFP) presented better results with a MMRE of 43 % in comparison to the 2012 Equal Size Bands Approach (MMRE = 63 %) and EPCU Size Approximation approach (cutoff at 16.4 CFP) with an MMRE = 45 %.

For last two approaches, it is possible to observe an underestimate of functional size using them; on the other hand, using the EPCU Improved Size Approximation approach (cutoff at 44 CFP), the results are above and below the real value.

In summary, in this 2015 case study, a cutoff at 44 CFP presents more realistic results, because it considers FP with a larger functional size (including a wide range of FP from the dataset), something that it is not happening using the cutoff at 16.4 CFP.

Planned further work includes the collection of a set of projects with their use cases or their functional process identified, in order to conduct a more in depth analysis of the EPCU Improved Size Approximation approach.

This will include a comparison of the behavior of the EPCU Improved Size Approximation approach, considering the output variable range using the defined quartile for each sector (Q-Size (sector$_i$)) and a more in depth analysis considering specific projects for each sector.

Appendix A: The Full Data Set of the Information Collected in This Case Study

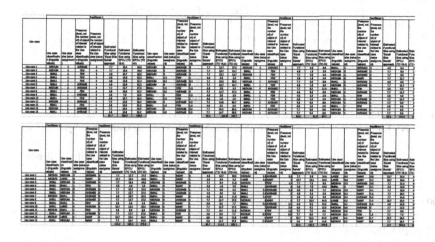

References

1. Morgenshtern, O., Raz, T., Dovir, D.: Factors affecting duration and effort estimation errors in software development projects. Inf. Softw. Technol. **49**(8), 827–837 (2007)
2. Valdés, F., Abran, A.: Industry case studies of estimation models based on fuzzy sets. In: Abran-Dumke-Màs (eds.) International Workshop on Software Measurement IWSM-Mensura 2007, Palma de Mallorca, Spain, pp. 87–101. UIB-Universitat de les Illes Baleares, 5–9 Nov 2007. ISBN 978-84-8384-020-7
3. Valdés, F., Abran, A.: Comparing the estimation performance of the EPCU model with the expert judgment estimation approach using data from industry. In: Lee, R., Ormandjieva, O., Abran, A., Constantinides, C. (eds.) SERA 2010. SCI, vol. 296, pp. 227–240. Springer, Heidelberg (2010). ISBN 978-3-642-13272-8
4. Valdés, F.: Design of a fuzzy logic software estimation process. Ph.D. thesis, École de Technologie Supérieure, Université du Québec, Montreal, December 2011
5. COSMIC Measurement Practice Commitee: The COSMIC functional size method version 3.0, advanced and related topics. http://www.cosmicon.com/portal/public/COSMIC %20Method%20v3.0%20Advanced%20&%20Related%20Topics.pdf (2007). Accessed 4 Sept 2010
6. COSMIC Measurement Practice Commitee: The COSMIC functional size measurement method, version 3.0.1, Measurement Manual, May 2009. www.cosmicon.com
7. Zadeh, L.A.: Is there a need for fuzzy logic? Inf. Sci. **178**(13), 2751–2779 (2008)
8. Vogelezang, F.W., Prins, T.G.: Approximate size measurement with the COSMIC method: factors of influence. In: SMEF 2007 Conference, Rome, Italy (2007)
9. Zadeh, L.A.: Fuzzy logic. IEEE Comput. **1**, 83 (1988)
10. Khelifi, A., Abran A., Symons, C., et al.: Proposed measurement etalon: C-Registration system, January 2007. http://www.cosmicon.com/portal/public/CRS_RUP_Case_ %20Study_version_Jan_04_2007_web_%20version_update_feb_2008.pdf. Accessed February 2008

11. Desharnais, J.-M., Abran, A.: Approximation techniques for measuring function points. In: 13th International Workshop on Software Measurement – IWSM 2003, pp. 270–286. Springer, Montréal, Canada, 23–25 Sept 2003
12. IFPUG: Function point practices manual, release 4.1. International Function Points User Group (IFPUG), Mequon, Wisconsin Release 4.1, January 1999
13. Santillo, L.: Early and quick COSMIC FFP overview. In: Abran, A., Dumke, R. (eds.) COSMIC Function Points Theory and Advanced Practices, pp. 176–191. CRC Press, Boca Raton (2011). ISBN 978-1-4398-4486-1
14. Conte, M., Iorio, T., Santillo, L.: E&Q: an early & quick approach to functional size measurement methods. In: Software Measurement European Forum SMEF 2004, Rome, Italy, 1–3 Jan 2004
15. Bock, D.B., Klepper, R.: FP-S: a simplified function point counting method. J. Syst. Softw. **18**, 245–254 (1992)
16. Jones, C.: Applied Software Measurement, Assuring Productivity and Quality, 2nd edn. McGraw Hill, New York (1997)
17. Santillo, L.: Early FP estimation and the analytic hierarchy process. In: ESCOM-SCOPE 2000 Conference, Munich, Germany, 18–20 Apr 2000
18. Meli, R.: Early function points: a new estimation method for software projects. In: ESCOM 1997, Berlin, Germany, May 1997
19. Mamdani, E.H.: Applications of fuzzy logic to approximate reasoning using linguistic synthesis. IEEE Trans. Comput. **26**(12), 1182–1191 (1977)
20. Mamdani, E.H., Assilian, S.: An experiment in linguistic synthesis with a fuzzy logic controller. Int. J. Man Mach. Stud. **7**(1), 1–13 (1975)
21. Valdés, F., Abran, A.: Case study: COSMIC approximate sizing approach without using historical data. In: 22nd International Workshop on Software Measurement & 7th International Conference on Software Process and Product Measurement – IWSM-MENSURA, Assisi, Italy, November 2012
22. Vogelezang, F., Symons, C., Lesterhuis, A., Meli, R.: Approximate COSMIC functional size guideline for approximate COSMIC functional size measurement. In: 23rd International Workshop on Software Measurement (IWSM) and 8th International Conference on Software Process and Product Measurement (Mensura), Ankara, Turkey, October 2013. IEEE doi: 10.1109/IWSM-Mensura.2013.14
23. Almakadmeh, K.: Development of a scaling factors framework to improve the approximation of software functional size with COSMIC - ISO19761. Ph.D. thesis, École de Technologie Supérieure, Université du Québec, Montreal, Canada, June 2013
24. Valdès, F., Abran, A.: COSMIC approximate sizing using a fuzzy logic approach: a quantitative case study with industry data. In: Joint Conference of the 24th International Workshop on Software Measurement and 9th International Conference on Software Process and Product Measurement - IWSM-MENSURA 2014, pp. 282–292. IEEE Press, Rotterdam, Netherlands, 6–8 Oct 2014. doi:10.1109/IWSM.Mensura.2014.44
25. De Marco, T.: Controlling Software Projects. Prentice Hall, Englewood Cliffs (1982)
26. De Marco, L., Ferrucci, F., Gravino, C.: Approximate COSMIC size to early estimate web application development effort. In: 2013 9th Euromicro Conference Series on Software Engineering and Advanced Applications, Santander, Spain, 4–6 Sept 2013
27. De Vito, G., Ferrucci, F.: Approximate COSMIC size: the quick/early method. In: 40th Euromicro Conference on Software Engineering and Advanced Applications, Verona, Italy, 27–29 Aug 2014

Author Index

Printed in the United States
By Bookmasters